D1008635

Dear Mr. Brooks Herman,

This small token of friendship is presential to you on your Seoul visit, Dec. 3-9, 2002.

Soon Jong Kim
Christmas 2002
Sambon, Korea
Dec. 3, 2002

Introduction to
KOREAN HISTORY AND CULTURE

OPPOSITE Footprints of a dinosaur in the fossilized sandy beach at Tŏngmyŏng, Kosŏng, South Kyŏngsang Province.

Hunting scene from a Koguryŏ mural, ca. 6th century.

ABOVE Roof tiles with surface design in Paekche period.

RIGHT A pair of earrings of Queen Muryŏng found inside the monarch's tomb, Paekche period.

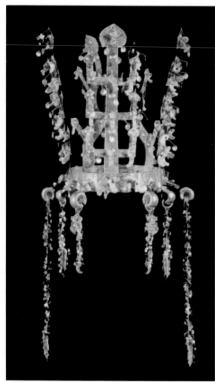

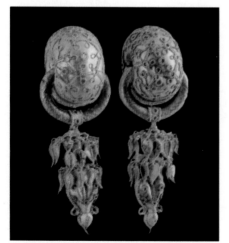

A golden crown with gold spangles and comma-shaped jades excavated from Shilla tombs, 5-6th centuries.

A golden girdle with pendents, of Shilla origin, circa 5-6th centuries, and gold bracelet of Ancient Shilla origin.

A pair of gold gilt-bronze ear pendants excavated from Shilla tombs, 5-6th centuries

A golden cap from the Tomb of the Flying Horse of Shilla, 5-6th centuries.

The Pulguk Temple built in the 8th century.

Three types of stone lanterns (left to right) : one located at the Pŏpchu Temple, one located at the Hwaŏm Temple ; and one formerly of the Kodal Temple, now at the National Museum.

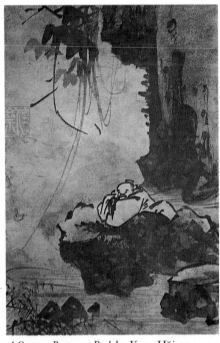

Part of *Clearing after the Rain on Inwang Mountain* by Chŏng Sŏn (Kyŏmjae, 1676-1759).

A Sage at Rest on a Rock by Kang Hŭi-an (Injae, 1419-64).

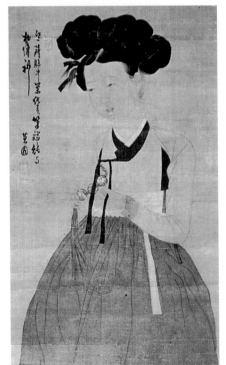

ABOVE *Diamond Mountains* by Chŏng Sŏn (Kyomjae, 1676-1759).

LEFT *Portrait of a Beautiful Woman* by Shin Yun-bok (Hyewŏn, 1758-1820)

Mirŭk Temple Pagoda of Paekche period, 7th century.

Ten-story stone pagoda of the Kyŏngch'ŏn Temple, 1348, now at the National Museum.

Ch'ŏmsŏngdae, star observation tower built in 647 in Kyŏngju.

ABOVE Koryŏ celadon ware: wine cup with stand with inlaid flower design.

LEFT Yi dynasty celadon ware depicting the simple naturalistic trends of the scholars of that time: bottle painted with plum flowers, one of the "four gentlemen" of flora.

Typical jade-green sanggam Koryŏ celadon bowls with inlaid design, 13th century.

11-headed Kwanŭm (Kuanyin) Posal made
of granite in Sŏkkuram grotto near Kyŏngju,
751 A.D.

Two figures accompanying the Buddha statue
in the Sŏkkuram grotto in Kyŏngju.

Gilt bronze Maitreya of the Three Kingdoms
period.

A gilt bronze Standing Buddhia with inscribed
date of 539, Koguryŏ. Ht. 16.2cm

Goblin Playing with a Toad by Shim Sa-jŏng (Hyŏnjae, 1707-69).

A folk painting of a mountain spirit.

A folk painting of a tiger.

A folk painting of lotus.

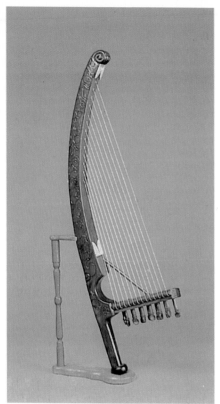

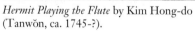
Hermit Playing the Flute by Kim Hong-do
(Tanwŏn, ca. 1745-?).

Some traditional musical instruments: FROM ABOVE TO BELOW Harp; Kkaenggwari; Kayagŭm, a 12-string zither.

Dancer of the Pongsan Masked Dance.

Musicians and a dancer performing the Farmers' Music (nong'ak)

Performance of the Lion Dance of Pukch'ŏng, South Hamgyŏng Province

The first Korean national flag created by the Progressives in 1882.

The ragtag insurgents of the Righteous Armies
who fought against modernized Japanese troops.

The Koreans celebrating the liberation and welcoming American troops.

Millions of North Korean refugees
fled into the South in search of
freedom during the Korean War.

Presidents of Korea

Syngman Rhee (1948-60)

Yun Po-sŏn (1961-63)

Park Chung-hee (1963-79)

Ch'oe Kyu-ha (1979-80)

Chun Doo-hwan (1981-88)

Roh Tae-woo (1988-93)

Kim Young-sam (1993-98)

Kim Dae-jung, 25 February, 1998
8th President of Korea

INTRODUCTION TO KOREAN HISTORY AND CULTURE

Andrew C. Nahm

新 韓 國 史 入 門

HOLLYM

Elizabeth, NJ · Seoul

Introduction to Korean History and Culture

Copyright © 1993
by Andrew C. Nahm

All rights reserved

First published in 1993
Slightly revised 3rd printing, 1994
Seventh printing, 2001
by Hollym International Corp.
18 Donald Place, Elizabeth, New Jersey 07208, USA
Phone: (908)353-1655   Fax: (908)353-0255
http://www.hollym.com

Published simultaneously in Korea
by Hollym Corporation; Publishers
13-13 Kwanchol-dong, Chongno-gu
Seoul 110-111, Korea
Phone: (02)735-7551~4   Fax: (02)730-5149, 8192
http://www.hollym.co.kr

Hard cover edition ISBN: 0-930878-08-6
Paperback edition ISBN: 0-930878-07-8

Library of Congress Catalog Card Number: 92-73743

Printed in Korea

TO MY WIFE, MONICA EUGENIA,
AND ALL THOSE FOREIGNERS
WHO MARRIED KOREANS

Contents

List of Maps

Preface

ALTHOUGH an eminent Indian Philosopher, Rabindra-nath Tagore, once said that "In the golden age of Asia Korea was one of its lamp bearers," Korea, an ancient nation with a long history and rich cultural heritage, had been by and large a *terra incognita* as far as most Western people were concerned. Early in this century a Western writer called Korea "the hermit kingdom."

It was not until the outbreak of the Korean War in 1950 that people in the West had a chance to become acquainted with Korea, but it was the hosting of the 1988 summer olympiad by Seoul, capital of South Korea, that aroused greater interests in the culture and social heritage of the Koreans and the ways in which the country, which had been economically backward only a short time ago, joined the industrialized nations of the world.

Korea is one of a handful of non-Western nations that has made the transition to full industrialization and modernization. However, Korea has preserved its self-identity and a considerable part of its traditional, pre-modern culture, despite the growing Western influence that has inundated the southern half since 1945. This ancient heritage and tradition, while constituting the strength of the people, created certain difficulties for the Koreans in coping with the problems of modernization.

At this time, Korea remains divided into two states, each attempting to modernize and enrich its economic power while endeavoring to bring about the reunification of the partitioned land and people. Be that as it may, the need to know more about Korea and its culture and people has steadily grown in the West.

Several English-language books of various kinds and authors have been published in the past, and many are now out of date, or are too short to provide an adequate picture of Korea's past and present, while others, including my own college text, are too bulky or complex for the general reader.

I was hesitant to agree to write a "simple," "brief," yet "comprehensive and interpretative" history of Korea for the general reader when asked to do so. The task of writing such a book is a difficult one: the selection of historical events and the makers of history for inclusion in a book such as this has to be arbitrary, depending on the author's value judgment, which may be different from that of others. Nevertheless, the task that was undertaken to meet such a need has resulted in this book.

Special efforts have been made to emphasize various aspects of the social and cultural development that shaped the outlook and habits of the Korean people, while offering narratives on the major historical developments in political, economic, and military areas. Efforts were also made not to include too many names of persons, although they played important roles in Korean history. Likewise, a minimum number of Korean terms are given in this book where it seemed necessary.

The author owes his gratitude to those scholars and writers who have published their works on Korean history, providing valuable sources and reference materials. He is also indebted to the many Korean scholars who provided him with valuable suggestions. He wishes to express his appreciation to his wife, Monica Eugenia, for her encouragement and editorial comments, as well as to Opal Ellis of the Department of History, Western Michigan University, who typed the manuscript.

The Romanization systems used in this book are those generally considered standards in the English speaking works: Wade-Giles for Chinese, Hepburn for Japanese, and the Ministry of Education's Romanization system, which is a modified system of the McCune-Reischauer Romanization method, for Korean. In cases of certain personal and place names, as well as the names of educational institutions and industrial firms, which are widely known and used by Western mass media, these systems were not applied.

Generally, the basic vowels, *a, e, i, o* and *u* are pronounced as in Italian and Spanish:

> *a as* in father   *e* as in end
> *i* as in India   *o* as in Ohio
> *u* as in rule

Two vowels, *ŏ* and *ŭ* are pronounced as below:

> *ŏ* as the o in ton   *ŭ* as the *oo* in foot

Some diphthongs (compound vowels) are pronounced as a single vowel:

> *ae* as the *a* in apple   *oe* as *ö* in German

But, each vowel in certain other diphthongs are pronounced separately:

> *ai* as the *ie* in tie   *oi* as the *oy* in toy

Generally, unaspirated consonants are pronounced softly:

> *ch* as j   *k* as g   *p* as b   *t* as d

When these consonants are aspirated by adding an apostrophe(') behind the letter, they are pronounced as in English words:

> *ch'* as ch   *k'* as k   *p'* as p   *t'* as t

An apostrophe is also used to separate two consonant sounds as in the cases of *Tan'gun* and *han'gŭl*, etc. Certain compound consonants are pronounced as follows:

> *ss* as the *s* in Sam   *tch* as the *j* in jam
> *tt* as the *d* in dam

Japanese vowels, *ō* and *ū* have long sounds as compared to short *o* and *u*.

Andrew C. Nahm

1
The Dawn of Korean History

KOREA is one of the oldest countries in the world. Her name, Korea, is derived from the Koryŏ dynasty, which ruled the land from 936 to 1392 as a unified kingdom. The other name of Korea, Chosŏn, more popularly known in the West as "the Land of the Morning Calm," came from the kingdom which the Yi dynasty established in 1392 and ruled over until 1910.

The Land, Climate, and People

The Geographical Setting. The Korean peninsula that projects due south from the Asiatic mainland toward the Japanese archipelago is about 621 miles long, and is 134 miles wide at its narrowest point and 150 miles wide at its widest point. It lies between 33° N and 43° N latitude, and from 124° to 131° longitude. The peninsula, a little over 85,000 square miles, is slightly larger than the state of Minnesota, and a little smaller than Great Britain. (See Map 1)

The peninsula is separated from Manchuria in China

by the Yalu (Amnok) and Tumen (Tuman) rivers, and it is surrounded by the Sea of Japan (East Sea), the Yellow Sea (West Sea), and the Korea Strait. Korea is also surrounded by three countries: the Soviet Union across the lower Tumen River, Japan across the Sea of Japan and the Korea Strait, and China across the Yellow Sea to the west and the Yalu and Tumen rivers to the north. Such a geographical location has had profound cultural and political implications throughout the ages. While playing the role of bridge for cultural transmission from Asia to Japan, the Korean peninsula itself became an object of competition among China, Japan and Russia in the late 19th and early 20th centuries.

Map 1. KOREA: IN THE HEART OF EAST ASIA

The Land. Korea is a mountainous country. Some 66 percent of the land area consists of gneiss and granite. Pushed-up sea floors, combined with prehistoric volcanic activity, created the rugged landscape of the Korea we know today. Such rugged yet scenic beauty of the land led the Koreans to describe their homeland as *kŭmsu kangsan,* or "rivers and mountains embroidered on silk."

The Changbaek Range and its branches cover an extensive area of both southeastern Manchuria and northern Korea. The highest mountain in this range is Mt. Paektu, (White Head, 9,000 feet) on top of which is a large crater lake. Mt. Paektu is the source of both the Yalu and Tumen rivers. Just south of the Changbaek Range are four rugged mountain ranges which occupy most of the northern regions of the peninsula. Linking these four ranges, the Kaema and the Pujŏn plateaus constitute the "roof" of Korea.

The T'aebaek Range, which constitutes the backbone of the peninsula, runs almost its entire length, paralleling the east coast, from the southern fringe of the Pujŏn Plateau. Located in this range are such scenic mountains as Mt. Kŭmgang (Diamond Mountain, 5,530 feet), Mt. Sŏrak (5,600 feet), and Mt. T'aebaek (5,100 feet). From the T'aebaek Range, several mountain chains branch out westward. The largest one of these is the Sobaek Range in southwestern Korea, in which Mt. Chiri (6,250 feet) is located.

Whereas the east coast, with the exception of the northeastern portion, generally has smooth shorelines with extremely narrow coastal areas, the western and southern coasts are characterized by lowlands and extremely irregular shorelines with numerous bays and inlets. Along the northeastern coast are a few bays, harbors, and wider coastal areas. Most of Korea's 3,400 islands are located near the western and southern coasts.

Among the main islands are Kŏjedo off the southeastern coast, Chindo and Wando off the southwestern coast, and the islands of Kanghwado and Yŏngjongdo near Inch'ŏn on the westcentral coast. The largest Korean island, Chejudo, is located some 100 miles off the southern coast. Its highest point is Mt. Halla (6,400 feet), an extinct volcano. Ullŭngdo and Tokto are located in the Sea of Japan.

All but four major rivers flow westward into the Yellow Sea: the Yalu, the Ch'ŏngch'ŏn, and the Taedong rivers in the north; the Imjin and the Han rivers in the center; and the Kŭm River in the southwest. The Tumen (Tuman) and the Sŏngch'ŏn rivers in the north flow into the Sea of Japan; the Naktong and Sŏmjin rivers in the south flow southward into the Korea Strait.

Only about 22% of the land is arable, and most of it is located in the western and southern regions. The major plains are those in the northwestern region along the Ch'ŏngch'ŏn and the Taedong rivers; those in the westcentral region along the Imjin, the Han, and the Kŭm rivers; and those in the southern region along the Naktong and the Sŏmjin rivers.

Climate. The climate of Korea is temperate, with four distinct seasons. Spring generally begins in early March, accompanied by warm breezes from the south, and lasts until the middle of June with light rainfall at regular intervals. Summer, the hot and humid season, begins in late June as the rainy season that lasts usually until the end of July. During the rainy season, the temperatures generally remain relatively cool, but following that period they may reach as high as 95°F in the south and 85°F in the north. Annual precipitation varies from about 24 inches in the north to more than 60 inches in the south.

Autumn, described by an ancient poet as the "season of

high sky and fat horses," generally begins around mid-September and ends toward the end of November. Autumn is the most colorful season, and it is also the busiest time of all for Korean farmers. Winter begins around mid-December and lasts until late February. January is the coldest month, with temperatures falling as low as 6°F in the north. Owing to the influence of the surrounding seas, the winter climate in the south is not as severe. The average January temperature in Seoul is 24°F, and in Pusan 33.6°F. Although the snowfall is heavy at times in the north, it is generally light in the southern half of the peninsula, and the extreme southern areas have only very light snowfall or none at all. The fauna and flora of Korea encompass subtropical, temperate and arctic species, and a semi-tropical climate prevails on Cheju Island.

The People. Ethnologically, Koreans belong to the Altaic family of races, which includes the Turkic, Mongolian and Tungusic peoples. Although Paleolithic man originated in Korea, it is believed that the Neolithic peoples, in the course of a long historical process, merged with one another as they combined with the new ethnic groups which arrived in Korea later, eventually becoming the ancestors of the present-day Koreans. Among the Neolithic peoples and the latecomers were the Tungusic tribes such as the Kaema (Koma), the Ye, the Maek, and the Puyŏ, which migrated to the peninsula from the Altai Mountain region, as well as from northeastern China via Siberia, Mongolia, and Manchuria, bringing with them the Neolithic cultures, the agglutinative and polysyllabic Ural-Altaic language, shamanistic religion, and a distinctive pottery culture.

Prehistoric Cultures

Korea's prehistoric period spans thousands of centuries from about 50,000 or 40,000 B.C. to 300 B.C. Some believe that it began more than 400,000 years ago. This prehistoric period includes the Paleolithic Age, the Neolithic Age, the Bronze Age and the Iron Age, each having its own distinctive sociocultural patterns.

Paleolithic Culture. A series of archaeological excavations carried out in Korea after 1963 produced abundant evidence that Korea's Paleolithic (Old Stone) culture developed in the northeastern corner of the peninsula and spread southward. Several Paleolithic culture sites, dating from 50,000 to about 30,000 B.C., have been excavated.

Evidence shows that Old Stone Age man lived first mostly in caves along the shorelines and river banks, and then built round-shaped, deep pit dwellings. Among the caves of the Paleolithic period are the Kŏmŭnmoru Cave and the Chŏmmal Cave. From these sites were found crude stone implements such as axes, quartz choppers, knives, points, side-scrapers, and harpoons. The discovery of fossils of the hyena, elephant, rhinoceros and monkey, which are no longer found in Korea, indicates that the climate during the Paleolithic period was much warmer than it is today. The discovery of a hearth at a dwelling site led to the conclusion that fire was used by Paleolithic man for both cooking and warmth. One of the upper layers of the Sŏkchang-ni site was estimated to have been 30,690 years old, and the charcoals unearthed from the hearth at this site were dated as 20,825 years old. Living mostly by hunting and fishing, Paleolithic man gathered fruit, berries, and edible roots.

Neolithic Culture. From about 5000 B.C., Neolithic (New Stone Age) people, who are believed to have been the ancestors of the present-day Koreans, appeared in Korea from the north, bringing a new, Scytho-Siberian pottery culture with them. Several Neolithic culture sites have been excavated in Korea.

The early Neolithic man, like Paleolithic man, lived along the coastal areas and on the banks of rivers, but they left caves and built houses of square or rectangular shape on shallow pits. These houses had both thatched roofs and heating systems. While hunting and fishing, the Neolithic people developed agriculture, grew millet-like grain, and produced grayish colored, round or pointed-bottom *chŭlmun* pottery with geometric (comb-marked) designs, as well as polished stone tools such as knive — including half-moon shaped knives — spears, hoes, arrow heads, mill stones, sinks for fishing nets, and sickles. They also produced stone mirrors and buttons, and with bone needles they produced clothing with animal skin first and then clothes of hempfibers as well as animal fur decorated with trinkets. They domesticated such animals as hogs, dogs, cows, and horses.

Late in the Neolithic period, cultivation began as the Neolithic people migrated southward and inland. It was also these Neolithic people who migrated to the Japanese islands of Kyūshū and Honshū, taking with them the *chŭlmun* pottery culture known in Japan as the *Jōmon* pottery. The comb-marked pottery of this new cultural period has been found not only in Korea, but also in Inner Mongolia, northeastern China, Maritime Province, and Japan, indicating that the people who inhabited these regions belonged to the same cultural group.

Neolithic society consisted of large tribal communities made up of several tribal units. Occasionally, each community had a large meeting place in its center, around

Chŭlmun
(*comb-marked*)
*pottery with pointed
bottom, Neolithic Age,
ca. 1500 B.C.,
excavated at
Amsa-dong, Seoul.*

which were built the dwellings of the members of the tribe. As sedentary life developed, a matriarchal family system was replaced by a patriarchal one as the authority of the tribal chieftain increased.

While honoring *hanŭlnim* ("Lord of Heaven"), often called *ch'ŏnji shinmyŏng* (the "God of the Heaven and the Earth"), as the supreme god, under whom the pantheon of lesser gods were believed to have existed, the Neolithic people practiced primitive animism, demonology and nature worship, which led to the rise of shamanism and the introduction of the magical power of shamans (*mudang*). The people worshiped the sun, the moon, and such natural objects as mountains, old trees, and aged rocks in unusual shapes — believing that these were the dwelling places of spirits of a benevolent as well as a malicious nature — and they regarded unfathomable phenomena of nature to be the workings of such deities. They also practiced ancestor worship, and erected totems (*changsŭng*) at the edge of villages to ward off evil spirits. They seem to have believed that all objects, including the mountains, the rivers and ponds, the wells, and the houses, as well as the earth itself, possessed spirits. They also held a spring festival to pray to heaven for a good harvest, and an autumn festival during which they gave thanks. Meanwhile, shamans (both male and female) developed a "magical formula" for establishing communication between the spirits and humans, the shamans themselves being the mediums. The shamans seem to have believed in the magical power of stars, especially the Big Dipper (*ch'ilsŏng*). Eventually, shamanistic ritual was called *yŏnggo*, and ancestor worship ritual was called *tongmaeng* in Koguryŏ, and a religious ceremony performed to honor Heaven was called *much'ŏn* by the people in Tongye ("Eastern Ye"). Music and dance developed in association with these religious practices and festivals. In addition, there is evidence that the Neolithic people also practiced a bear cult (bear totemism).

Bronze and Iron Cultures. Influenced by the Scytho-Siberian and Chinese cultures around 1,000 B.C., a bronze culture developed in the Liao River region of Manchuria and spread into the Taedong River region in northwest Korea around the seventh century B.C., moving southward, and gradually replacing the Neolithic culture. Perhaps it was at this time that the people in northeastern China, known as Tung-i ("Eastern Barbarians"), migrated to the Korean peninsula, bringing the black pottery culture with them. With superior bronze weapons and a high degree of political organization, the people who brought this new culture to Korea established their domination over the early Neolithic people. Remains of the designless black pottery have been found all over the peninsula, and in the Liao and the Sungari river regions of Manchuria, as well as in Maritime Province.

With the rise of the new culture, a new flat-bottomed *mumun* (designless) pottery replaced the comb-marked and v-shaped pottery of the early Neolithic period. At the same time, red pottery, painted with oxidized iron, appeared.

Bronze implements unearthed in Korea included swords, daggers of various shapes, spear points, knives, bells, mirrors, and various farm implements such as hoes and sickles. Cooking vessels as well as decorative objects such as buttons and rings have also been found. With bronze tools, they produced grooved stone axes as well as highly polished stone tools used to cut down the larger timber for the construction of dwellings. One uniquely Korean item produced with these tools was bronze mirrors. These are different from the Chinese bronze mirrors in that they had two and sometimes three knobs on the back, instead of just one, and the backs were decorated with geometric designs.

Significant among the remains of the late Neolithic and Bronze culture periods were dolmens and menhirs, which were found in nearly all parts of Korea with the exception of the northeastern area. Whereas the purpose behind the menhirs (*sŏndol*), giant stone pillars, is not clear, the dolmens (*koindol*) were tombs of leading members of this age. The tombs of the northwestern area consisted of two parts: burial chamber and

Bronze bells, probably a harness ornament, 8th-7th century B.C.

protective roof. The burial chamber was constructed with four or more large stone slabs, on the top of which was placed a huge flat stone as large as 24 feet by 18 feet and weighing several tons. While some dolmens were located in isolated areas, 40 or 50 dolmens in a group have been found in some northwestern parts of Korea. The southern type of dolmen tombs had a large, flat boulder placed on four or more rocks.

As the bronze culture advanced in the fourth century B.C., iron culture emerged first in the north and then in the southern regions of Korea in the third century B.C. Among the iron implements unearthed have been daggers, picks, swords, spear points, axes, plows, hoes, and sickles, which increased both the military and the economic power of the people of the developing iron culture. During the Iron Age, the prototype of the present-day *ondol* (a device to heat the floor) was adopted.

During the late bronze and iron culture periods, the styles of tomb-building underwent a considerable change. Dolmen were replaced by three types of tombs. The first was a subterranean, rectangular, stone chamber constructed of four or more stone slabs; the second was a 12 feet by 3 feet earthen pit grave; and the third consisted of tombs where two or three large earthenware coffins, containing the dead, were buried. The tombs were covered with varying sizes of stone or earthen mounds, according to the political and social status of the buried.

Discovered in these tombs have been bronze and iron tools, such as weapons, mirrors, belts, armbands, and necklaces, along with other implements. It seems that the recasting of old bronze tools for new ones was commonly practiced due to the scarcity of iron.

From the late Neolithic period onward, various new tribal groups such as the Ye, the Maek, and the Tung-i people migrated to the Korean peninsula, joining other peoples who had already settled there. As a result, considerable political and social changes took place, particularly during the late bronze and iron periods when mounted horseman with iron weapons arrived. Meanwhile, an agricultural economy developed with the cultivation of millet, barley, maize, and rice, as well as the introduction of stock-breeding and cottage handicrafts.

A clay figurine of a woman and several small human figures made of bone have been found, and although it is not clear as to when these were produced, it is believed that they date back to the bronze period. Drawings incised on rocks, believed to be those of the late bronze and iron periods, have also been discovered. A drawing discovered at Yangjŏn-dong in Koryŏng county in North Kyŏngsang Province (formerly the Tae Kaya area) consists of a number of concentric circles in a geometric design, crosses, and human masks. Other drawings discovered at Ch'ŏnjŏn-ri and Pan'gudae in Ulchu county in South Kyŏngsang Province (formerly the Chinhan area) present a variety of geometric designs such as circles, triangles, and diamonds. They also contain drawings of animals such as tigers, deer, boars, and rabbits in pairs, and hunting and fishing scenes showing pictures of whales, tortoises, and other marine life. The meaning behind these rock drawings is not clear, but it is speculated that they had religious significance and were the symbols of the procreative process since a picture of the sun appears with pictures of animals in pairs.

Early Nationhood — Myth and History

Like the histories of other ancient nations, Korea's antiquity is shrouded in clouds of mythology and ambiguity.

Details of petroglyphs incised on Pan'gudae Rock, South Kyŏngsang Province. Top: a tiger at the right, a leopard in the center and the tail of a whale at the left; bottom: a whale at the top and a wolf (upside down) at the bottom.

Primitive rock carvings.
ca. 1200 B.C. Ulchu, North
Kyŏngsang Province.

Scarcity of source material makes the study of its early history difficult and the writing of a factual history almost impossible. Traditionally, Korean history dealing with the northern area before the Christian era has been divided into the Tan'gun Chosŏn, the Kija Chosŏn, and the Wiman Chosŏn periods, covering the time span from 2333 to 108 B.C., which was then succeeded by the period of Chinese domination. Korean history dealing with the southern area generally dates back to the third century B.C.

Myths and legends associated with the founding of early Korean kingdoms are abundant. Marriage between celestial beings and humans, the role played by light in connection with the birth of a leader, the birth of boys from large eggs or chests are all elements of stories to explain the origins of founders of early Korean dynasties or nations.

Old Chosŏn. Much more archaeological and documentary evidence are needed to substantiate the traditional Korean notion regarding Old Chosŏn, which was said to have been established in 2333 B.C. This notion was based on a story in the section dealing with "Ancient Records" in *Memorabilia of the Three Kingdoms (Samguk yusa)* written by the Buddhist Monk Ilyŏn (1206-1289). According to this mythology, Hwanung, son of Hwanin (the God of Creation), descended upon a mountain with three sacred seals and three thousand followers, establishing there a Sacred Town. Thereupon, he commanded the Lords of Wind, Rain and Clouds, attended the planting of grains, regulated the lives of the people, healed sickness, and administered justice, directing more than three hundred and sixty affairs and civilizing human society as he regulated the workings of nature.

Ilyŏn wrote that when a bear and a tiger prayed to

Hwanung to make them human beings, Hwanung gave them each a stalk of mugwart and twenty cloves of garlic (both are used by Koreans as purifying agents) and commanded them to eat them and shun the sunlight for one hundred days. Both followed his instructions, but the bear managed to become a damsel after twenty-one days, while the tiger failed because it could not stay in the cave that long. When the damsel wished to be married, Hwanung changed his form to human and married the woman. She then gave birth to Tan'gun Wanggŏm, who established a kingdom named Chosŏn with its capital at Asadal, in the fiftieth year (2333 B.C.) of the reign of Emperor Yao of the Hsia dynasty of China.

Tan'gun Wanggŏm is said to have ruled Chosŏn as priest (*tan'gun*) and secular ruler (*wanggŏm*) for 1,500 years. Ilyŏn wrote that when the emperor of Chou sent Kija (*Ch'i-tzu* in Chinese) to Korea as king, Tan'gun retired, becoming a mountain deity at the age of 1,908. According to *Historical Records* (*Shi-chi*) of Ssuma Ch'ien of Han China, Kija was a scion of the royal house of the Shang (Yin) dynasty who fled to Korea when the Shang was overthrown by the Chou dynasty around 1122 B.C. Kija then became the king of Chosŏn.

Such a myth as that of the birth of Tan'gun and the founding of Chosŏn, which Ilyŏn included in his book (along with many other myths and legends), may be related to the rise of the tribe with the bear totem, as well as the origin of the belief in the mountain deity. Whereas Tan'gun became the mountain deity, according to legend the tiger became his guard, and over a hundred stories related to benevolent tigers have been created.

Lacking historical and documentary sources, it is impossible to verify any facts that might have been the basis for Ilyŏn's story. Likewise, the story related to Kija cannot be substantiated for lack of evidence. Up to the time of occupation of North Korea by the Communists, there existed a "tomb of Kija" in the vicinity of modern Pyongyang. However, after the partition of Korea, the Communists in the north are said to have excavated Kija's tomb finding nothing inside this huge earthen mound, which resembled those of Shilla kings in modern Kyŏngju.

At the hazy dawn of Korean history, a leader of the tribe with bear totems may have consolidated power and formed a tribal nation named Chosŏn sometime around 2333 B.C. in the modern Liaotung region in southwestern Manchuria with himself as a high priest (*tan'gun*) and secular ruler (*wanggŏm*), and expanded his territory into the Korean peninsula north of the Taedong River. Around 1122 B.C., a Chinese refugee named Kija, from the fallen Shang (Yin) state, may have come to this state and taken over power, thus becoming the new ruler.

Be that as it may, several Chinese sources indicate that there existed in the seventh century B.C. a state named Chosŏn whose territory covered southern Manchuria and northwestern Korea. Its capital was at Wanggŏmsŏng. It had border clashes in the Liao River region with the Chinese state of Yen and traded with another Chinese state named Ch'i during the Spring and Autumn period (770-481 B.C.) and the Warring States period (481-221 B.C.) of China. Whereas some Korean historians believe that the capital of Chosŏn was located in the southern tip of the Liaotung peninsula, others believe that it was located near modern Pyongyang. Whichever the case may be, the fact that there existed a state named Chosŏn with its territory in southwestern Manchuria and northwestern Korea cannot be denied. This state of Chosŏn is given the name of Old Chosŏn by Korean historians in order to distinguish it from the Kingdom of Chosŏn which the Yi dynasty established in 1392.

From about the fourth century B.C., there existed three large tribal states in Manchuria, sharing their borders with Chosŏn. They were Puyŏ in the Sungari River basin, Hsienpei in the west, and Ye in the T'ungchia River basin along the middle reaches of the Yalu River. Ye was a tribal state formed by the Yemaek tribes which migrated out of Puyŏ into southern Manchuria sometime around 300 B.C. Chinese sources indicate that Puyŏ, Ye, and Chosŏn had stern criminal laws, superior military power, and considerable economic strength. Meanwhile, sometime in the second century B.C., two small tribal federations emerged in Korea, namely Imdun in the eastern region and Chinbŏn in the west-central region of the peninsula.

Due to a long period of warfare, first with the Yen and then with the Ch'in states of China, Chosŏn became a smaller kingdom as it lost its territory in Manchuria. In the second century B.C., it was a purely Korean kingdom, bordering Imdun to the east, and Chinbŏn to the south. With the migration of a large number of refugees from the north into the southern regions of Korea, both bronze and iron cultures developed there from the fourth century B.C. Meanwhile, although documentary sources are lacking, it seems that there emerged in the second century B.C. a large, loosely federated state, Chin, consisting of some seventy-eight Han tribes. (See Map 2)

Wiman Chosŏn. When the state of Ch'in overthrew the state of Yen in 222 B.C. in its process of unification of China and the building of the first Chinese empire, a warrior named Wiman fled from Yen to Chosŏn with a large number of troops, becoming a military commander of King Chun of Chosŏn. Wiman, whose true identity is yet to be established, was given a high military post by King Chun to defend the northwestern border of Chosŏn. How-

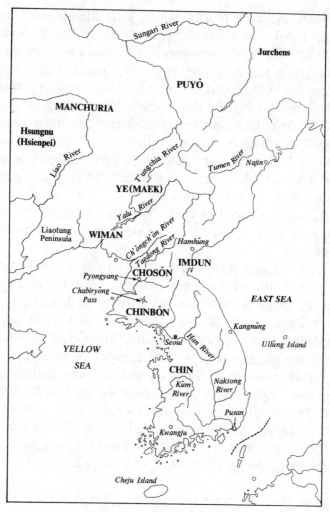

Map 2. KOREA AND MANCHURIA AT THE TIME OF
WIMAN CHOSŎN (2nd Century B.C.)

ever, sometime between 194 and 180 B.C., Wiman
usurped the throne of Chosŏn and became its king, forcing King Chun to flee to the state of Chin in the south.

With its superior military and economic power, Wiman

Chosŏn subjugated its neighboring states of Imdun to the east and Chinbŏn to the south. At the same time, it adopted a hostile policy towards China, now under the rule of the Han dynasty, having overthrown the Ch'in dynasty in 202 B.C. Meanwhile, the ruler of the Ye state voluntarily surrendered to Han China, and the Chinese established a short-lived Ts'anghai Commandery in that region in 128 B.C., which was replaced by the Hsüant'u Commandery in 107 B.C. The extension of Chinese territory in this region antagonized Wiman Chosŏn more, causing it to disrupt China's trade with the Chin state in southern Korea, which then increased tension between Chosŏn and China.

Chinese Invasion of Korea and Its Impact. Emperor Wu of the Han dynasty, facing the hostile policy of Chosŏn, and being fearful of a possible alliance between Chosŏn and the Hsungnu tribes on the northern Chinese frontiers, invaded Chosŏn in 109 B.C., overthrowing Wiman Chosŏn one year later.

Immediately after the fall of Chosŏn, the Han dynasty of China established the three commanderies of Lolang (Nangnang), Chenfan (Chinbŏn), and Lint'un (Imdun), and a year later a fourth, Hsüant'u (Hyŏndo) Commandery in the former territory of the Ye, thus controlling all of Korea north of the Han River except the northeast, as well as southern Manchuria. Each of these commanderies, which were divided into prefectures, was put under a Chinese viceroy, and administered by Chinese officials. Of these, Lolang was the most important with its center of power at Wanggŏmsŏng, militarily and economically in the most strategic location.

These commanderies, while safeguarding China's frontiers, served China's economic interest well by exploiting the natural resources and manpower of the local

regions. In addition to salt and iron ore, timber, agricultural and marine products, and a labor force were
exported to China. In order to minimize local resistance
to Chinese rule, the Chinese government granted Chinese
official titles to local leaders, as well as to those engaged
in trade, encouraged trade between Korea and China, and
indoctrinated the local inhabitants with Chinese culture.

However, as internal disunity grew in China, resistance
of Koreans, as well as challenges from various nomadic
peoples to the north of China, increased. Finally, in 82
B.C., the Chenfan and Lint'un commanderies were
abolished and the Hsüant'u Commandery was relocated to
northwest Manchuria. In Lolang itself, a rebellion took
place when Han China was in political turmoil in the
wake of Wang Mang's usurpation of power (8-23 A.D.).
The rebellion in Lolang was subjugated by 20 A.D., but
its existence became precarious.

In the second century A.D., when Chinese commanderies in Korea were abolished, except for Lolang, the
tribal units of the Yemaek people in the former Imdun region formed two separate states, Okchŏ and Tong'ye
(Eastern Ye). At this juncture, the Chinese victory of
Liaotung put Lolang under its control and established a
new T'aifang (Taebang) Commandery in the former
Chenfan region to protect Lolang. Meanwhile, the
Hsüant'u Commandery in Manchuria was removed
further north, leaving the southern part of Manchuria to
the rapidly rising Koguryŏ. Koguryŏ eventually took over
the Lolang Commandery in 313, and the T'aifang
Commandery shortly thereafter, ending Chinese domination in the north.

The expansion of Chinese control in Manchuria and
the establishment of Chinese commanderies in Korea had
an enormous impact in both regions. To be sure, the
areas dominated by the Chinese were economically

exploited, but the cultural benefits of China that they received were a significant factor in Korean development. Chinese language, philosophy, political concepts and systems, laws, social structures, and art spread in these areas, marking the beginning of a Chinese sphere of cultural influence.

As we shall see later, Chinese influence grew in Korea while such political institutions as kingship, hereditary succession of power from father to son, bureaucracy, and administrative districts were adopted by Puyŏ and Koguryŏ as the usage of coinage and the construction of walled towns spread.

Lolang was by far the most Sinicized. Its administrative center was at Wanggŏmsŏng, a small but well-planned walled city with paved streets, a drainage system, and a cemetery. The roof tiles and bricks it produced had artistic designs and Chinese characters, and the tombs the Chinese built in the present-day Kangsŏ area have left a rich cultural heritage. Meanwhile, far-reaching social changes in Korea resulted from the increase of large clan and tribal solidarity, the intermarriage between Koreans and Chinese, and the migration of Chinese families with clan names.

The Chin State and the Three Han Federations. It is not clear when the Chin state emerged and what its territory was, but it is assumed that sometime in the third century B.C. a loosely formed federation, consisting of some seventy-eight tribal communities, developed and sought direct contact with Han China. It is generally assumed that the Chin state had its center of power at present-day Kwangju, Kyŏnggi Province, which is located in the lower region of the South Han River.

With the influx of an ever-growing number of refugees from the north who brought with them more advanced political skills and metallurgical culture, the political and social structure of the Chin state deteriorated. Out of this process there emerged the three separate political entities of Mahan, Chinhan, and Pyŏnhan, which are collectively known in Korean history as the *Samhan*, or the Three Hans. (See Map 3)

Each Han was a federation of tribal units. Mahan, with fifty-four tribal communities, was located in the central region of the Korean peninsula, just south of the Han River, with its center of power at Hansŏng (now Kwangju), and its territory extended into the southwestern region of the peninsula. Chinhan was made up of twelve tribal communities and located in the southeastern region of Korea, east of the Naktong River, with its center of power in the area called Sŏrabŏl (now Kyŏngju area). Pyŏnhan, made up of twelve tribal communities, occupied the southern end of the peninsula between the Sŏmjin and the Naktong rivers with its centers of power at modern Kimhae and Koryŏng.

Whereas each federation was an alliance of many tribal units, each tribal unit consisted of several clans sharing the same lineage. Each unit had its own chieftain, and chieftains of tribal units in each federation formed a council of chieftains and elected the head of the federation, practicing a rotation system. However, in the first century B.C. with the penetration of Chinese influence from the north and facing a Chinese policy of aggression, these tribal federations increased their solidarity, bringing about a rapid political evolution. Out of this process, the two kingdoms of Paekche and Shilla emerged: Paekche from Mahan and Shilla from Chinhan. Only Pyŏnhan failed to become transformed into a unified kingdom.

The Han federations had a separation of power between secular and religious leaders. While secular leaders were called *shinji* or *ŭpch'a*, religious leader was called *ch'ŏn'gun,* a priest who had his own separate territory, called *sodo,* which enjoyed extra-territorial rights. On *sodo* was erected a tall wooden pole decorated with bells and a drum, indicating that the Han people practiced

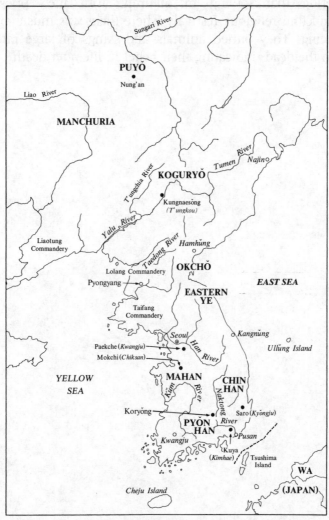

Map 3. CONFEDERATED KINGDOMS IN KOREA AND MANCHURIA
(ca. 3rd Century A.D.)

shamanism. As they developed an agricultural economy, they produced silk, precious metals, and decorative stone jewels. They celebrated spring and autumn festivals, praying to the heaven in spring for a good harvest, and offering thanksgiving in autumn, with the "priest" conducting religious festivals where there was music and dancing. They buried animals and wings of large birds with the dead, indicating their belief in life after death.

2

The Three Kingdoms and Unified Shilla, 57 B.C.-936 A.D.

TRADITIONALLY, Korean history from 57 B.C. to 936 A.D. is divided into two sub-periods: the Three Kingdoms period, (See Map 4) which ended with Shilla's unification of the three kingdoms in 668 A.D., and the Unified Shilla period that ended in 892 A.D. This was followed by a brief Later Three Kingdoms period from 892 to 936 A.D.

The Emergence of the Three Kingdoms

The Rise of the Kingdom of Shilla. The traditional date for the founding of Shilla is 57 B.C., and according to afore-mentioned *Memorabilia of the Three Kingdoms* by Ilyŏn, the legendary founder of Shilla was Hyŏkkŏse. The story goes that he was found in a large egg guarded by a white horse, and he became the progenitor of the Pak clan of the Saro tribe, one of the twelve tribes in Chinhan. When he was found, the council of six tribal chieftains (*Hwabaek*) of Saro elected him to be the first ruler of the

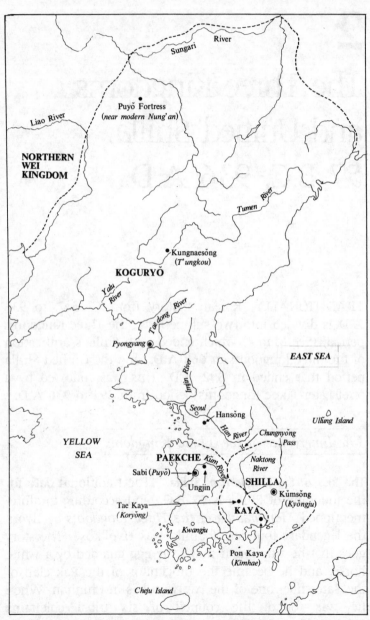

Map 4. KOREA IN THE THREE KINGDOMS PERIOD (ca. 450 A.D.)

Saro state. The same legendary source indicates that the founding ancestor of the Kim clan was Alchi, who was found in a large golden chest guarded by a mysterious bird, and the ancestor of the Sŏk clan was T'alhae, who was found in a chest on a boat drifting along the shores of Sŏra. Both Alchi's descendants and T'alhae and his descendants became rulers of the Saro state. Thus, these men of reputed divine origins became the founders of the three royal clans that ruled Shilla on a rotation basis until 356.

Claiming such divine origins, these clans appropriated unique, privileged status, increasing their political power. Thus, of the fifty-five rulers of Shilla, eleven were from the house of Pak, eight from the Sŏk clan, and the remaining thirty-six (including three queens) were from the house of Kim. Hyŏkkŏse was the first Shilla ruler, T'alhae was the fourth ruler, and the first ruler from the house of Kim was Alchi's grandson, who was the thirteenth Shilla "king."

The Saro tribe of six clans, armed with such mythology and being situated in the fertile region of Sŏrabŏl, increased its power, and, conquering its neighboring tribes, brought about the end of Chinhan and the rise of the state of Saro (later renamed Shilla). Instead of being called "kings," the rulers of the Saro state employed such titles as *kŏsŏgan, ch'ach'aung, isagŭm,* and *maripkan* in the early period of Shilla.

The Rise of the Kingdom of Paekche. The traditional date for the founding of the Kingdom of Paekche is 18 B.C., and a total of thirty-one kings ruled up to 660 A.D. In accordance with Ilyŏn's book, the founder of Paekche was Onjo, a son of Chumong (founder of Koguryŏ), of the Puyŏ lineage of the Kyeru tribe, who fled from Koguryŏ to Mahan. During the period between 28 and 234 A.D., his successors increased both political and military power, nurturing the strength of the Paekche tribe located in the fertile region of the South Han River basin. By 235 A.D., its power was greater than that of Mahan itself.

Situation in Pyŏnhan. Of the three Han federations, Pyŏnhan was the only one that did not emerge as a unified kingdom. However, Pyŏnhan, which had twelve tribal units, was consolidated into six separate Kaya (Karak) states. The two most developed among them were Pon Kaya at the mouth of the Naktong River and Tae Kaya in its middle reaches. These two joined with others forming the Kaya federation.

Kaya, like Paekche, was much more advanced than Saro. It produced more and better iron goods, its food supply was abundant, its weaving industry was prosper-

Stoneware duck-shaped vessel excavated from a Kaya tomb.

ous, and its pottery was superb. It had advanced art and music, producing such musical instruments as a twelve-string *kayagŭm* ("Kaya zither"). It traded with Koguryŏ, which emerged in Manchuria and extended its territory in the Korean peninsula, as well as Japan, promoting close cultural ties with Japan. But Kaya states neglected the development of military art and spirit. As a result, caught in the power struggle between Paekche and Saro, it was harassed by both until Pon Kaya fell to Saro in 532 A.D., and Tae Kaya and other Kaya states succumbed to Saro in 562 A.D.

The Rise of Koguryŏ and Its Becoming a Korean Kingdom. According to Ilyŏn, the Kingdom of Koguryŏ was founded in 37 B.C. by Chumong, who had lived in Puyŏ. Chumong is given magical origins by the legend that tells that he emerged from an egg.

Chumong later fled from Puyŏ south to the Ye area, and with the help of those five tribes who followed him established a new nation named Koguryŏ, and became its first king (Tongmyŏng). The people of Koguryŏ honored Chumong as the founder of the kingdom by observing the harvest festival named *tongmaeng*.

Establishing his center of power at T'ungkou (T'onggu in Korean, later renamed Kungnaesŏng) in the north side of the middle reaches of the Yalu River, Chumong and his immediate successors built a strong foundation for the new monarchy and nation and expanded the territory of Koguryŏ, first by conquering the Chinese-held Liaotung region in the first century A.D., then Okchŏ and Tong'ye (Eastern Ye) in the northeast littoral of Korea in the second century, making Koguryŏ a Korean kingdom.

Unlike the state of Puyŏ, which was located in the Sungari River region in Manchuria, older and economically developed by virtue of being located in the region where arable and pasture lands were plentiful, Koguryŏ was located in the mountainous regions, south of Puyŏ. In order to survive and grow, Koguryŏ needed to develop strong military power, becoming an aggressive state.

Political Development and External Affairs of the Three Kingdoms

The early rulers of the newly emerged kingdoms carried out aggressive nation-building plans, and by the middle of the third century all three kingdoms in Korea became full-fledged nations, bringing a long period of warfare. In the end, Shilla, in collaboration with T'ang China, overthrew Paekche and Koguryŏ, unifying the three kingdoms.

Political Change and External Affairs of Koguryŏ. The monarchical power was strengthened by the sixth ruler, King T'aejo ("Great Progenitor," reigned 53-146 A.D.), who elevated the Kyeru clan to the royal house, adopted hereditary kingship, and expanded its territory into the Korean peninsula. The ninth ruler, King Kogukch'ŏn (reigned 179-196) strengthened the central bureaucracy, and improved the administration of the kingdom by dividing it into five provinces. He replaced the brother-to-brother succession system with that of the father-to-son system.

Between 219 and 300 A.D., Koguryŏ faced serious threats from the Chinese states of Wei and Chin, as well as from the Hsienpei nomads. But when King Mich'ŏn (reigned 300-331) took the throne, Koguryŏ not only removed these threats successfully, but also conquered the Chinese commanderies of Lolang in 313, and T'aifang shortly thereafter. After the conquest of these regions, however, Koguryŏ suffered a severe blow first at the hands of the Earlier Yen (a state established by the Hsienpei in northern China) in 342 when its troops sacked the capital of Koguryŏ, and then at the hands of Paekche when its troops invaded the Koguryŏ territory and killed its king in battle in 371.

Between 371 and 491 the two kings, Kwanggaet'o and Changsu, strengthened national defense and expanded the territory, relocated the capital of the kingdom in 472 from T'ungkou to Wanggŏmsŏng (modern Pyongyang) in Korea and improved the political structure by adopting the twelve-grade official rank system. Some 170 garrison towns were constructed during this period as economic growth was brought about, more food was produced and salt and fish were exported.

Koguryŏ was ruled by eight kings between 491 and 660, but they were mediocre rulers and the power of the kingdom began to decline. It lost the Han River basin, as well as the southeastern region, to Shilla in 551, as it faced the growing Chinese threats. At this juncture Koguryŏ made peace with Paekche, and entered into a period of warfare with Shilla.

In the wars with the forces of the Sui dynasty of China in 589 and 612, Koguryŏ successfully blocked Sui expansionism, thanks to a decisive military victory won by a Koguryŏ commander Ŭlchi Mundŏk at the Battle of the Salsu (now Ch'ŏngch'ŏn River) in 612. However, Koguryŏ faced the ambitious T'ang dynasty that succeeded the Sui dynasty in 618. Despite the bloodshed that the king brought against his opponents in the 620s, and a military *coup* of commander Yŏn Kaesomun in 642, which dethroned the king and exercised the military dictatorship that he had established, Koguryŏ was able to win a series of military victories against the T'ang forces that invaded Korea several times between 645 and 656.

These victories against the Chinese prevented certain conversion of the entire Korean peninsula into a Chinese colony by the T'ang dynasty, but these wars depleted the national strength of Koguryŏ as it faced hostile Paekche and Shilla to the south. It should be remembered that neither Paekche nor Shilla alone was able to repel Chinese armies in the middle of the seventh century.

Political Development and Foreign Affairs of Paekche. Paekche maintained peaceful ties with Chinese states, and quickly borrowed Chinese patterns. Thus, in 260 King Koi (reigned 234-286), who was regarded as the founder-king of Paekche by its people, established a Chinese-type bureaucracy with six ministries as he adopted a system of ranking officials into sixteen grades and designated the colors of robes of these officials. As he promoted the power of Paekche, expanding its territory, Mahan moved its capital to modern Iksan, North Chŏlla Province, leaving Paekche free to strengthen its power in the central region of Korea with its capital at Hansŏng (modern Kwangju) in the lower Han River basin.

The national power of Paekche grew during the reign of Kŭnch'ogo (346-375), who established the system of father-to-son succession of kingship on a permanent basis. He had a scholar named Ko Hŭng compile a history of Paekche known as *Sŏgi*. With the help of the Wa (Japanese) people on northern Kyūshū, he absorbed Mahan in 369 and in 371 he sacked Wanggŏmsŏng, killing the Koguryŏ king in battle. He also prevented the take-over of the Kaya region by the Wa people.

The Paekche kings of the period between 375 and 385 improved Paekche's relationship with Japan by sending to that country books, artisans, musicians and Buddhist monks, making Buddhism a state religion in 384. However, their successors, most of whom had short reigns, lacked ability and foresight. In 475, Koguryŏ launched its aggressive war in the Han River region, during which the Paekche king was captured and beheaded. When Koguryŏ took over the capital of Hansŏng, Paekche moved its capital to Ungjin (modern Kongju) in present-day South Ch'ungch'ŏng Province.

During the 479-523 period, Paekche regained its national strength, and it concluded a marriage alliance with Shilla against Koguryŏ, constructed more military defense structures, reorganized the nation's administrative districts into twenty-two, conquered the island of T'amna (now Chejudo), and strengthened its relations with Japan. However, after 523, as Paekche faced ever-increasing hostility from Koguryŏ, it moved its capital further south to Sabi (modern Puyŏ), dividing the kingdom, whose size was reduced, into five provinces.

With a noble but unrealistic notion, the Paekche kings after 523 attempted to regain the national strength based on a spiritual (religious) foundation, instead of military and economic power. Buddhism flourished, many beautiful statues of Bodhisattva Maitreya were produced, and many famous temples and pagodas were constructed, but the nation did not become stronger while Shilla grew increasingly aggressive. When in 554, Shilla, breaking its marriage alliance, drove Paekche out of the lower Han River region, the Paekche king struck back, only to be killed in battle. From this point, Paekche's decline was rapid.

Political Change and the Growing Strength of Shilla. Shilla, which had been far behind Koguryŏ and Paekche in terms of national development, rose rapidly during and after the reign of the seventeenth ruler, Naemul Maripkan (reigned 354-402). It was he who strengthened the monarchical authority and the power of the house of Kim, and in alliance with Koguryŏ checked Paekche's expansion into Kaya. When Koguryŏ grew too powerful, in 433 Shilla allied this time with Paekche against the northern foe, while establishing a friendly tie with Japan by sending some eighty-eight musicians to that country. This was followed by the conclusion of a marriage alliance between the houses of Kim of Shilla and Puyŏ of Paekche.

Between 458 and 600, the authority of the central government was strengthened when the six Saro tribal communities in Sŏrabŏl were replaced by six administrative districts. The establishment in 487 of post stations improved the networks of communication and transportation between the capital and key points in the kingdom.

When the twenty-second ruler Chijŭng (reigned 500-514) took the throne, he adopted the title of king (*wang*), discarding the previously used titles such as *maripkan* and others. In 512, he subjugated the island of Ullŭng in the Sea of Japan. At this juncture, Shilla was officially adopted as the name of the kingdom, with Kŭmsŏng (now Kyŏngju) as its capital.

The process of nation-building advanced during the reign of King Pŏp'ŭng (reigned 514-540). It was he who established the Ministry of Defense in 516, adopted a new code of administrative laws in 520, along with the seventeen-grade official rank structure of the central government, including the color of official robes, and instituted the Bone Rank (*kolp'um*) system which was applied to the aristocracy. He was the first Shilla ruler to adopt the reigning era name of *Kŏnwŏn* ("Initiated Beginning") in 536. His adoption of Buddhism in 527 was a milestone in Shilla's cultural development. By conquering Pon Kaya in 532, he expanded the territory of Shilla in the fertile region of the lower Naktong River.

During the reign of King Chinhŭng (540-576), Shilla further expanded its territory when it took over the

Koguryŏ domain in the upper Han River basin. Then, in 562, Shilla overthrew Tae Kaya in the fertile region in the middle reaches of the Naktong River, where a huge amount of iron was produced. King Chinhŭng pushed the northern frontiers of Shilla far into northeastern Korea, taking away the former Okchŏ and Tongye regions from Koguryŏ. After conquering the region that is now in the southern part of South Hamgyŏng Province, where a large amount of fish and salt was produced, he erected two large stone monuments and fortresses along the new frontiers of his kingdom as he had done elsewhere. (See Map 5) Finally, in 584, the marriage alliance with Paekche was broken and Shilla took over the lower Han River area.

As territorial expansion took place, the government structure of Shilla underwent further change. Four new ministries were established in the late sixth century, followed by the establishment in 651 of the Royal Chancellery as the top organ of the government, overshadowing the Council of Nobles (*Hwabaek*).

One of the significant developmental aspects of Shilla in the sixth century was the rise of its military strength. Early Shilla military consisted of a small number of royal guards whose primary function was to protect the ruler and the capital, and to serve as a striking force in time of war. However, as the frequency of war with both Koguryŏ and Paekche increased, six garrisons were established, one in each district, and in 583 the royal guards were reorganized into six units of sworn banners, or *sŏdang*. In 625, another *sŏdang* was organized. Local defense and security was maintained by garrison soldiers under the command of local governors.

The rise of *hwarang* or "flowery youth" units was another important aspect in connection with the rise of the military strength of Shilla. Although the origins of

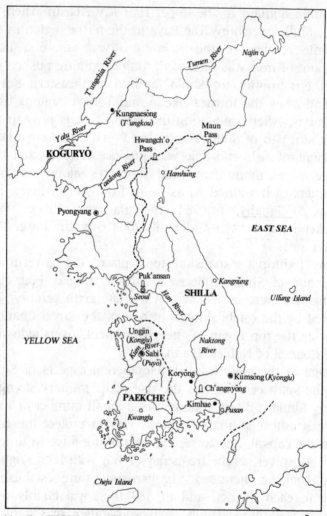

Map 5. TERRITORIAL EXPANSION OF SHILLA UNDER KING CHINHŬNG
(ca. 570) (⌂ Location of Stone Monuments)

hwarang groups are obscure, they were comprised of unmarried sons of aristocratic families who had formed
social groups for the purpose of training their minds and
bodies. Practicing nature worship, these bands of youths

roamed the land in search of the right places for mental and physical training, loving wine, women, and song. At the same time, they developed a martial spirit and military skills.

In 576, the king converted these social groups into elite military units and gave them a variety of military training. After that they were indoctrinated with the "Five Injunctions for Mundane Life," written by a Buddhist monk, which stressed loyalty to the sovereign, filial piety to one's parents, fidelity toward one's friends, bravery and high sense of mission, and respect of the sanctity of life (avoidance of indiscriminate killing). These injunctions consisted of what is known as *Hwarang-do*, or "The Way of Hwarang."

In 642 Shilla suffered a military defeat when Paekche launched a last desperate war against Shilla, taking some forty fortresses in the former Kaya region from Shilla. At this juncture, Shilla sought Koguryŏ's assistance by dispatching its crown prince, Kim Ch'un-ch'u, who later became King Muyŏl, to the capital of Koguryŏ. His mission, however, failed when Koguryŏ demanded a large territorial concession of Shilla in the Han River region. Shilla also sought assistance from China, and the T'ang government dispatched a peace-making envoy to Korea, but he was caught and imprisoned in Koguryŏ.

Muyŏl took over the throne as T'aejong ("Great Progenitor") in 654 after the reign of two queens, and strengthened the dynastic rule of the house of Kim by abolishing the stipulation that the king's mother had to be a member of the house of Pak. Meanwhile, he strengthened the military power of the kingdom in collaboration with his brother-in-law, Kim Yu-shin. His plans were continued by his son who succeeded to the throne and prepared for the conquest of both Paekche and Koguryŏ.

The Rise and Fall of Unified Shilla

Shilla's Unification of the Three Kingdoms. After suffering a defeat at the hands of Paekche in 642, Shilla strengthened its military posture while securing China's agreement to provide military assistance against both Paekche and Koguryŏ.

A full-scale war against Paekche commenced in 660 when China sent its forces against Paekche as the Shilla forces under Kim Yu-shin launched their offensive on land from the east. Paekche, although it received Japanese military assistance, was unable to counter the invading forces, and the king surrendered to the commanders of the joint forces. After the fall of Paekche in 660, futile efforts were made between 660 and 663 by the royalities of Paekche, in cooperation with the Japanese, to restore Paekche.

While fighting the Paekche revivalists, in 661 the T'ang forces attacked the capital of Koguryŏ for the purpose of reclaiming northern Korea for China. The Chinese alone were unable to take the capital and it was not until the Shilla forces arrived, fresh from the victory against Paekche, that a joint attack began in 667, forcing the last Koguryŏ king to surrender to the allies in 668. The fighting continued, however, for another two years when those who refused to surrender fought a futile war to save their nation. With the help of China, Shilla was able to bring about the destruction of both Paekche and Koguryŏ.

Shilla-T'ang Conflict. Shilla and T'ang China were subsequently to become entangled in a struggle for territorial control. The T'ang government displayed unmistakable signs that it had no desire to see the emergence or a unified Korea under Shilla, or allow Shilla's frontiers to reach the Yalu-Tumen River region, let alone extend into Manchuria.

The clash of interests between Shilla and China took place in the former Paekche area, even before the fall of Koguryŏ, when the Chinese established the Ungjin Commandery of China in occupied Paekche with a former Paekche prince as its governor, and forced the Shilla king to conclude a treaty of friendship with him. Not only that, the T'ang government attempted to reduce the Kingdom of Shilla to the status of a Chinese commandery. After the fall of Koguryŏ, the Chinese created nine Chinese commanderies in Koguryŏ's former territory, and then they established the Protectorate-General to Pacify the East at the former Koguryŏ capital of Pyongyang, giving it jurisdiction not only over these nine commanderies, but also over Shilla and the former Paekche region as well. Needless to say, none of these were acceptable to Shilla. In the end, Shilla launched an all-out war against the T'ang forces and their puppets, driving them out of Korea in 676.

Meanwhile, taking advantage of an insurrection by the Khitans against T'ang, a former Koguryŏ general, who had been taken to the Liao area as a prisoner of the T'ang forces, escaped to eastern Manchuria, leading a band of followers. Then, in 698 he established a new state of Chin (renamed in 713 as Parhae), with himself as king, in the former territory of Puyŏ which had been taken over by Koguryŏ in the fourth century. Parhae's subjects included the Koguryŏ people, the Khitans, and a large number of Malgals (predecessors of the Jurchens, later Manchus).

Thus, in the process of Shilla's unification of the three kingdoms, Koguryŏ's former territory in western Manchuria was lost to China while its eastern region and northeastern Korea became the territory of Parhae. The area north of the Taedong River in northwestern Korea became the region where a large number of the Malgals resided.

Shilla After the Unification of Korea. After unifying the three kingdoms, Shilla's legal code was revised, the monarchical authority was further strengthened, many aristocrats were purged, and the power of the president of the Council of Nobles was weakened by the kings of the late seventh and eighth centuries.

The structure of the central government was also expanded by the addition of new ministries and departments. In 674, the system of grading the provincial officials into eleven ranks was adopted, and in 685 the kingdom was redistricted into nine provinces—three in the former area of Shilla-Kaya, three in the former area of Paekche, and three in the former Koguryŏ area. Each province was divided into prefectures, each prefecture into counties, and each county into villages. Below the village level were smaller districts called *hyang, so,* and *pugok* where slave laborers were settled. At the same time, five sub-capitals were established to increase the administrative control of the central government over the enlarged kingdom. (See Map 6) When these sub-capitals were established, aristocratic families of the conquered areas were relocated in those places as prisoners-of-war as other rebellious people were forced into unfree status or became slaves.

In 689, the Shilla government abolished the system of granting "stipend land" to local officials, replacing it with the new "office land" system whereby local officials were given smaller amounts of land as their source of income by collecting only grain tax from the peasants in those areas, rather than owning the land themselves. Then in the early eighth century, the king began to distribute farmlands to free farmers between the age of 20 and 60. Such steps were taken with clear intentions to increase the direct taxing power of the central government while reducing the increase of privately-owned lands. Among the taxes collected by the central government were grain and military taxes in goods, and labor tax. The old

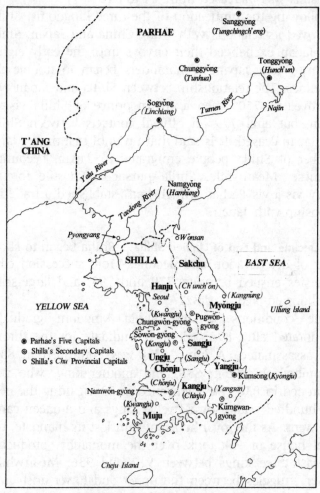

Map 6. ADMINISTRATIVE DIVISIONS OF UNIFIED SHILLA

system of granting a sizeable amount of land to meritorious persons was maintained for a while, but it too was to be abolished toward the end of the Shilla period.

The defense structure was also reorganized with the increase of the number of royal guards (sŏdang) in the capital from two to nine units, and the number of local garrisons was increased from six to ten.

Following the unification of the three kingdoms, Shilla improved its relations with T'ang China and Japan. Shilla and Japan exchanged their envoys until the early eighth century when Japanese marauders began to trouble the coastlines. The relationship between Shilla and Japan was improved in 750 when a crown prince of Shilla visited Japan, but after 779 all official contacts between Shilla and Japan ceased. It is said that up until that time a large number of Shilla people emigrated to Japan, becoming Japanese. Meanwhile, Shilla pursued a hostile foreign policy vis-à-vis Parhae, which had established a trade relationship with Japan.

The Decline and End of Unified Shilla.   Shilla began to show signs of deterioration and decline. More succession controversies ensued between 779 and 798, and large-scale rebellions erupted after 822.

The conditions in the Shilla kingdom gradually deteriorated after 836, when a candidate for the throne was assassinated. A king, who was enthroned in 836, committed suicide in 838, and another king, who was enthroned in 838, was dethroned in 839. During the next one hundred years, some twelve kings and a queen came and went. As the royal house of Kim lost its mandate, the royal house of Pak took over the monarchy, producing the last three kings between 912 and 936. Meanwhile, power struggles between the upper and lower aristocrats increased in intensity. Seeing the chaotic situation arising in the capital, the peasants revolted under certain bandit leaders. The kingdom was doomed. Meanwhile, Shilla's foreign trade, which had flourished under the leadership of Chang Po-go, collapsed with his assassination in 846 in a power struggle.

Taking advantage of the prevailing conditions, and plagued by tax increases by the central government, the number of bandits increased, and in 839 Shilla witnessed the eruption of a large-scale rebellion in the former Paekche area. The Shilla government was unable to deal with the situation, and in 892 a rebel established the Kingdom of Later Paekche. At the same time, another rebel, Kung'ye, established the Kingdom of Later Koguryŏ in 901 in the central region of Korea, bringing the Later Three Kingdoms period.

In 918, Wang Kŏn, a leading subordinate of Kung'ye, rebelled against his master, overthrowing the Kingdom of Later Koguryŏ. When Wang Kŏn took over the throne, he changed the name of the kingdom to Koryŏ, and established his capital at Song'ak (renamed Kaegyŏng, now Kaesŏng).

Warfare among Shilla, Later Paekche, and Koryŏ ensued. In 927, the king of Later Paekche sacked the capital of Shilla, killing the Shilla king. At the request of the new king of Shilla, Wang Kŏn of Koryŏ dispatched his troops against the troops of Later Paekche in 935. In that year, the last Shilla king voluntarily surrendered to Koryŏ, ending the long history of the Kingdom of Shilla. In 936, Wang Kŏn overthrew the Kingdom of Later Paekche by force, thus uniting Korea, this time without foreign military assistance.

3

Social, Economic, and Cultural Development, 57 B.C.-936 A.D.

DURING the Three Kingdoms and Unified Shilla periods, significant social and economic changes took place as a profound cultural transformation occurred on the Korean peninsula. As time passed, tribes were divided into clans, and clans into family units as communal living gave way to an entirely new social structure. As the population increased, and political and social conditions changed, economic activity expanded and was diversified. With the influx of Chinese cultural influences, the cultural patterns of the people likewise underwent fundamental changes.

New Social Patterns

The rise of aristocracy and the institutions that developed in each kingdom were among the most significant social changes. In Koguryŏ, the five tribes that built the new nation constituted the aristocracy. While some conquered people were given commoner status, most of them—as well as criminals—were enslaved. In Paekche, a similar social structure emerged with the Paekche tribal members and those of their allies constituting the aristocracy. As the Paekche tribe increased its power and subjugated other tribes, some of the conquered people became commoners while some others were incorporated into the aristocracy. The majority of the conquered people, however, and all criminals were enslaved.

In Shilla, the members of the six tribes that occupied the area known as Sŏrabŏl and built the new kingdom became aristocrats, and most of the members of other tribes that were subjugated by them became "ordinary people," although some of them were given low ranks in the aristocracy. In Shilla, as in Koguryŏ and Paekche, many of the conquered people and criminals became slaves, who resided and worked in restricted areas called *hyang, so,* and *pugok.*

Most of the slaves were under the direct control of the government in all three kingdoms, and many of the established families, as well as some commoners, owned slaves and domestic servants. In all three kingdoms, these unfree people (slaves, as well as butchers, grave-diggers, and others who were engaged in manual labor) were called the "low-born" people.

Another important aspect of social change was the rise of clan names. During the tribal period, and up to the end of the three Han federations period, Koreans were identified by their given names and the names of the tribes to which they belonged. However, with growing contact with China and the influx of Chinese, new clan names of the aristocratic families appeared. Although some clan names had two Chinese characters, most Korean clans adopted single Chinese character surnames. Buddhist monks abandoned their original names, adopting religious names, but the commoners and the "low-born" people were not permitted to adopt surnames.

As has been discussed earlier, the founders of the three kingdoms and certain early kings of Shilla were known by clan names that originated in mythology. Among the royal clans of Shilla were such names as Pak, Sŏk, and Kim. In Koguryŏ, in addition to the royal clan surname of Ko, such Chinese-style surnames as Yŏn and Tae were adopted, and in Paekche such surnames of aristocratic families as Kuk, Mok, Paek, and Sa appeared, in addition to the surname of the royal house Puyŏ.

Following the adoption of clan names by the royal houses of Shilla, in 33 A.D. the king gave new clan names to the remaining three Saro tribal units and others, and such clan names as Yi, Ch'oe, Chŏng, and Sŏl appeared. After that, the kings gave certain meritorious individuals new surnames, giving rise to new clan names such as An, Kwŏn, Nam, and Wang. Meanwhile, more Chinese with different clan names immigrated to the peninsula, influencing other Koreans to adopt these Chinese clan names. As a result, many Korean clan names identical to those of the Chinese appeared after 580 A.D. Therefore, it became necessary for the Koreans to identify themselves by blood line. The identification of blood relationships was usually associated with the locality (*pon'gwan*) where the clan name originated. Marriage between a man and a woman who had the same *pon'gwan* was prohibited, no matter how distantly they were related by blood.

The Bone Rank system that was instituted in 516 in Shilla classified the Shilla aristocrats into several categories. It consisted of two divisions: the "bone" rank and the "quality" rank. The bone category consisted of the Sacred Bone group and the True Bone group. The "quality" rank was divided into six "head-ranks," with the sixth head-rank at the top, followed by the fifth and the fourth ranks, which were assigned to lesser aristocrats. Although it is not certain, the head-ranks three, two and one may have been assigned to the other free peoples who were not given the privilege to secure government offices. Only those who held the True Bone status and those in the head-ranks six, five, and four were qualified to hold certain ministerial posts, as the following chart shows:

Bone Rank Grades	The 17 Office Ranks																
	1	2	3	4	5	6	7	8	9	10	11	12	13	14	15	16	17
True Bone Head-rank	─	─	─	─	─	─	─	─	─	─	─	─	─	─	─	─	─
Six						─	─	─	─	─	─	─	─	─	─	─	─
Five										─	─	─	─	─	─	─	─
Four												─	─	─	─	─	─
Government Posts																	
Yŏng	─	─	─	─	─												
Kyŏng						─	─	─	─								
Taesa										─	─	─	─				
Saji											─	─	─				
Sa												─	─	─	─	─	─

RELATIONSHIP OF BONE RANK GRADUATION TO OFFICE RANKS AND POST

Evidently, the population in Shilla after 688 was registered in six categories based on age and sex—these included able-bodied men and women, adolescents, pre-adolescents, small children, the aging, and the aged—for the purpose of mobilizing them for labor service, as well as allocating farmlands for them to cultivate for the aristocrats. Apparently, the Shilla government took a triennial census after 668, wherein households in the villages were classified into nine categories in accordance with the number of able-bodied adults they contained.

An important aspect of social development was the rise of a class of artisans and skilled workers, such as gold and silversmiths, metal workers, carpenters, masons, painters, and ceramic workers.

Patterns of Economic Development

As the aristocratic social order emerged in all three kingdoms, the pattern of land ownership changed. With the new concept of the ownership of all lands by the throne, each government made land grants to members of the royal house and to those individuals who rendered meritorious services to the founding and strengthening of the new dynasty. The royal house itself in each kingdom kept a large amount of land as its own source of income, while a sizable amount of land was kept in the hands of the government as its source of tax revenue. Later, in Paekche and Shilla, the land-grant systems known as the "tax village" and the "stipend village" were adopted. A "tax village" was a large area of land that included several villages given in perpetuity to a meritorious subject; a "stipend village" was a small area of land entrusted to a government official as his source of income for the duration of his official appointment. In 689, Shilla's "stipend land" system was briefly replaced by the "office land" system, which allowed the grantee to collect only grain tax from the inhabitants of the area.

Buddhist temples and monasteries in Paekche and Shilla also received large land grants. Their land holdings increased when an increasing number of aristocratic families who were Buddhists donated lands. In addition, aristocratic families made land donations in order to escape the tax burden. As a result, in 662, a Shilla king issued an ineffective edict prohibiting such donations.

Land reclamation was carried out by both the government and individuals in all three kingdoms. Those lands reclaimed by individuals became privately-owned land. Food production increased with the expansion of farmland, coupled with the introduction of plowing by oxen in 562 in Shilla, and the construction of irrigation systems in both Shilla and Paekche. It appears that in all three kingdoms there was a large number of wandering farm hands who were called "floating farmers."

Whereas the establishment of post stations in Shilla in the latter half of the fifth century improved communication and transportation, the increase of products such as iron and leather goods manufactured by the unfree people in *hyang*, *so*, and *pugok* areas improved the economy of Shilla. Stock raising, leather works, and manufacturing in general were done at these localities. The establishment of markets and shops in 490 in the capital of Shilla clearly showed that a market economy was developing in that kingdom.

Although all three kingdoms were engaged in foreign trade in the form of government tribute missions, it was Shilla that promoted foreign trade as such, allowing private trade with China and Japan. Despite the issuance of a ban by the T'ang court against private trading in the late eighth century, private trade between Korea and China grew steadily. Some thirty or forty ports on the south and west coasts of Korea were engaged in foreign trade. Korea imported books, hand-crafted goods (art work, decorative objects), and high-quality silk from China, while exporting to both China and Japan such items as raw materials, gold, silver and iron goods, salt, textile fabrics including hemp cloth, and ginseng.

Until his death in 846, Chang Po-go of Shilla dominated the trade between Korea and China as well as between Korea and Japan. In 828, Chang established the Ch'ŏnghae Garrison of 10,000 men on the Island of Wando, off the southwest coast of Korea, as well as colonies of Koreans (called Shilla Quarters) in the Shantung and Kiangsu areas of China, a Buddhist temple in Shantung, and also a maritime empire, while reducing piracy in the sea lanes of the Yellow Sea and the Korea Strait. After his death, the Ch'ŏnghae Garrison was abolished and Shilla's foreign trade collapsed.

Cultural Development

Profound change occurred in Korea during the Three Kingdoms and the Unified Shilla periods as societies became more organized and economic conditions improved. Confucianism, Taoism, Buddhism and other cultural influences that arrived from abroad found a fertile soil and flourished in Korea. While Confucianism, and to a certain degree Taoism, found adherents in the ruling class, Buddhism became the religion of the majority.

The Arrival and Development of Buddhism. Although Buddhism may have entered Koguryŏ and Kaya sometime in the first century A.D., the official date of the arrival of Buddhism to Koguryŏ is said to be 372 A.D. when a Chinese monk arrived. Be that as it may, evidence shows that it did not make any significant impact in that kingdom, although a few renowned Buddhist monks and scholars emerged and some temples were built. Evidently, all Buddhist temples of Koguryŏ were constructed of wood, and so were eventually destroyed by war and other causes.

Buddhism, which migrated southward, became a strong religion in Paekche following the arrival of a Chinese monk in 384. The first Buddhist temple in Paekche was built in 385, and Buddhism became the state religion of the country. Buddhism was introduced to Shilla by a Koguryŏ monk in the fifth century, but it did not receive official sanction until after the martyrdom of Ich'adon in 527. With the arrival of more Koguryŏ monks in Shilla after 551, Buddhism became the religion of the ruling class. In 553, the Pulguk Temple and other renowned temples were built, followed by the construction of many others in the seventh century.

Buddhism grew in popularity as it promised the faithful not only salvation in the land of the Western Paradise, but also provided answers to many questions regarding birth and rebirth and the causes of pain and the ways to eliminate it, as well as protection for the state and the well-being of the people. It brought about intellectual growth, the Festival of Eight Vows, and the Assemblies for Sutra Recitation by One Hundred Monks. Moreover, with the development of Buddhism in Paekche and Shilla, new forms and styles of music and musical instruments and art and architecture developed, while countless elegant and graceful statues of Buddha and Maitreya were produced, witnessing the rise, not only of religious zeal, but also artistic tastes and metallurgical and engineering skills.

As intellectual activities and religious studies grew rapidly, many eminent monks emerged in Korea, and many Korean monks who traveled to China and India brought new Buddhist doctrines, establishing various sects. Among those monks were Shilla monks such as Hyech'o, who traveled to India and authored *Record of the Journey to the Five Indian Kingdoms*; Hyŏn'gwang, who brought the doctrine of *Ch'ŏnt'ae* (*T'ient'ai* in Chinese); Ŭisang, who studied in China and brought the *Hwaŏm* sect to Shilla; and Wŏnhyo, who propagated the doctrine of the

Chǒngt'o ("Pure Land") sect, and authored many books, including *Treatises on the Harmonization of Disputes among the Ten Schools of Buddhism,* which pleaded for the unity of all Buddhist sects. Much like Christianity in Europe after the fourth century, Buddhism in Korea became a force that formed the cultural unity of the people in all three kingdoms.

The golden age of Buddhism arrived following Shilla's unification of the three kingdoms as new sects emerged, joining other sects that had already been established. Among these new sects were the *Sǒn* (*Zen* in Japanese), the *Chin'ǒn* ("True Word"), and the *Chǒngt'o* ("Pure Land"). Eventually, the *Sǒn*, or "Contemplative School," and the *Kyo*, or "Textual School," became the two divisions of Korean Buddhism. Whereas the *Sǒn* emphasized sudden enlightenment through individual efforts, the *Kyo* branch, which included the *Chǒngt'o* and other sects, emphasized the observation of rules and dependence on the mercy of Buddha for the salvation of souls.

The construction of such temples as Pǒmǒ in 671, the reconstruction of the Pulguk Temple and the construction of the Sǒkkuram grotto temple in 751-790, and the construction of the Pongdǒk Temple in 771, to mention only a few, clearly reflected the strength of Buddhism and the devotion of the people to it. In 807, the renowned Haein Temple on Mt. Kaya was built as a combined headquarters of the *Sǒn* and the *Kyo* branches of Buddhism, but the merger of the two did not take place at that time.

It is said that at one time on the South Mountain near the capital of Shilla there were over one hundred small Buddhist temples, eighty outdoor statues of Buddha, and sixty small pagodas. Most of these temples and pagodas have perished, but there still remain many statues of Buddha. Some of them are free standing, but many of them were sculptured in the face of large rocks. It is believed that when the synthesis between Buddhism and the primitive practice of rock worship took place, "more human-like" faces of Buddha were sculptured on rocks of unusual size and shape.

In addition to many temples, hundreds of stupas were constructed to honor certain monks, and many huge bronze bells were cast and dedicated at these temples. Among the renowned pagodas built were the Lion Pagoda of the Hwaŏm Temple, and the elegant Tabo ("Many Treasures"), the Sŏkka (Sakyamuni), and the Muyŏng ("Shadowless") pagodas standing on the grounds of the

A frontal view of the statue of Buddha in the Sŏkkuram grotto temple, Mt. T'oam.

The stone Pagoda of Many Treasures on the grounds of the Pulguk Temple.

Pulguk Temple.

Unfortunately, many of the original temple buildings and some pagodas were destroyed by fire, as well as by the Mongol invasions of the mid-thirteenth century and the Japanese invasions of the late sixteenth century. Pulguk Temple, whose wooden buildings were burned down, was reconstructed in 751 only to be destroyed again by foreign invaders. Hwangryong Temple, built in 553 and completely burned down by the Mongols leaving only some foundation stones, has not been rebuilt.

The Rise of Confucian Studies and Scholarship. Confucianism was introduced to Koguryŏ in the fourth century, and a national academy for Confucian studies, known as T'aehak, was established in 372, followed by local schools called kyŏngdang. However, Koguryŏ refused to be Sinicized, and like Buddhism, the impact of Confucianism in Koguryŏ was minimal. Be that as it may, Confucian influence was reflected in the production in the early period of a 100-volume historical record of Koguryŏ known as Yugi, ("Extant Records"), and its revised version in five volumes called Shinjip, ("New Compilation"), published in 600.

Although it is not known if Paekche established a Confucian school, Confucian influence nevertheless was strongly felt. The Chinese-style *Sŏgi* ("*Documentary Records*") of Paekche was produced in the fourth century, and the nation saw the rise of many eminent Confucian masters (*paksa*) such as Wang In and Ko Hŭng. Paekche also dispatched Wang In (Wani in Japanese) and other Confucian scholars, Buddhist monks, and artisans to Japan.

Although Confucianism entered Shilla much later than in the other two kingdoms, Shilla's *National History* had already been written by 545. The establishment of a government office in charge of Confucian studies and the National Academy (*Kuk'hak*) in 682 marked milestones in Confucian studies as well as intellectual growth. Notably, it produced many outstanding Confucian scholars such as a master calligrapher Kim Saeng and Kim Tae-mun, who authored many books such as *Miscellaneous Records of Shilla, Biographies of Eminent Monks*, and *Chronicles of the Hwarang*. In 717, portraits of Confucius and many of his disciples were brought from China and installed at the National Academy, where not only Confucian classics, but also Chinese history and literature were taught. A Confucian scholar, Ch'oe Ch'i-wŏn of the late ninth century had the title of Superintendent of Learning and directed the studies of the *Five Classics of Confucianism* and Chinese history.

Adoption of a Writing System. Due to the lack of a written Korean of their own, the scholars of the Three Kingdoms period produced books and documents in the Chinese language. The use of written Chinese increased during the fourth century, while monks were also engaged in studies in Sanskrit.

The adoption of the *idu* system in Shilla was a significant cultural development in the early seventh century. It enabled the transliteration of Korean words using Chinese characters. After that additional methods were adopted, making the reading of Chinese writing and the writing of Korean sentences easier. Shilla's *idu* system was adopted by the Japanese scholars who developed the early Japanese writing system called *Manyōkana*.

Native Songs and Poetry. Ancient Chinese sources described Koreans as "a people who enjoy singing and dancing." Songs and dances were involved in spring and autumn communal religious events. The early Koreans honored heaven and thanked the earth with their songs and dances.

Korean native songs called *hyangga* ("native songs") or *saenaenorae* ("new songs of the land") developed in Shilla. Ancient songs and dances were religious in nature, and they were the means of communion with the deities and spirits. However, many *hyangga* were secular in character. With the introduction of the *idu* system, native songs that had been transmitted by oral tradition were written down. A catalog of songs of the three generations called *Samdaemok*, compiled in 888, is said to have included between 1,000 and 1,500 such songs. A few *hyangga* of the Shilla period were preserved in Monk Ilyŏn's *Memorabilia of the Three Kingdoms*. Some examples are given below:

> Princess Sŏnhwa
> Hoping for a secret marriage
> Went away at night,
> With Mattung in her arms

> * * *

> Here now I sing the flower strewing song—
> As offering of flowers, do you
> As my pious heart commands:

> *Attend and bring the Maitreya Buddha*
> *From the distant Tusita Heaven.*

*   *   *

Shin Ch'ung, a poet of the mid-eighth century, wrote a poem entitled "Regret," and said:

> *You said you would no more forget me*
> *Than oaks would wither before the fall.*
> *O that familiar face is there still,*
> *The face I used to see and admire.*

*   *   *

A monk named Kwangdŏk of the seventh century wrote the following poem entitled "Prayer to Amitabha."

> *O Moon*
> *Go to the West, and*
> *Pray to Amitabha*
> *And tell that there is one*
> *Who adores the judicial throne, and*
> *Longs for the Pure Land,*
> *Praying before Him with folded hands.*

The "Songs of Ch'ŏyong," written in the ninth century, is said to be one of the best examples of the *hyangga*.

Following the arrival of Buddhism, many songs and dances associated with it developed. The *hyangga* cited above is a good example. Buddhist chants and dances became an integral part of Korean culture. At the same time, Confucianism also fostered new music and dance associated with its rituals. Many Chinese musical forms and instruments, along with dances, were appropriated by the Koreans, enriching their cultural life. Meanwhile, Koreans created new musical instruments, among which were the *kŏmungo*, a six-string zither of Koguryŏ, and the *kayagŭm*, a twelve-string zither of Kaya. One of the dances, which was performed around the pagodas on the temple grounds, symbolized the life of the moon (waxing and waning) and expressed the human desire to have an everlasting life. Meanwhile, shamanic rituals known as *kut* (chanting, dancing, and exorcism) were widely performed.

Art, Architecture, and Sculpture. A variety of remains of the Three Kingdoms and those of Unified Shilla show a high degree of aesthetic achievement by the artists and craftsmen of the periods. Many of remains are works of great magnitude, manifesting the characteristics in aesthetic propensity of the early Koreans, including Buddhist temples, pagodas and stupas, statues of Buddha, Bodhisattvas, Maitreya, mural and fresco paintings, tombs, and ceramic and earthen ware, and figurines.

Art and architecture of Koguryŏ were best represented by the tombs and fresco paintings on the walls and ceilings of the burial chambers of the tombs built from the fifth to early seventh centuries, most of which were constructed near the old and new capitals of Koguryŏ.

Two types of Koguryŏ tombs have been found. One is pyramidal in shape, and constructed by placing large slabs of stones one atop the other; the other is stone-chambered tombs covered by earthen mounds with the entrance on ground level. The former is represented by the Tomb of the General, and the latter by several Koguryŏ tombs discovered near modern Pyongyang. Among them are the Tomb of Four Spirits, the Tomb of Wrestlers, and the Tomb of the Dancers which contained masterpieces of Koguryŏ art treasures. Murals on the walls of some of these tombs depicted the life of warrior-aristocrats, official functions, and religious concepts and other beliefs and customs of the time. Furthermore they were painted with deep red, green, yellow, blue, and black colors, which may have had some ties with shamanism. Highly decorative geometric and floral designs were employed by the artists who painted the ceilings, beams, and pillars of these tombs.

There is only a handful of historic remains of Paekche with which to study its art and architecture. Among them are the tomb of King Muryŏng, and a tomb discovered near Puyŏ. However, it is said that the best examples of Paekche art are found on the wall of the Golden Hall of the Hōryūji temple near Nara, Japan, believed to be the works of the Paekche painter Ajwa, and the Koguryŏ monk Tamjing.

The brickwork tomb of King Muryŏng with its semi-circular ceiling, and the stone-chambered tomb discovered at Nŭngsan-ri near Puyŏ provide some glimpse of Paekche architecture. However, the architectural art of Paekche is best represented by a five-story, stone pagoda on the grounds of the Chŏngnim Temple in Puyŏ, and an immense multi-storied stone pagoda standing on the grounds of the Mirŭk Temple in Iksan, North Chŏlla Province.

Shilla painters must have painted the temple walls. It is said that the painting of a pine tree by Solgŏ on the wall of the Hwangnyong Temple was so realistic that birds mistook it to be a real tree and attempted to fly into it. However, all original wooden structures and paintings on the walls of these temple buildings have been destroyed, and there is no way of knowing the true style of Shilla painting. The only original painting that has survived was found in the Tomb of Heavenly Horse. It was a "heavenly horse" painted on a mud guard made of birch tree bark.

The growth of Confucian learning in Shilla brought about the rise of scholars with refined calligraphy skills. Among them were Kim In-mun, Kim Saeng, and Ch'oe Ch'i-wŏn.

Many tombs of pre-Buddhist age Shilla are located in

and around Kyŏngju, and some of them have been excavated, revealing Shilla's tomb-building style. Like the tombs of Koguryŏ and Paekche, Shilla tombs had burial chambers, but unlike the others, they were small and had no entrance. Moreover, Shilla tombs had earthen mounds of enormous size on top of the huge stone mounds that covered the burial chambers. Some of these mounds are 200 feet in diameter and 60 feet in height. Many art treasures have been unearthed from such tombs.

The finest examples of Shilla architecture are found at the Pulguk Temple and the Sŏkkuram grotto temple. The Pulguk Temple, built in 553, was rebuilt in 751 on a larger scale, only to be destroyed by the invading Japanese troops in 1592. It was again rebuilt on a smaller scale. Although all original buildings of the Pulguk Temple were destroyed, ample evidence of the highly developed architectural art and technology of Shilla is displayed in its stone structures, such as the Bridge of White Clouds and its upper flight, the Bridge of Azure Clouds, that leads up to the entrance gate, the stone supports for the two front pillars of the Floating Shadow Pavilion, and stone pagodas (the "Many Treasures," the "Shadowless," and the "Sakyamuni") in the inner courtyard. These stone pagodas, along with the Lion Pagoda on the grounds of the Hwaŏm Temple, are regarded as the finest examples of stone monuments built by Shilla artists.

The Sŏkkuram grotto temple on the hills of Mt. T'oam behind Kyŏngju was constructed in 751-790. It is a man-made stone grotto with a rectangular antechamber and a circular inner chamber with a domed ceiling formed by cut blocks of stone. A large stone statue of Sakyamuni Buddha, the best of all statues of Buddha, is placed on top of a lotus flower shaped stone platform in the center of the inner chamber.

The only surviving secular architectural works of Shilla are the Star Observation Tower (Ch'ŏmsŏngdae) and the water channel (P'osŏkchŏng). Ch'ŏmsŏngdae, which was constructed during the reign of Queen Sŏndŏk (630-646), is a bottle-shaped, twenty-nine-foot-high stone tower, which may or may not have been an observatory. P'osŏkchŏng is a large abalone-shaped, narrow, winding water channel under an ancient tree. It is said that kings and their guests sat around the stone channel and had poetry composition contests, wherein a person was to compose a poem before a cup floating on the water reached him. The Imhaejŏn, or the "Pavilion on the Sea," which was burned down, was a complex of banquet halls built out onto the water of a man-made lake called Anapchi. Only the stone foundations of the pavilions remained after the Japanese invasion. Recently, some new buildings have been built on these foundation stones.

The people of Cheju Island (formerly T'amna), who might have migrated from the South Pacific region or from south China, produced stone statues of various sizes called *harubang*, perhaps symbolizing their phalic culture. Be that as it may, the history of Korean sculpture began with the introduction of Buddhism.

Among the finest Buddhist statues produced in Korea were the gilt bronze statues of Takagata Buddha around 539. In Koguryŏ and Paekche many gilt bronze statues were also produced. It is known that the nine-foot-tall wooden statue of Bodhisattva Kwanŭm (the Goddess of Mercy) was carved and erected on the grounds of the Hōryūji temple near Nara, Japan in the sixth century. Shilla craftsmen also produced many elegant gilt bronze statues of Buddha and other Buddhist saints. However, the finest artistry of Shilla iconographic art is represented by stone wares. Among them is a large stone statue of Sakyamuni Buddha in the Sŏkkuram grotto temple. The craftsmen who worked on the Sŏkkuram also sculptured various Bodhisattvas and ten disciples of Buddha in relief on the face of a semi-circular stone wall, as well as two "Heavenly Kings" on the wall of the antechamber, and Four Deva Kings standing guard along the passageway. Together with these Buddhist statues, stone lanterns, stone stupas and pagodas, and stone water basins associated with Buddhist architecture were also produced in Shilla.

The largest bronze bell of Shilla. This one, often called "Emille Bell" cast in 771, was originally hung at the Pongdŏk Temple.

Other Arts and Crafts. During the bronze culture period, small hanging bronze bells called *tongt'aek* were cast. Inheriting this tradition, and with the rise of Buddhism, more temple bells of all sizes were cast. Among the largest Shilla bells is that of the Pongdŏk Temple, which was cast in 771. This bell, often called "Emille Bell," which currently hangs in the National Museum of Kyŏngju, is eleven feet high, seven feet and six inches in diameter, nine inches thick, and weighs 150,000 pounds. On its surface is a relief lotus flower motif and the "flying angel-Buddha," praying amidst waving diaphanous draperies and clouds.

With the rise of tomb culture, craftsmen in both Paekche and Shilla produced ornamental and other tiles. A piece of ornamental brick unearthed at the site of a temple in Puyŏ showed the stamped design of a landscape of Taoist mode. The Shilla craftsmen produced roof tiles with various designs such as flowers and animal figures. Among those which survived intact are the twelve tiles, each with a relief of a Chinese zodiac animal, in the stone fence around the tomb of Kim Yu-shin in Kyŏngju. Meanwhile, they produced tomb figurines made of clay, such as figurines of humans, horses, carts, houses, men on horseback, and various animals.

It is evident that both Paekche and Shilla artisans produced ornaments in gold and precious stones, but it was Shilla that had the richest gold deposits and produced the most gold ornaments. Unfortunately, most of the gold jewelry produced in Paekche was buried in the tombs that were plundered. However, the gold crowns and the ornamentation of gold crowns unearthed from the tomb of King Muryŏng amply demonstrate the artistry of the Paekche craftsmen.

Some pre-Buddhist age Shilla tombs yielded many art treasures, including gold crowns, shoes, belts, earrings, fingerrings, and bracelets that were made of pure gold, and a large number of gemstones and molten glass, all testifying to the high artistic quality of Shilla crafts.

The Rise of Geomantic Theories. While Buddhism came into vogue, the growing Chinese cultural influence in Shilla also brought about the rise of the geomantic theories called *p'ungsusŏl*, or the "water and wind theories," which "explained" nature's workings and the relationship between cause and effect on the basis of certain cosmic principles such as *yin* and *yang* and the five elements (fire, water, wood, metal, and earth).

Applying such principles, masters of geomancy analyzed topographic features to find balanced land configurations on which to place houses and tombs. They advanced a theory that the natural features of a land area and their configuration directly affect the fortunes and misfortunes of the people as well as the country. If a favorable site was selected for a house, a tomb, a shrine, or even a capital of the nation, it would bring good fortune to the individual or to the kingdom. An unfavorable site meant sure disaster. In addition, the four directions of the universe were also believed to have a certain relationship to creation, prosperity, degeneration, and death. The east and the south were favorable directions to face, and facing the west and the north was to be avoided. At the end of the Unified Shilla period, a monk named Tosŏn popularized the geomantic theories by combining primitive beliefs with Buddhist ideas as well as Taoistic theories. Superstitious or not, such concepts took deep root in the consciousness of the Koreans, influencing their decision making.

4
The Society and Culture of Koryŏ, 918-1392

THE new dynasty and the Kingdom of Koryŏ that Wang Kŏn established in 918 lasted until 1392, and Koryŏ was the origin of the modern Western name of Korea. During this period, thirty four kings ruled the nation, the territory of the kingdom expanded, and new political, social, and economic patterns emerged as cultural progress was brought about. Despite Wang Kŏn's admonishment that the Koreans lived in a land quite different from that of the Chinese, that the characters of the two people were different, and that there was no reason to copy too excessively the Chinese ways, Koryŏ nevertheless borrowed heavily from China, accelerating the process of Sinification which had begun in the earlier period.

New Political and Military Patterns

Claiming that Koryŏ was the successor to Koguryŏ, Wang Kŏn, who was given the posthumous title of T'aejo ("Great Progenitor," reigned 918-943) established Song'ak (renamed Kaegyŏng, now Kaesŏng), which was his home base as the new capital of the kingdom. The location of many palaces and Buddhist temples and monasteries which were built in the capital were carefully selected in accordance with the geomantic theories propagated by Monk Tosŏn.

As he pushed the northwestern frontiers of the kingdom as far north as the Ch'ŏngch'ŏn River, he rebuilt Pyongyang, which had been laid in ruins, and made it the Western Capital. When the last king of Shilla and its noblemen voluntarily surrendered to him in 935 he treated them well. In the following year, he destroyed the Later Paekche by military force, reunifying Korea, this time without foreign assistance. In 938 he conquered Cheju Island where the Kingdom of T'amna had existed.

T'aejo had three queens and twenty-six consorts from various powerful local gentry families, thus establishing marriage alliances with them and gaining their support. When he died, he left the Ten Injunctions for his posterity to observe faithfully for the sake of the well-being of the kingdom and prosperity of the people. By the time he died, the Sacred Bone rank of Shilla was completely demolished and many members of the sixth head-rank grade of Shilla were recruited into the new government.

In 949, following the brief period of power struggle within the Wang clan and political instability, Kwangjong, one of the sons of Wang Kŏn, took the throne, established a stable royal authority and a new political structure, and constructed more palace buildings. In 956, he adopted the nine official rank system from China, each rank divided into "senior" and "junior" categories, making a total of eighteen ranks, and the colors and style of official attire were also designated. The two other important actions taken by him were the restoration under the Slave Review Act of free status to a large number of commoners who had been enslaved during the chaotic late Shilla period (many slaves were freed also), and the adoption of the Chinese civil service examination system in 958 in order to recruit well-educated civilians into the government in place of the old military officials, laying the foundation for the rise of a new aristocracy. The reform measures initiated by Kwangjong were completed by his successor who reigned between 981 and 997.

Political Structure. The central government patterned after that of China was headed by three top organs: the Royal Chancellery, which was a king's council involved in policy making, the Royal Secretariat, which drafted royal degrees and transmitted them, and the Secretariat of State Affairs, an executive branch which consisted of six ministries of Personnel, Military Affairs, Revenue, Punishment (Justice), Rites (Ceremonies), and Public Works. The first two organs were collectively called the Directorate of Chancellors, and its head was a *de facto* prime minister. Below the six ministries were nine agencies (*kushi*) that handled financial affairs of the court.

The Privy Council was another important organ of civil officials which was an advisory body to the king dealing with national security. The Censorate was a scrutinizing organ of the government involved in the matters of appointment of officials and changes in status, as well as checking the conduct of the monarch and government officials.

The top military organs were the Council of Generals, a counterpart of Privy Council of the civil officials, consisting of generals, and the Council of Commanders consisting of regimental commanders. T'aejo's personal army was reorganized into two Royal Guards and all private armies of local gentry were either disbanded or incorporated into the national defense force which was formed in 947. It was reorganized into a six division army in 995. The rank and file of the Two Guards and Six Divisions were professional military men from families belonging to the "soldiering order," whose social status and military service obligation were hereditary.

The government also established the East and West Infirmaries to care for the indigent sick, a public dispensary, the Charitable Granaries that stored grain for public relief purpose, and the Stabilizer Granaries to maintain the steady price of grains.

Administrative Districts and Local Government. In the beginning the kingdom was divided into twelve provinces, but in 1018 it was redistricted into the Capital Region (Kyŏnggi), five circuits (*to*), and two border regions (*kye*). In addition to Pyongyang, which had been named the Western Capital, two other sub-capitals — the Southern Capital (Hanyang, now Seoul) and the Eastern Capital (now Kyŏngju) — were established. Kaegyŏng, the capital of the kingdom, was called the Central Capital. There were five regional military command headquarters.

Each circuit was divided into provinces, each province into counties, each country into prefectures, and each prefecture into villages. Below the village level were units called *hyang*, *so*, and *pugok* where slaves and other unfree people lived and worked. Each regional military command headquarters had several garrisons.(See Map 7)

All heads of these local administrative units were appointed by the central government on fixed terms of office, and no officials could serve in their home districts. In order to check the abuses of power, or prevent treason, the central government dispatched inspectors-general to local areas, and all those local officials were ordered to send young members of their families to the capital to serve in certain assigned posts as *kiin* in the capital. *Kiin* were in fact hostages.

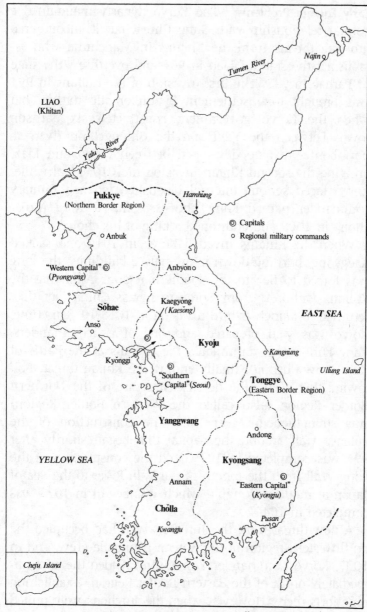

Map 7. KOREA DURING THE KORYŎ PERIOD

Early Foreign Problems. The Koryŏ dynasty maintained a cordial relationship with Sung China, but it encountered growing threats from the Khitans in Manchuria who established the state of Liao in 907 and overthrew the state of Parhae in 925. The first invasion of the Khitans in 993 was brought to a settlement by diplomatic means, but when the Koryŏ government constructed six garrison towns between the Yalu and the Ch'ŏngch'ŏn rivers, a new border dispute developed between Koryŏ and Liao, bringing the second Khitan invasion in 1010. Meanwhile, Koryŏ faced serious internal bloodshed when a military commander named Kang Cho assassinated King Mok-chong in 1009 and enthroned a king of his choice.

When the Khitans invaded Korea in 1010 and sacked Kaegyŏng, burning down many palace buildings, the king was forced to flee to the southern region. After that the Khitans withdrew from Korea to harass China, but they returned to launch a third invasion in 1018-19. This time, Koryŏ was well prepared and one of its commanders, Kang Kam-ch'an, annihilated the Khitans at the Battle of Kuju (now Kusŏng), finally ending the Khitan threat. Following this event, the defense structure of the Northern Border Region (also called the Western Border Region) was strengthened. Meanwhile, the construction of the defense wall around the capital that began shortly after 993 was completed in 1019, and the construction of the Long Wall from the mouth of the Yalu River to the Sea of Japan at modern Yŏngp'o which was begun in 1033 was completed in 1044.

A new threat from the Jurchens who had occupied the northwestern region of the Korean peninsula grew, and in 1007, Koryŏ Commander Yun Kwan invaded the area immediately north of the Eastern Border Region, establishing nine forts there. However, when the Jurchens were united into the state of Chin in 1115 under their new leader,

Akuta, Koryŏ submitted to its demand and accepted the status of vassal to Chin which eventually ruled north China until 1234.

Social and Economic Patterns

With the rise of an elite group of men of gentry origin who contributed to the establishment of the Wang dynasty, and when the members of the sixth head-rank of Shilla were recruited into the Koryŏ government, a new social structure emerged in Korea. Needless to say, the Bone Rank system of Shilla was discarded and the men of the True Bone rank lost their former status and power.

Social Structure and Practices. In general, the new social structure of Koryŏ consisted of the aristocracy, the commoners, and the "low-born" class. The aristocracy included the high-ranking civil officials who were collectively called the "literati branch" or the "eastern branch," and the top military officials were collectively called the "military branch" or the "western branch," thus both groups were collectively called *yangban*, or "both branches." Between the *yangban* aristocracy and the commoner class were the petty court functionaries who were called the "southern branch." The hereditary low-ranking military men were included in the "soldiering order," and the commoner class called "good people" included peasants. Below the commoner class were the "low-born" people, most of whom were slaves, domestic servants, tanners, leather workers, butchers, wicker workers, traders, the manual workers, and public entertainers. Social status was hereditary.

Among the new powerful aristocratic houses that emerged were the Kim clan of Ansan, the Yi clan of Inju (now Inch'ŏn), the Yun clan of P'ap'yŏng, the Ch'oe clan of Haeju, and the Kim clan of Kyŏngju. After the Kim clan of Ansan enjoyed power monopoly by providing queens, the house of Yi supplied queens to seven successive kings during the period of some eighty years from 1046. The aristocrats who held positions in the central government were permanent residents of the capital.

Economic Change. An important change in the economic system of Koryŏ was the nationalization of the land. With this, royal estate land was set aside to defray expenditures of the court, and public land was set aside as a source of revenue to defray the expenditures of the government. In 940, the king distributed the "merit lands" in perpetuity to those who rendered meritorious services to the founding of the new dynasty, regardless of their official ranks, and under the Farm and Fuel-land Law of 976, land grants were made to the officials in the top five official ranks.

As the Confucian bureaucracy emerged the Farm and Fuel-land Law was modified in 998 as the Stipend Land Law (readjusted in 1034 and 1076), and land grants were made to the officials in the eighteen ranks for the duration of their tenure. The Stipend Lands were managed by the state, which also collected land rent (25% of the harvest) and a land tax (10% of the harvest) from the peasants who cultivated these lands. Those who owned merit lands paid no land tax, but collected 50% of the harvest from their tenants as rent. Under this system, those peasant families enrolled in the "military order" were given "soldiers land," those who were in local government were given "local service land," and Buddhist temples were also given land grants. The land grants were also made to families of deceased civil officials and soldiers, as well as war widows. The main crops grown were rice, millet, and barley, and a large amount of land was used to cultivate hemp and mulberry trees whose leaves were used to feed silkworms.

With the rise of the nobility and the deterioration of government management, the number of large estates grew from the twelfth century, particularly during the period of Mongol domination, landholdings therefore being concentrated into the hands of a small number of powerful families of high officials. Thus, the size of privately owned lands grew vastly as a growing number of formerly free peasants became tenant farmers or serfs. There were some 360 such large estates in the early twelfth century, and the number steadily grew despite efforts made by the government to curtail the abuses of power by the nobility. In such a situation, a growing number of hopelessly poverty-stricken peasants and over-burdened slaves fled from their localities into mountainous regions. The *Green Mountain Song*, which was written at that time, reflected the economic realities of the peasantry. The song begins as follows:

> *Let us live, let us live,*
> *Let us live in a green mountain.*
> *Eating with grapes and vine berries,*
> *Let us live in a green mountain.*

During the Koryŏ period, the property owned by the nobility was divided among the children, including female off-spring, more or less equally. Widows enjoyed the right to inherit the property from their husbands.

Manufacturing was largely in the hands of the government that established manufactories at *hyang, so,* and *pugok* throughout the country where slaves worked. These manufactories were engaged in the production of raw materials and gold, silver, iron, thread, silk cloth, ornaments, charcoal, salt, inkstone, oil, and ceramics.

Public slaves contributed the bulk of workers at these manufactories.

Because commerce in general had not developed significantly, there was no great need for currency. However, iron coins were minted in 996, copper coins in 1097, and in 1101 silver money in the shape of an urn was produced, and in 1102 new copper coins called *Haedong t'ongbo* were minted. Meanwhile, Chinese coins were brought in for circulation.

The government collected several kinds of taxes. A land tax was imposed on all land except the land owned by the merit subjects, public land, temple land, and land granted to families of deceased civil officials and soldiers, or widows. The land was classified into three grades according to its productive capacity, and one-tenth of the harvest was collected as land tax. A head tax was collected according to the number of taxable adults in the household. A corvée tax was paid by male adults of the peasantry between the ages of sixteen and fifty-nine in various forms of labor service. A salt tax, a business tax, and tax on ships were also collected. All taxes, except the corvée tax, were paid in goods.

A limited foreign trade was maintained with China after the collapse of Korea's foreign trade following the death of Shilla's Chang Po-go in 847. However, the ports of the Yesŏng River near Kaegyŏng where Chinese as well as Arab merchants traded played an important role. Guest houses were built in the capital as well as in other places for diplomats and merchants from China. Korea's main export items were gold and silver utensils, raw copper, ginseng, hemp cloth, paper, inkstone, felt, folding fans, and swords. Korea imported tea, lacquerware, books, dye stuff, and medicine.

When cotton was introduced from China in 1362, cotton was cultivated and the production of cotton cloth began. However, the production of hemp cloth and silk remained the major textile industry carried out by the peasantry. Gunpowder, which was introduced to Korea around 1370, led to the production of firearms, but it did not contribute much toward economic growth as such.

As economic activity and society simultaneously developed, the number of various guilds called *po* and public inns increased. A *po* was similar to an association: some of them were mutual aid associations while others were money lending institutions. There were charitable *po*, and some *po* were established for the promotion of education.

Cultural Development

Korea's growing contact with China brought about her cultural development in a variety of ways. To be sure, Buddhist culture continued to flourish, but secular culture became increasingly popular.

Art and Architecture. Korea's painters and calligraphers were heavily influenced by the Sung culture of China first, and subsequently by the new styles developed in Yüan China that exerted some influence over them. While Buddhist painters produced their works at the newly established Buddhist temples, secular painters promoted literary painting. Unfortunately, nearly all their works, including "Yesŏng River Scene" by Yi Yŏng of the twelfth century, who established a new school of landscape painting, were destroyed during the rebellion or wars. The Koryŏ painters painted with brush and black ink on silk or paper, their subjects being such items as bamboo, chrysanthemum, orchid, and plum, which were called "four gentlemen." Such other paintings as "Bodhisattava Avolokitesvara Holding a Willow Branch" by Hyehŏ and "Hunting on Mt. Heaven," assumed to be that of King Kongmin, were among a few masterpieces of the Koryŏ period.

The calligraphic art was further promoted by such masters as Yu Shim and Ch'oe U, and a monk named T'anyŏn, who together with Kim Saeng of Shilla are known as the "Four Worthies of Divine Calligraphy." Yi Am, who emerged in the fourteenth century, replaced the Sung style with that of the Yüan style, establishing the calligraphic style which became prominent during the following centuries after his death.

The sixty-foot stone Maitreya and the twenty-foot stone lantern that were dedicated in the late tenth century at the Kwanch'ok Temple in Nonsan, Yanggwang Province (now South Ch'ungch'ŏng Province) and the clay Amitabha on the grounds of the Pusŏk Temple built in 1330 in Yŏngju, Kyŏngsang Province are the most outstanding sculptural works of the Koryŏ period. Along with these, the ten-story marble pagoda which was dedicated at the Kyŏngch'ŏn Temple in Kaep'ung, Kyŏnggi District in the early fourteenth century, the eight-foot stupa (Shilsangt'ap) erected for the National Preceptor Hongbŏp around 1017, and the stupa (Hyŏn-myot'ap) erected for the National Preceptor Chigwang around 1085 represent the finest sculpture of the period. The marble pagoda of the Kyŏngch'ŏn Temple, the stupas of Hongbŏp and Chigwang are now standing in the grounds of the Kyŏngbok Palace, which has become a part of the new National Museum.

Most early architectural works of Koryŏ, including all the palaces built on the Full Moon Terrace (Manwŏltae) in the capital, were destroyed during the rebellion or foreign invasions. Be that as it may, a large number of magnificent Buddhist temples were constructed during the Koryŏ period. Among them was the Hŭngwang Temple, the largest (99,000 square feet of floor space) Buddhist temple ever built in Korea in 1067. The Hall of Paradise of the Pongjŏng Temple built in the thirteenth century in Andong, Kyŏngsang Province, and the Hall of Eternal Life and the Hall of the Founder of the Pusŏk Temple built in 1330 in Yŏngju, Kyŏngsang Province, are said to be the best examples of Koryŏ architecture in wood that survived. These Buddhist temples, pagodas, and stupas, together with those of Paekche and Shilla, made Korea, particularly the southern part, one of the largest open museums of fine art in the world.

Buddhism in Koryŏ. The legacy of the Golden Age of Buddhism of Shilla was carried over to the Koryŏ period. As King T'aejo made Buddhism the state religion, he stated in the first of his Ten Injunctions that "The successful outcome of the great enterprise of founding our dynasty is entirely owing to the protection of many Buddhas." As Buddhism became "Buddhism for the Protection of the Nation," T'aejo built many Buddhist temples, encouraged harmonious development of Buddhism and native religious tradition, and proclaimed that both the Lantern Festival and the traditional harvest festival called *P'algwanhoe* should be observed in earnest.

The Lantern Festival was observed on the fifteenth day of the first month of the lunar calendar, and the *P'algwanhoe* (thanksgiving festival) was observed on the fifteenth day of the eleventh month of the lunar calendar, honoring the various Buddhas and Buddhist saints as well as the spirits of heaven, earth, and wind to bring tranquility to the nation and the well-being of the royal house and the people. In order to solicit the blessings from Buddha, the birthday of Buddha was celebrated on the eighth day of the fourth month of the lunar calendar, and the Inwang Assembly of a large number of monks was held to pray for peace in the nation.

Buddhism flourished in Koryŏ under state sponsorship. First of all, the government built many temples, made land grants to the temples and monasteries, and bestowed such high ranks as the Royal Preceptor and the National Preceptor upon eminent monks. Many members of the royal house, including some kings, became monks. Buddhism was also subscribed to by the aristocracy, and many aristocratic families donated land to the temples and monasteries. With the institutionalization of the examination for the clergy patterned after that of the civil examination, monks were given clerical ranks, receiving land grants and exemption from corvee duties.

Buddhism in Koryŏ was split into two main branches, of the *Kyo*, or Textual School and the *Sŏn*, or Contemplative School. Whereas the Textual School was supported by the ruling dynasty and the aristocracy, the Contemplative School was supported by local gentry. Needless to say, each school was divided into various sub-sects.

One of the important developments in Buddhism was the publication of the *Tripitaka* ("Three Baskets"), which was a complete collection of Buddhist scriptures. The carving of tens of thousands of woodblocks for the *Tripitaka* began in the early eleventh century as an effort to secure Buddha's protection for the kingdom against the Khitans who invaded Korea. The carving of these massive woodblocks was completed in 1087 and the first edition of the *Tripitaka* was published. These woodblocks, which were stored at the Puin Temple in Taegu, were destroyed in the thirteenth century Mongol invasions.

The carving of the new set of 81,137 woodblocks for a new edition of *Tripitaka* began in 1236 and was completed in 1251 while the Koryŏ court had taken refuge on Kanghwa Island, and the *Tripitaka Koreana* (*Koryŏ Taejanggyŏng*) was printed. These new woodblocks were

Detail of a wooden printing block; 81, 258 wooden printing blocks carved to print the Tripitaka Koreana stored at the Haein Temple.

preserved at the Haein Temple on Mt. Kaya near Taegu. Meanwhile, Monk Ŭich'ŏn, a brother of the king, who established the Directorate for Buddhist Scriptures, published the *Supplement to the Tripitaka* and others as he founded the Ch'ŏnt'ae (T'ient'ai in Chinese) sect.

One of the most important aspects of Koryŏ Buddhism was the effort made to unite the Textual (*Kyo*) and the Contemplative (*Sŏn*) schools. Such attempt had been made by a king in the middle of the tenth century, but it was Monk Ŭich'ŏn (1055-1101) as a National Preceptor who made positive efforts to unite the many Buddhist sects. Although he gained many adherents to his ecumenical movement, there was considerable opposition from some of the sects that launched a strong counter movement. Ŭich'ŏn died without achieving his goal.

However, in the fourteenth century, the Contemplative

School, which had been divided into Nine Mountain Sects, was united into the *Chogye* sect. The *Chogye* sect eventually incorporated the doctrines and practices of the Textual School. As a result, Korean Buddhism, unlike the Japanese, became broader in concepts and less sectarian.

Educational Development, the Civil Service Examination System, and Scholarship. Although T'aejo established the school in Pyongyang, Koryŏ's educational development began with the adoption in 958 of the Chinese civil service examination system and the establishment of the Superintendent of the National Academy in 992 for Confucian studies in the capital.

In the first half of the eleventh century, before the state school developed fully, an eminent scholar by the name of Ch'oe Ch'ung, who is known as the "Korean Confucius," established a private academy for Confucian studies known as the Nine Course Academy. This school was joined by a dozen other private academies, producing well-educated scholars who passed the civil service examinations and entered into government services.

Encountering competition from these private academies, King Yejong (reigned 1105-1122) reorganized the National Academy into six colleges. Two of these colleges were for Confucian studies, one was the College of Literary Studies, one was the College of Law, one was the College of Calligraphy, and the sixth was the College of Accounting. He also established the military college, local academies, and the Fund for Nurturing Worthies as a foundation to promote academies, and set up two study centers in the palace, recruiting scholars and collecting books. Although the military college was abolished by his successor (Injong), an increasing number of books were imported from China. Meanwhile, removable metal type was invented in 1232, making possible the printing of more books.

Following the adoption of the civil service examination system, entry into the government services depended primarily on one's educational attainment and passing various examinations. Such systems, which were in full operation toward the end of the twelfth century, consisted of three divisions: the literary, the classics, and the miscellaneous. The Literary Examination selected candidates on the basis of their ability to compose in sets of Chinese literary forms such as poetry, prose, ode, and essays, while the Classics Examination tested knowledge of such Confucian canons as the *Book of History, Classic of Changes, Classic of Songs, Spring and Autumn Annals,* and *Analects.* The Miscellaneous Examination was to select professional and technical specialists in such areas as law, accounting, medicine, divination (astrology), geography, and geomancy.

Three levels of examinations were conducted. The first level examination was given at the county office to select thirty candidates to be presented at the provincial examination. The provincial examination selected thirty candidates as "presented scholars" to take the final examination conducted at the palace. The palace examination selected thirty candidates to be appointed to the key positions in the central government.

Although these examinations were theoretically open to all except the "low-born" people and the children of monks, in reality only the sons of aristocratic families were able to obtain education to qualify themselves to take these examinations. The sons of the officials of the fifth rank and above enjoyed the special privilege of receiving government appointments without taking any examinations under the system called *ŭmsŏ.*

The rise of Confucian studies, of course, meant the development of studies of Chinese culture, including language, literature, and poetry. Thus such disciplines as the study of Chinese literature and the writing of Chinese-style poetry developed. The most important aspect of the newly rising culture was reflected in the scholarship and publication of a large number of historical works between 1145 and 1317. Among these were the *Historical Records of the Three Kingdoms(Samguk sagi)* compiled by Kim Pu-shik and others in 1145, and the Monk Ilyŏn's *Memorabilia of the Three Kingdoms (Samguk Yusa)*, published in the early thirteenth century. These two constitute the basic sources for the study of early Korean history. Many of the books that were published before the Mongol invasions were destroyed during the Mongol wars.

Music and Dance. Although Buddhism had lost its creative qualities and the lucidity of the Shilla period, with the increase of Chinese influence and the state sponsorship of Buddhism, together with the rise of the new aristocracy, both secular (ceremonial) and religious music and dance developed.

Many Chinese musical books, notes, and instruments and dance forms collectively called the *Tang-ak* or *a-ak* in Korea were imported, and they were used in Confucian rituals, court ceremonies, and various occasions at the residence of aristocrats. The observance of such Buddhist festivals as the Lantern Festival in early spring, and the celebration of the *P'algwanhoe* in autumn, together with other religious and secular festivals promoted music and dance. Certain melodic chanting of Buddhist scriptures and dance forms that had developed during the Shilla period were kept. In the Grand Festival of One Hundred Seats, some 30,000 Buddhist monks and 4,000 musicians performed music and dance.

The two unique poetic forms that developed during the

Koryŏ period were *changga* ("long songs") and short poems called *shijo*, or "occasional verses." Whereas the long songs were similar to Western epic poems and ballads, *shijo*, which is highly structured and has several forms, is similar to the Western ode in character, and structurally akin to Japanese *haiku*. The most commonly used form of *shijo* is that in which forty-five syllables are arranged in three lines.

While the Confucian *literati* composed long Kyŏnggi-style long songs (*changga*) called *pyŏlgok*, such as *Hallim pyŏlgok* and *Kwandong pyŏlgok*, the commoners composed such *changga* as *The Green Mountain Song*, and *The Song of Chŏng'ŭp* in which the life of the peasants is depicted. Some long songs expressed love themes, and such songs as *The Turkish Bakery* depicted licentious scenes, making the Koryŏ songs radically dissimilar from those of Shilla.

The art of *shijo* was to develop fully later, but the poet U T'ak (1262-1342) left the following *shijo* behind:

> *East winds that melt the mountain snow*
> *Come and go, without words.*
> *Blow over my head, young breeze,*
> *Even for a moment, blow.*
> *Would that you could blow away the grey hairs*
> *That grow so fast around my ears?*

With the establishment of the Mongol domination, Mongol musical and dance forms were brought in, enriching the cultural life of the kingdom. Meanwhile, mask dances such as the Lion Dance became popular.

Ceramic Art. Perhaps the greatest cultural achievement of Koryŏ was in ceramic art. The potters of Koryŏ improved the technology of pottery making that was imported from Sung China, producing the artistic and elegant Koryŏ celadon which was the demonstration of their creativity and innovativeness. The "restless inventiveness" of the potters of Koryŏ at such kilns as Puan and Kangjin brought about a remarkably high degree of achievement in ceramic art represented by masterpieces of *sanggam* jade-green ware, of exquisite color and quality, as well as white and black celadon ware, and bronze wares inlaid with silver, with willow tree, lotus and floral, and other designs.

A wide variety of shapes of celadon ware was produced for various purposes. They included such items as brush holders, cups, flasks, flower vases, incense burners, water droppers to make black ink, wine bottles, pitchers, and tea pots. These took on a variety of plant or animal shapes such as bamboo shoot, chrysanthemum, fish, lotus, mandarin duck, melon, monkey, parrot, pomegranate, rabbit, and turtle. The halcyon glaze of Koryŏ ware was described by a Korean poet as having "the radiance of jade...the crystal clarity of water...as if the artists had borrowed the secret from heaven."

Typical jade-green sanggam *Koryŏ celadon ware with inlaid design, 13th century.*

Incense burner with a reticulated ball lid, 12-13th century.

The potters of Koryŏ also produced brown wares of elegant quality and style as if they were competing with the
potters of the bygone days of Shilla. However, the
Mongol invasions in the middle of the thirteenth century
destroyed Koryŏ ceramic art almost completely as many
kilns were smashed and potters were killed or taken captive to China. Thus the secrets of Koryŏ celadon that had
been jealously guarded by certain families of potters were
totally lost.

Rebellion, Power Struggle, and Uprisings

All was not well with the Koryŏ dynasty. The autocratic
rule of Koryŏ was based on civil supremacy, and military

officials were put in an inferior position, often suffering humiliation at the hands of civil officials. As a result, the hostilities of military men against the civil officials led to open warfare in the twelfth century, creating an extremely unstable political situation. To make matters worse, treason and rebellion came in succession, accompanying popular uprisings, bringing about a rapid decline of the Koryŏ dynasty.

Treason and Rebellion. The first serious internal disturbance came when King Mokchong was assassinated in 1009 by Kang Cho, the military commander of the Northwest Frontier Region. Shortly after that, Kang Cho was in turn killed during the Khitan invasion, and political stability was restored as Koryŏ fought wars first with the Khitans and then with the Jurchens in the early twelfth century.

The treason of Yi Cha-gyŏm in the early twelfth century created a serious domestic crisis. The Yi clan of Inju had taken away power monopoly by the Kim clan of Ansan, and during the period between 1046 and 1122 the Yi clan monopolized power by supplying queens to seven kings.

Yi Cha-gyŏm, who was the father-in-law of the king, became ambitious, and he removed the king by contrivance, putting his grandson on the throne in 1122, and he plotted to make himself king. The king's counter-plot to eliminate his father-in-law failed. The king was put under house arrest, and his supporters were put to death. During the counterattack of Yi's forces, many buildings in the royal palace were destroyed by fire. As Yi contemplated to kill the king, one of his henchman betrayed him in 1127, and Yi was sent into exile and died. With this the power of the Yi house collapsed.

King Injong, who survived Yi's treason and fled to Pyongyang, issued a fourteen-point reform decree, and returned to Kaegyŏng. However, he faced another threat to his dynasty when several men of Pyongyang attempted to seize power. To do so, these men, led by Monk Myoch'ŏng, and evoking various geomantic theories, urged Injong to abandon Kaegyŏng, whose "vital forces were exhausted," and make Pyongyang the new capital "for the sake of rejuvenation of the dynasty."

When Injong refused to do so, they proposed other things first and then in 1135 Myoch'ŏng rebelled, creating a new state named Great Accomplishment (*Taewi*), and adopting a reign title of Heavenly Commencement (*Ch'ŏn'gae*). However, a royal force led by Kim Pu-shik, who had opposed the transfer of the capital to Pyongyang earlier, overthrew Myoch'ŏng's state, restoring peace.

Coup d'État of Military Officers. In 1170, unhappy military officers, led by Chŏng Chung-bu, brought about a bloody coup d'état against civil officials, dethroning the king and putting a new king on the throne, exhibiting power with his private guards unit called *Tobang*. In the process, many civil officials were massacred. An attempt made to restore the deposed king failed, bringing more bloodshed.

Meanwhile, in 1172, there were bloody peasant uprisings, first in the Northern Frontier Region when the local people who were politically oppressed and heavily burdened with taxation rose in armed rebellion. It was followed by uprisings in the Kongju area in the Yanggwang Circuit in 1182. The latter was the most serious because it was brought about by soldiers, joined by slaves.

In such an unsettled situation, a power struggle developed among Chŏng's men who had arrested power from the civil officials. Chŏng became a victim of the struggle and was assassinated in 1179 by one of his own men. Another military officer who had replaced the man who murdered Chŏng was also assassinated in 1197 by Ch'oe Ch'ung-hŏn and his brothers, who established the dictatorship of the Ch'oe house.

Ch'oe Ch'ung-hŏn ruthlessly eliminated other challengers, including his own brothers and a nephew. After establishing the Office of Flourishing Tranquility, Ch'oe Ch'ung-hŏn overshadowed the monarchy. In 1209, when he uncovered a plot to overthrow his dictatorship, he established another organ named the Directorate of Decree Enactment as the top organ of the government under his personal control.

The dictatorship of the Ch'oe house lasted for over 60 years to 1258, and during this time four members of the house of Ch'oe ruled the kingdom as dictators. They were Ch'oe Ch'ung-hŏn himself, his son U, and U's descendants Hang and Ŭi. Within the short span of sixteen years from 1197 to 1213, the Ch'oes deposed two kings and enthroned four. As the kings became puppets, Ch'oe broke down the power of the Buddhist temples and monasteries, and crushed the army of the monks that stormed the capital to overthrow the military dictatorship of the Ch'oe house.

Ch'oe U, the second dictator, established another new organ named the Personnel Authority at his own residence, handling all matters related to government personnel and subjugated the peasant and slave uprisings of 1193 in Kyŏngsang Circuit, of 1198 in the capital, of 1199 in the Eastern Border Region, of 1200 in the Chinju, and of 1202 in the Kyŏngju areas in Kyŏngsang Circuit. In the Miryang uprising in Kyŏngsang Circuit of 1193 alone, some 7,000 rebels were killed. Ch'oe U also set up six private guard units, increasing the number of units in his private army to thirty-six. In addition, he formed a private cavalry unit called the Elite Horse, and the Three Elite Patrols (two Night Patrols and the Army of Transcendent Righteousness for Combat) known in Korean as *Sambyŏlch'o*. The financial needs of the Ch'oe dictatorship and military were met by income from a large area in the Chinju area in Kyŏngsang Circuit granted by the king to the Ch'oe family, as well as from national revenue.

Ch'oe U improved the relationship with the royal government. He even returned to the former owners the properties his father had confiscated by force, gaining the legitimacy of the dictatorial regime. At no time did the Ch'oe house attempt to abolish the Wang dynasty per se, but merely reduced it to virtual puppet status.

The Mongol Invasions and the Fall of Koryŏ

Koryŏ was able to protect its newly gained northwestern territory from the Khitans after winning the victory at the Battle of Kuju in 1019, and prevented the invasion of the Jurchens, who had established the state of Chin in Manchuria, destroyed the state of Liao of the Khitans in 1215, and overthrew the Northern Sung in China in 1127. But in the early thirteenth century it encountered the growing demands of Mongols who overthrew the state of Chin in 1215.

The Mongol Invasions. When Koryŏ refused to meet various demands of the Mongols, including large annual tributes, and when a Mongol envoy to Koryŏ was killed in 1225 on the way back from his mission from Koryŏ, the Mongols launched their first invasion in 1231, forcing the Koryŏ court to sue for peace. But when the Ch'oe dictatorship resolved to resist the Mongols and relocated the Koryŏ court to Kanghwa Island in 1232, the Mongols invaded Korea again. During the next thirty year period, the Mongols invaded Korea six times, causing tremendous destruction of historic structures and national treasures, as well as farms and dwellings. In 1254 alone, some 200,000 Koreans were taken away as captives and the number of people who died during the course of the Mongol invasions was said to be approximately half a million. It was during these invasions that the first set of woodblocks for the *Tripitaka* was destroyed along with many temples. The second set of woodblocks for the *Tripitaka* was carved while the Koryŏ court was staying on Kanghwa Island as an offering of prayer to Buddha for his protection of the country. But Korea's ability to resist the Mongols did not improve.

When Korea, including its capital, was under Mongol occupation, the civil officials who favored making peace with the Mongols were able to assassinate the last Ch'oe dictator in 1258, and concluded a peace treaty with the Mongols, accepting Korea's vassalage to the Mongol empire. However, a military leader who opposed pro-Mongol policy eliminated the pro-Mongol civil officials and deposed the king, who had implemented the pro-Mongol policy.

In this situation, in 1270 the Mongols intervened, restored the king who had been deposed, and put to death several military officials who were anti-Mongol. With this the Koryŏ court returned to Kaegyŏng, ending its struggle against the Mongols.

The Rebellion of the Sambyŏlch'o. When the Koryŏ king capitulated to the Mongols and moved back to Kaegyŏng, the leaders of the Three Elite Patrols (*Sambyŏlch'o*), which had been stationed on Kanghwa Island, refused to obey the royal order to disband the units. In 1270, under the leadership of Pae Chung-son, they established a new government with a royal kinsman named Wang On as king, and brought about what is known as the Rebellion of the Three Elite Patrols against the Koryŏ court and the Mongols. In order to strengthen their position, the rebels moved to the island of Chindo, off the southwest coast of Chŏlla Circuit. In 1271, a combined force of Koryŏ and Mongols forced the rebels to flee to Cheju Island where they constructed a fortification. However, the rebels fell in 1273 after a series of bloody battles.

The Mongol Domination and Its Effects. Although Koryŏ was able to maintain its independence, it remained a vassal to the Mongol empire and suffered a long period of domination by the Mongols.

To be sure, the royal house of Koryŏ and that of the Mongol empire were allied by marriage (the son of Wŏnjong married a daughter of Khublai Khan and other crown princes married Mongol princesses and remained in Peking as hostages until they were enthroned), and Koryŏ kings often visited the capital of the Mongol empire. In order to signify that Koryŏ was a subordinate nation, Koryŏ kings were prohibited from using the title *chong* ("progenitor") or *cho* ("ancestor"); instead they could call themselves merely "loyal king" (*wang*) such-and-such. Thus all Koryŏ kings from 1274 to 1351 had monarchical titles of "loyal such-and-such king," meaning they were loyal to the Mongol empire. Moreover, Koryŏ kings took Mongol names, had Mongol-style hairdos, wore Mongol costumes, and used the Mongol language.

The government structure of Koryŏ was also remodeled to differentiate it from that of the Yüan dynasty. Thus the three chancellors were merged to form a single Council of State, and the Royal Secretariat was renamed Milchiksa, whose name suggests diminished importance. Meanwhile, the Mongols put northeastern Korea and Cheju

Island under their direct administrative control. The six boards were reduced to four offices: Personnel and Rites were combined into an Office of Properties, the Board of Revenue became the Office of Census, the Board of Military Affairs was renamed the Office of Military Rosters, the Board of Punishment was renamed the Office of Legal Administration, and the Board of Public Works was abolished.

Korea was also forced to send a large amount of tribute goods to the Mongol court. These included gold, silver, textile fabrics, grain, ginseng, celadon ware, falcons, and eunuchs and young maidens, worsening the economic situation of the people, particularly that of the peasants. During the period of Mongol domination, powerful families that allied with the Mongols gained political privileges, such as participation in the deliberation of the Privy Council, as they enlarged their land holdings and increased the number of slaves owned by them. Many of the members of these powerful families became government officials, securing large areas of land under the salary land system which had replaced in 1271 the original office rank land system under the Stipend Land Law.

The unsuccessful Mongol invasions of Japan in 1274 and 1281 brought about disastrous results to Koryŏ. When the Mongols launched their first invasion in November 1274 with 25,000 troops, Koryŏ was forced to supply 7,000 soldiers and all the ships to carry troops. Bad weather and stiff resistance of the Japanese forced the invading forces to withdraw after losing some 13,000 men, mostly by drowning.

Meanwhile, in 1280 the Mongols established the Eastern Expedition Field Headquarters in Korea in order to launch the second invasion. In the second invasion that was launched in June 1281, the Mongols sent 140,000 troops from China and Korea to Japan. Again, Koryŏ was forced to supply 900 ships, 15,000 seamen, 10,000 soldiers, and a large number of carpenters to repair the ships, as well as a large quantity of provisions, equipment and weapons. The second invasion was met by well-prepared Japanese troops and resulted in bloody battles on land and sea near the shores of northwestern Kyūshū. Then came the typhoon in the midst of fierce fighting in the middle of August, destroying nearly all the ships. It was a total defeat in which some 100,000 invaders were reported to have been killed, half of them by drowning. After the failure to conquer Japan, the Eastern Expedition Field Headquarters was kept as a liaison organ of the Mongols, interfering in the internal affairs of Koryŏ.

Nationalistic Movement. Although Korea suffered many disasters and was dominated by the Mongols, some positive accomplishments were made. King Ch'ungyŏl (reigned 1275-1308) expanded the National Academy and established the Institute for the Teaching of Classics and History for the sons of the officials below the seventh rank. He even made an attempt in 1298 to regain national sovereignty and implement reform measures. His successor, King Ch'ungsŏn (reigned 1308-13) established a royal library called the Hall of Ten Thousand Volumes as Neo-Confucianism of Chu Hsi was introduced to Korea by a Korean scholar, An Yu, who studied in China in the late thirteenth century, arousing a new academic interest. Meanwhile, the printers used movable metal type, and between 1234 and 1313 many books on history and medicine, as well as poetry, were published.

It was King Kongmin (reigned 1351-74) who launched a national recovery movement. His first act was the abolition of the Yüan liaison organ (the Eastern Expedition Field Headquarters), purging the pro-Yüan faction. After that, he restored the former government structures, and recovered the northeastern territory and Cheju Island, which had been administered by the Mongols. By attacking the Mongol military base in Manchuria, he provoked the pro-Mongol faction, which attempted to assassinate him. As the Chinese were overthrowing the Mongol dynasty of Yüan, and establishing the Ming dynasty in 1368, King Kongmin immediately declared a pro-Ming policy.

King Kongmin abolished the Personnel Office, which the Ch'oe dictatorship had established, restoring the authority of the monarchy over personnel matters. Appointing a monk named Shin Ton as a National Preceptor and Prime Minister-Plenipotentiary, Kongmin had him carry out a sweeping reorganization of the government and implement reform measures. Shin Ton ousted all pro-Mongol officials, employed new men in the government, and carried out land reform under the direction of the newly created Directorate for Reclassification of Farmland and Farming Population, returning lands and slaves seized by the powerful families to their original owners. A large number of free men who had been enslaved regained their former status and many slaves were set free. Shin Ton's reform acts aroused strong reactions from the powerful families, bringing not only his own downfall and death, but the assassination of King Kongmin at the hands of the reactionaries.

The Fall of the Koryŏ Dynasty. The Japanese marauders who began to raid the south coast of Korea from the early thirteenth century became increasingly troublesome after 1350 as the entire coastal area of the south and west was affected. The problems that the Japanese pirates created were not brought under control until their base on Tsushima Island was destroyed by a Korean expeditionary force in 1389.

Meanwhile, Korea was invaded in 1359 and 1361 by Chinese bandits called the Red Turbans. They even seized the capital in 1361, forcing the king to flee to Andong, Kyŏngsang Circuit. The Red Turbans were finally driven out but many properties that had survived the Mongol invasions were destroyed.

The political controversy that developed within the Koryŏ court regarding the Mongols and the Chinese created a crisis that signaled the end of the dynastic rule of the Wang clan. Whereas the king was advised by a high military official, Yi In-im, to discard the pro-Ming and revert to the pro-Mongol policy, two other powerful military leaders, Ch'oe Yŏng and Yi Sŏng-gye, vehemently opposed Yi In-im's policy and they collaborated in ousting him from power. However, when in 1388 the Ming dynasty made its intention to establish a Chinese commandery in the northeastern Korea, Ch'oe Yŏng and Yi Sŏng-gye parted ways. Ch'oe launched a military expedition with the king's approval against the Chinese military base in the Liaotung region, and Yi Sŏng-gye was appointed one of the two deputy commanders of the expedition under Ch'oe. Yi took his troops as far as Wihwa Island in the mouth of the Yalu River, but, although he was outraged by the intention of the Ming dynasty to establish its commandery in Korea, he was not fully in favor of the anti-Ming policy and had opposed the expedition plan from the start. Yi led his troops back to Kaegyŏng and ousted the king and Ch'oe, seizing political control for himself.

With the help of many outstanding civil officials such as Chŏng To-jŏn, Yi Sŏng-gye put two kings of his choice on the throne in 1388 and 1389, and carried out a sweeping land reform as he eliminated his opponents one by one. In 1391, after burning all the existing registers of public and private land in 1390, he installed a new Rank

Land Law, redistributing only the land in the Kyŏnggi district to incumbent and former officials, according to the ranks they had in the government, for the lifetime of the recipients. It also allowed the widows of officials who did not remarry to keep a portion of their husband's land as "fidelity land." All other lands were put under state control. Such a sweeping reform brought about the downfall of the powerful families of the literati, and it also gave rise to the anti-Yi movement. Facing such a situation, Yi resolved to overthrow the Koryŏ dynasty, and in the process many royalists, including the highly respected scholar Chŏng Mong-ju, were assassinated. In 1392, Yi Sŏng-gye brought about the end of the Koryŏ dynasty, which had been plagued by rivalry and internal uprisings, as well as foreign invasions for some three hundred years.

5

The Sinified Korea of the Yi Dynasty, 1392-1860

THE Yi dynasty of the Kingdom of Chosŏn which Yi Sŏng-gye established in 1392 lasted until 1910. During this long period, a total of twenty-seven kings ruled the kingdom, converting Korea completely into a Sinified state which was dominated by an aristocratic social group called *yangban*. In this chapter, we will discuss various aspects of the development of the Yi society up to the dawn of the modern age of Korea that arrived in the middle of the nineteenth century.

New Political and Military Patterns

Yi Sŏng-gye, who became T'aejo ("Great Progenitor," reigned 1392-98) of the Yi dynasty, named the new kingdom Chosŏn ("The Land of the Morning Calm"), thereby linking it with the first Korean state. Hanyang was selected as the new capital of the kingdom in accordance with geomantic theories in the hope that the kingdom would last ten thousand years. Hanyang, renamed Hansŏng, eventually became commonly known as Seoul, which means "capital" in Korean.

After selecting the new capital site, T'aejo proceeded to construct magnificent palaces and inner and outer defensive walls, with large and small gates, around the capital Ch'angan, one of the ancient Chinese capitals, was used as a model for the construction of the new capital. Meanwhile, T'aejo subjugated the northwestern region of Korea inhabited by the Jurchens, and the northwestern region north of the Taedong River — which had been a disputed territory — thus making the Yalu and the Tuman rivers the new northern boundary lines of Korea. T'aejo also established Korea's vassalage to Ming China, and sent a mission to Japan, establishing a new relationship with that country.

In the process of the founding of the new dynasty, T'aejo's successor adopted the *Administrative Code of Chosŏn* in early 1400, and the *Six Codes of Governance* with the help of scholars such as Chŏng To-jŏn. The *Six Codes of Governance* was also revised and expanded by his successor, King T'aejong (reigned 1400-1418) into the *Basic Six Codes* and the *Supplemental Six Codes*. Other national codes also adopted by T'aejo's successors were the *Orthodox Code* during the reign of Sejong (1418-1450) and the *National Code* by King Sŏngjong (reigned 1469-1494). Following the publication of a Confucian manual of ethics called *Conduct of the Three Bonds* in 1432, the manual for state ceremonies entitled the *Five Rites of State* was published in 1474. A political handbook entitled *Exemplar for Efficient Government* was published in 1441 to provide guidance for officials.

Political Structure. The top state organ was the Council of State, a policy-making body consisting of three councillors. Its president, called *Yŏng'ŭijŏng*, was a *de facto* prime minister. The Royal Secretariat drafted and transmitted the king's decrees and documents, and transmitted communications to and from the king. In order to prevent abuses in the exercise of political and administrative authority, the Office of Special Lectures, Office of the Inspector-General, and the Office of the Censor-General were created. These were collectively called *Samsa*. Administrative functions were invested in the six ministries of personnel, revenue (taxation), rites (ceremonies), war (military affairs), punishment (justice), and public works. Gradually, the heads of these six ministries also functioned as the king's advisers, overshadowing the Council of State. All important government posts were first held by subjects of merit, but later on, all government officials were selected from those who passed civil service examinations. The top military organ was the Headquarters of the Three Righteous Armies.

Administrative Districts and Local Governments. The kingdom was divided first into seven provinces, and then into eight when the province, which had included all conquered northern areas, was divided into two. (See Map 8)

In addition to provincial capitals, the kingdom had four special magistrate areas, four headquarters for security, and forty-four sub-headquarters for security. Each province was divided into prefectures, each prefecture was divided into counties, and each county into districts. Under the district level were villages and hamlets, and below the village level were areas where slaves resided and worked.

All magistrates, including governors and garrison commanders, were appointed by the central government on fixed terms of office, and village chiefs were selected from local gentry families. Like Koryŏ, the Yi dynasty also disallowed magistrates to serve in their home districts.

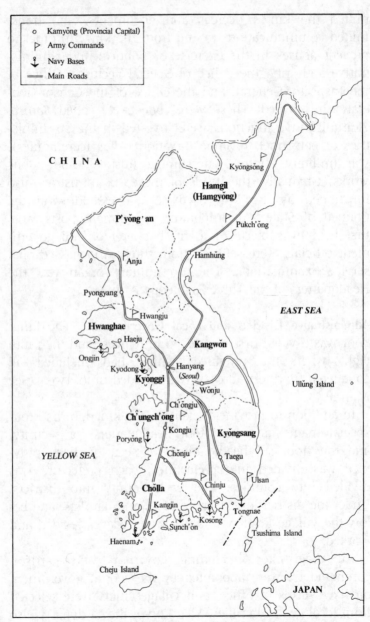

o   Kamyŏng (Provincial Capital)
▷   Army Commands
⚓   Navy Bases
——   Main Roads

CHINA

Kyŏngsŏng

**Hamgil
(Hamgyŏng)**

P'yŏng'an

Pukch'ŏng

Anju

Hamhŭng

Pyongyang

Hwangju

EAST SEA

Hwanghae

Haeju

Kangwŏn

Ongjin

Kyodong

Hanyang
(*Seoul*)

Kyŏnggi

Ullŭng Island

Wŏnju

Ch'ŏngju

Ch'ungch'ŏng

Kongju

Kyŏngsang

Poryŏng

Chŏnju

Taegu

YELLOW SEA

Chinju

Ulsan

Chŏlla

Kangjin

Kosŏng

Tongnae

Sunch'ŏn

Tsushima Island

Haenam

Cheju Island

JAPAN

Map 8.   EIGHT ADMINISTRATIVE DISTRICTS FROM 1392 TO 1896

Each county had its own agency of the local aristocrats who assisted the county superintendents, called "shepherds of the people." The petty functionaries in the local governmental units were called *ajŏn* or *hyangni*.

As in Koryŏ, the nine official rank system for high-ranking officials was adopted, each rank divided into "senior" and "junior" grades, bringing the total number of official ranks to eighteen. These ranks were assigned to those *yangban* members who passed the civil service examinations and were given high administrative positions. No government officials who worked as functionaries (technical workers) or petty officials were given these ranks.

Military Organizations. It took some time to eliminate private armies of merit subjects and others that were formed toward the end of the Koryŏ period. But in 1400, these private armies were either abolished or incorporated into the national army, and the Headquarters of Three Righteous Armies was established as the top military organ of the state. This was followed by the establishment of the Five Military Commands in 1464. In 1530, six garrison forts were built in the lower Tumen River region and four military outposts were constructed in the middle Yalu River region. Subsequently, regional army command headquarters and naval command headquarters were established at key locations as many local garrisons were installed.

The personnel of the military force consisted of officers who passed civil service examinations, professional soldiers, and the peasants who were drafted into military service as "conscript soldiers" (*Pubyŏng*) on a rotation basis. In order to facilitate rapid communication between the capital and regional military command headquarters, a network of beacon fire stations and post (pony) stations was set up.

Early Domestic Disturbances and the Japanese Problem. The auspicious beginning of the Yi dynasty was marred by bloody power struggles among the members of the royal house. The first of such events took place when T'aejo named his successor. T'aejo had eight legitimate sons by two of his queens, and his eighth son, not content with the selection of his half-brother to be the successor, rebelled, killing two of his half-brothers, including the crown prince and an eminent scholar named Chŏng To-jŏn. Shaken by the bloodshed, T'aejo abdicated in 1398 in favor of his second son and retired to a Buddhist monastery.

The new king (Chŏngjong), following advice given by his astrologers who also practiced geomantic theories, abandoned Seoul and took the court to Kaegyŏng but he too faced an internecine feud among his brothers, which brought about his abdication in favor of his brother, who became King T'aejong.

T'aejong ("Great Ancestor") was an able king who reigned 1400-1418. He brought the court back to Seoul, strengthened the authority of the monarchy, improved the government structure, reduced the power of the Buddhists by decreasing the number of temples and monasteries, and confiscated land from evil officials, freeing all the slaves they had possessed. His successor, known as Sejong the Great, accomplished many great deeds as we shall see later.

When Sejong died, he was succeeded by a king whose reign lasted only two years. In 1452, Tanjong, a young son of that king was enthroned under the shadow of his ambitious uncles. Seventeen months later, one of his uncles, Prince Suyang, carried out a bloody plot, forcing his nephew to abdicate and sending him into exile, as he killed all key officials whom he regarded as his enemies. Suyang then took the throne in 1455 as Sejo. The counter-coup of six eminent scholars in 1456 to restore Tanjong met with disaster, producing the "martyrdom of six." Meanwhile, the Yi government which had faced the Jurchen uprising in Hamgil Province in the 1420s, continued to suffer unrest in that region when Yi Ching-ok led a rebellion in 1453. A local magistrate, Yi rebelled against being replaced. This rebellion was followed by another in Hamgil brought about by Yi Shi-ae in 1467, who with the support of a large number of peasants attempted to establish his own state there. These rebellions were crushed, but the problems of the Jurchens became serious in the 1580s, especially in 1583.

Problems in the north were compounded by the presence of Japanese pirates. Although an expedition sent to Tsushima in 1419 destroyed the bases of these pirates, and Korea opened its three ports in the south to the Japanese for trade, Japanese marauders continued to trouble the coastal areas. Finally in 1510, the Japanese residing at the three ports carried out armed uprisings, resulting in the closing of these ports and suspension of trade with Japan until 1572. It was at this juncture that a new Border Defense Council was set up.

Social and Economic Patterns

The Yi dynasty brought about a stratified society whose class lines were clearly drawn and rigidly maintained, creating a social heritage which was sharply influenced by Confucian concepts.

Social Structure. At the top of the social structure was the dominant class called *yangban*, or "both orders," which included the members of the officialdom who served in the ranked positions in the civil and military bureaucracy. Most of the officials were the holders of academic degrees, and they and their family members constituted the *yangban* class. As in Koryŏ, the military order (*muban*) enjoyed less prestige than the civil order (*munban*). All members of the *yangban* class were exempted from performing corvée or military duties. Not allowed to be engaged in any manual labor, they were restricted to government work or to the intellectual and cultural professions. Members of the *yangban* families married among themselves, and they even refused to have any non-*yangban* families as their neighbors. Under social codes that began to be adopted in 1470 women of the upper class had to cover their faces and heads with various types of head coverings when they went out. Widows of the *yangban* families were even forbidden by law to remarry, and sons and grandsons of remarried widows were not eligible to hold any government posts. In the capital of Seoul, the northern and southern sections were reserved for the residences of the *yangban* families.

Below the *yangban* class was the "middle people" (*chung'in*) group which included petty functionaries such as medical staff, language and technical specialists, and military cadre members. These hereditary functions were reserved for the members of this group.

The commoners, called *sang'in* or *sangmin*, were classified into three social categories with the peasants at the top, followed by the artisans and the merchants. Below the commoner class was the "low-born" (*ch'ŏnmin*) group which included slaves, domestic servants, butchers, tanners and leather workers, gravediggers, entertainers, prostitutes, and others who were engaged in "undesirable professions." This social structure dominated by the *yangban* class remained almost intact until the eighteenth century, when new social and economic forces brought about the inevitable evolutionary changes as we shall see later.

The peasants were much like serfs who were bound to the soil, each carrying an identification tag at all times and having no freedom of movement. Under the law, they were not free to relocate their residence, and the law organized five peasant households into a unit that was collectively responsible for the enforcement of the law and fulfillment of their responsibilities, such as paying taxes.

Like Koryŏ society, Yi society had a large slave population. Most of them were public slaves who either tilled the public land or worked at government factories. A majority of private slaves were those who had their own households and tilled the land owned by their owners as if they were serfs, and others were domestic slaves who also tilled some land. Slave status was hereditary, and slaves were bought and sold. There were some 350,000 slaves in the early period of the Yi dynasty, but the number declined to less than 200,000 in the late seventeenth century, following the Japanese and Manchu invasions. Many slaves gained freedom by either paying taxes in lieu of labor service, or by serving in the military. Some bought their freedom from private owners, while others simply ran away, becoming bandits. In 1801, most of the government slaves were freed.

As the influence of Confucianism grew, Korean social patterns became Sinicized according to Confucian precepts. Thus Confucian social ethics and social institutions were transplanted, and the observance of the five Confucian principles which govern human relationships was stressed. These five principles were: absolute loyalty of the subject to the sovereign; filial piety, that is, obedience and respect of children for the father (parent); love between husband and wife; respect of the juniors for the elders; and trustworthiness between friends. Women were indoctrinated to be silent and obedient, and above all chaste. Submissiveness was regarded as a woman's supreme virtue, and her life was governed by the principle of three obediences: to her father as a child, to her husband as a wife, and to her first son as a widow. Her value was judged by her ability to perpetuate the family line and provide care for her husband and his parents. To be a "wise mother and good wife" was to be her supreme goal in life. Under such a social pattern, the status of women declined, and by 1470 they had even lost the property rights which they had previously enjoyed.

No tombs of the Yi period have been excavated. However, it is believed that previous tomb-building style was discarded while the size of the earthen mounds on the burial grounds of the kings and queens, as well as commoners became smaller.

Early Economic System. Like Koryŏ, the economic foundation of Chosŏn of the Yi dynasty was agriculture, and an individual's wealth was measured by the amount of farms and fire-wood land which he owned. As time passed, the number of free artisans and craftsmen who were engaged in manufacturing industries increased, bringing commercial growth and changes in the economic structure of the kingdom.

When the Yi dynasty came into being, land grants were made to meritorious subjects while the Rank Land Law, which Yi Sŏng-gye had put into operation in 1391. Both incumbent and former officials were allocated land in the enlarged Kyŏnggi district according to their ranks. Although the rank lands were granted for the lifetime of the recipients only, a large amount of these lands became private properties of their families. Much of the land was kept to raise revenue to meet the need of the court and the central government, and land allocations were made to local governments and educational institutions to raise revenues to defray their expenditures. Each garrison was also given a certain amount of land to meet its financial needs.

In 1466, the Rank Land Law was replaced by the Office Land Law, under which land grants were made only to incumbent office holders. This was abolished in 1556 and after that officials were paid salaries in cash and goods rather than land. Up until 1556, land grants to meritorious subjects and the allocation of territory to military officers as hereditary property were made, but gradually the system of salary payment replaced the system of land allocation. A clear trend was the steady decrease of state-owned land as the amount of land owned by the *yangban* families gradually increased. All farms, whether they were public property or owned by civil and military officials and the *yangban* families, were cultivated by the peasants who paid a land tax equal to one-tenth of the harvest. The land tax rate was reduced to one-twentieth under the Tribute Tax law enacted in 1444 and farmlands were classified into six grades according to their fertility. The number of *kyŏl*, or productivity units, was determined in accordance with the fertility of the land, and the tax rate was based on the number of *kyŏl*, not on the size of the land.

In addition to land tax, the peasants who cultivated land as tenants paid rent, which was fifty percent of the harvest, to private landlords. In cases of government property, the rent was twenty-five percent of the harvest. However, the landlords usually collected more than a half of the harvest from their tenants. Furthermore, the peasants were obligated to pay local tax in goods as well as a corvée (labor) tax, and also performed military services as conscript soldiers on a rotation basis. In order to make the peasants collectively responsible for their duties to the state, peasant households were organized into units of five.

In order to improve their livelihood, the peasants made improvements in technology, dug reservoirs, and increasingly used fertilizers. At the same time, they reclaimed marsh lands, converting them into rice paddies. They also produced cotton and hemp cloth as well as silk.

The production of farm implements, brass ware, furniture, brush pens and paper, and weapons also increased, meeting the growing demands. At one point, some 6,300 skilled workers were employed by the government in Seoul and in the provinces.

Although commercial growth was discouraged under certain Confucian concepts, large merchant firms grew in the capital, establishing wholesale and retail shops in certain designated areas in the city. Among them were the Six Licensed Stores, which were authorized by the government to deal in silk, cotton cloth, writing brushes, paper goods, ramie cloth, and marine products such as dried fish and seaweed. Certain grain dealers became agents for the government and the *yangban* families.

Local periodic markets came into being where retail merchants and peddlers sold their goods to local inhabitants. At the same time, wholesale markets emerged here and there in the southern regions where large quantities of medical herbs and oxen were traded.

Early Cultural Development

Confucianism and Buddhism. Neo-Confucianism became the orthodox state creed of Yi Korea. It was introduced by An Yu, who had studied in China and returned to Korea in the early fourteenth century. Intolerant and highly theoretical and doctrinary in concept, Neo-Confucianism was a branch of Confucianism that dealt with the nature of man and kingly authority, and it attempted to explain the universal order in metaphysical terms. In political ethics, it emphasized the kingly authority and absolute loyalty of the subjects to the ruler. In its social doctrine, it stressed the observance of the five ethical principles in human relations previously mentioned. Observance of ceremonial rites such as ancestor worship was regarded as a cardinal virtue. The rise of such a doctrine eventually brought about bitter controversies among Confucian scholars, resulting in four purges of scholars (*Sahwa*) between 1498 and 1545.

Among the dominant Neo-Confucian scholars were Kim Chong-jik (1431-92) and his main disciple, Kim Il-son, who was executed in the second purge of scholars in 1504. Other leading Neo-Confucian scholars were Cho Kwang-jo(1482-1519), who promoted the Village Code (*hyang'yak*) Movement shortly before he was executed in 1519; Yi Hwang(T'oegye, 1501-70), who stressed the importance of a principle called *i*, which he believed governs human nature and behavior; and Yi I (Yulgok, 1536-84), who emphasized the principle of the energizing element called *ki*. Represented by Yi Hwang and Yi I, the *i* and *ki* schools of Neo-Confucianism consisted of numerous outstanding groups of *literati*, called *sarim*, of the sixteenth and seventeenth centuries, who were engaged in active scholarly debate. Some of them championed the observance of family rituals stressed by Chu Hsi in his essay entitled *Family Rites*.

The Confucianization of Korea led to the sudden decline of Buddhism. King T'aejong had already inaugurated in 1406 an anti-Buddhist policy, drastically reducing the number of temples and monasteries, and confiscating

• *The portrait of Yi I and his calligraphic work.*

their lands and slaves. The culturally tolerant King Sejong and one of his successors whose personal faith was Buddhism tolerated Buddhism, resulting in the famed Wŏn'gak Temple being built in Seoul in the 1450's. However, after 1468 a policy of suppression was pursued, leading to the complete abrogation of the monk registration system and a total ban on anyone entering the priesthood.

In the middle of the sixteenth century, Buddhism recovered its strength somewhat as the Pong'ŭn Temple was made the headquarters for the *Sŏn* School and the Pongsŏn Temple that of the *Kyo* School. But the Buddhist revival was short-lived and Buddhism became the religion of mostly the uneducated, rural population.

Educational Development and Civil Service Examinations. In order to promote education, the national Confucian academy called *Sŏnggyun'gwan* was established in Seoul. Below it were four schools in Seoul for Confucian studies. In the local areas county schools, called *hyanggyo*, were established. Primary schools, called *sŏdang*, where basic

Chinese characters and some Confucian classics were taught, were also established in the villages by individual scholars. All these schools were for the sons of the *yangban* families. Primary education began at the age of four, and at the age of seven selected students advanced to the four schools in Seoul or to the county schools. A small number of graduates of these secondary schools were admitted into the national academy in Seoul.

The civil service examination system which was

Sŏdang*(village school) by Kim Hong-do (Tanwŏn, ca. 1745-?)*.

imported from China conducted two levels of examinations: the licentiate (lower level) and the erudite (higher level). For each examination a quota of thirty-three was set. Successful candidates were then permitted to take a palace examination in the presence of the king. The candidate who passed the palace examination with the highest grade was given the coveted and prestigious degree of *chang'wŏn* and accorded special treatment with an assumed chance to advance to a high rank on the bureaucratic ladder. These examinations were conducted once every three years, but occasionally special examinations were given, diminishing the importance of the triennial examinations.

Three categories of civil service examinations were given: the classics licentiate examination, the military examination, and the general information examination. Whereas the classics licentiate examination dealt with Confucian subjects and literary qualifications, the military examination tested skills in military arts, as well as knowledge of Confucian classics and military text. The general information examination was given in foreign languages, medicine, astronomy (including divination and geomancy), and law.

Needless to say, the classics examination had higher prestige, followed by the military examination and the general information examination in descending order. Whereas those who took the upper two divisional examinations were from *yangban* families, those who took the general information examination came from the "middle people" (*chung'in*) group and remained in that social class.

Although educational opportunities were limited primarily to sons of the *yangban* class, many sons of the families of the "middle people" group and some of the commoner families received formal educations. After the sixteenth century this phenomenon became more apparent as some of the sons of the commoner families secured lower positions in government services. Young girls of the *yangban* families received education at home, mostly under the supervision of their father or grandfather.

King Sejong and the Cultural Development. During the reign of King Sejong (1418-50) great cultural and scientific advancement was brought about. The most important advancement was the creation of the Korean alphabet, commonly called *han'gŭl*, by scholars of the Hall of Worthies who had been commissioned by the king to do so. Sejong, who believed that Koreans ought to have their own written language, adopted the new Korean script and promulgated it in 1446 as *Hunmin Chŏng'ŭm*, or the "Correct Sounds to Instruct the People." The language itself consisted of vowels, diphthongs(double-vowels), consonants and double-consonants.

Although conservative, pro-Chinese *literati* officials called it *ŏnmun*, or "vernacular language," and refused to use it, King Sejong established the Office for Publication in Han'gul, which published such works as the *Songs of Dragons Flying to Heaven*, a tribute to the virtues of the royal ancestors, and the *Dictionary of Proper Pronunciation of Korean*. The new, simple writing system enabled the women of the *yangban* families and the commoners to be literate, contributing to the rise of a new culture in Korea as will be seen later.

In addition, Sejong built an observatory on the grounds of the palace in 1434, and encouraged scientists to invent new tools, resulting in the creation of the rain guage in 1442, astronomical clocks, sundials, and water clocks. A year after his death, a projectile-launching vehicle was invented, followed by the invention of rocket projectiles, and instruments to measure land elevation and distance.

Early Scholarship. With the development of education under state sponsorship, and by the efforts made by scholars who had retired from government offices and established private schools, scholarship rapidly developed. With the production of improved removable copper printing types beginning in 1403, numerous books authored by these scholars were published, enriching the national culture. Many of these were historical studies, such as the *Annals of King T'aejo*, published in 1413. Following the publication of this book, a series of annals (*shillok*), which recorded court and national events covering the entire Yi period, was published.

The adoption of the new Korean written language stimulated the growth of native studies. Thus between 1432 and 1485, many books of the history and geography of Korea were produced. Among them were *Precious Mirror for Succeeding Reigns*, a new *History of Koryŏ*, *Essentials of the History of Koryŏ*, *Comprehensive Mirror of Korea*, *Geographical Description of the Eight Provinces*, and *Augmented Survey of the Geography of Korea*. At the same time, such books as *Straight Talk on Farming*, *Compilation of Native Prescriptions*, *Exemplar of Korean Medicine*, *Calculation of the Motions of the Seven Celestial Determinants*, and *Records on Gunpowder Weaponry* were published.

Poetry and Song. While the Confucian *literati* were involved in writing Chinese-style poetry (*Hanshi*), new two, four-syllable semantic units of Korean lyric verse called *kasa* were being written by such poets as Chŏng Ch'ŏl of the sixteenth century, who created such poems as the new *Kwandong pyŏlgok* and *Samiin gok*. Meanwhile, such poets as Pak Il-lo and Yun Sŏn-do of the late sixteenth and early seventeenth centuries refined and popularized the *shijo* poetry that had developed at the end of the Koryŏ period. Among the masterpieces of *shijo* were Yun Sŏn-do's *Song to Five Companions* and *New Songs from My Mountain Fast.* Yun's *Song to Five Companions* reads as follows:

> *How many friends have I?*
> *The streams and rocks, the pines and bamboo;*
> *You too I welcome,*
> *Moon rising over eastern mountain.*
> *What need is there for more*
> *Beyond these five companions?*

Not only men, but also women, such as Shin Saim-dang, mother of the eminent Confucian scholar Yi I (Yulgok) became accomplished *shijo* composers. A *kisaeng* (female entertainer) of the sixteenth century, Hwang Chin-i, who lived in Songdo (Kaegyŏng), wrote the following *shijo*:

> *I would cut the waist of*
> *The long November night,*
> *And roll up one half*
> *And keep it under my coverlet*
> *Of the spring breeze.*
> *And when my love returns to me*
> *I would unroll it inch by inch.*

While traditional short *shijo* was composed, many long, descriptive poems (*kasa* and *sasŏl shijo*) were also produced. An anonymous poet left behind the following long poem:

> *Pass where the winds pause before crossing over,*
> *Pass where the clouds too pause before crossing,*

> *High peaks of Changsong Pass where*
> *Wild hawks and trained hawks*
> *And highest soaring falcons*
> *All must pause before crossing over.*
> *Were it my love awaiting me across yonder pass*
> *I would pause not once in my crossing over.*

Some *shijo* poems were instructional by nature, but most of them revealed inner feelings and convictions. Some expressed egalitarian concepts or a carefree lifestyle while others were satirical in character.

Kim Ch'ŏn-t'aek, who was an accomplished *shijo* poet himself, compiled a catalog of songs entitled *Enduring Poetry of Korea* in 1728, and Kim Su-jang, another *shijo* poet, published an anthology entitled *Songs of Korea* in 1763. The *Anthology of Korean Poetry*, which was compiled by Pak Hyo-kwan and An Min-yŏng, was published in 1876.

Painting. Ink and brush drawings, mostly landscapes known as "literary painting" – which had developed in Koryŏ, were increasingly popular among the *yangban* scholars of the Yi period who became fine painters by avocation. Among them was Kang Hŭi-an(1419-64). In addition, government artists such as An Kyŏn of the mid-fifteenth century, Ch'oe Kyŏng of the late fifteenth century, and Yi Sang-jwa of the early sixteenth century, made names for themselves. They drew mostly idealized Chinese-style landscape paintings. Of these, An Kyŏn's "Dream of Strolling in a Peach Garden" is the most famous. At the same time, the painting of what the painters called the "four gentlemen" became increasingly popular. These "four gentlemen" were the plum, the orchid, the chrysanthemum, and bamboo. In addition, paintings of other flowers such as the peony, palms and

Punch'ŏng*("powder-green")bottle of the Yi period; white porcelain jar with an angler in underglazed blue, Yi period.*

banana plants, birds such as sparrows and magpies, and animals, especially cats and dogs, became popular.

Along with literary and other painters, famous calligraphers emerged as painting and calligraphy were regarded as a single form of fine art.

Ceramic Art. The potters of the Yi period developed a new ceramic art, producing a particular ware known as "powder green"(*punch'ŏng*) of various sizes and shapes which was rustic and unpretentious in appearance. The "powder-green" tea cups were valued highly not only in Korea, but also in Japan.

White porcelain ware (*paekcha*), which replaced the jade-green celadon ware of the Koryŏ period, was simple in form and had underglaze designs of birds, fish, flowers, bamboo, orchids, and landscapes in cobalt blue. In the early Yi period, white porcelain and "powder-green" ware were produced mostly for the *yangban* class.

Unfortunately, however, the ceramic industry was totally destroyed during the Japanese invasions at the end of the sixteenth century as major kilns were smashed and a large number of ceramic workers were taken captive to Japan. It took a long time for this industry to revive. When it did, the art of "powder-green" ware was missing and the production of white porcelain ware dominated the ceramic industry. For the commoners, brown ceramic ware of various shapes and sizes was produced.

Confucian Ritual Music and Dance. The Chinese music known in Korea as *Tang-ak* or *a-ak*, meaning graceful music, developed rapidly with the adoption of Chinese-style Confucian and court ceremonies. Chinese music and dance were employed for Confucian shrine rituals and court ceremonies. While using Chinese musical notes and instruments, Korean musicians composed music including the now well-known *The Ball Throwing Dance, A Nightingale Singing in a Spring Eve*, and *The Boating Dance*.

In addition to *a-ak*, which was used mostly for rituals, another form called *chŏng-ak*, or authentic music, developed for the enjoyment of the *yangban*. Needless to say, the shamans, masked dancers, and public entertainers perpetuated the native music and dance while the Buddhist monks maintained their traditional religious music and dance.

The Decline of the Yi Dynasty

The Literati Purges and Their Aftermath. The conflict between the king and the officials in the Censorates and the Office of Special Lecturers, and the power struggle between the meritorious elite and the Neo-Confucian *literati* brought about a series of bloody tragedies known as *sahwa*, or "literati purges," between the years of 1498 and 1545. These purges resulted in a chaotic political situation which contributed to the decline of the Yi Dynasty.

The first two such purges were brought about by the mentally unbalanced king Yŏnsan'gun in 1498 and 1504, when a large number of Neo-Confucian *literati*, as well as many meritorious elites, were put to death. The third purge came in 1506, when the new king, in alliance with the merit subjects, eliminated many Neo-Confucian scholars. The fourth purge came in 1545, when a young king who was under his mother's strong influence purged more Neo-Confucian scholars. Thus within a half century, many outstanding Neo-Confucian scholars became victims of purges, while the kings themselves became less effective in ruling their kingdom. Needless to say, these purges weakened the foundation of the Yi dynasty considerably.

Although the Neo-Confucian *literati* suffered greatly in these successive purges, their power in the local regions continued to grow as many of them retired from the government and established private academies. Thus they were able to regain their former strength by the middle of the sixteenth century.

The first prominent private academy (Sosu Sŏwŏn), which was founded in 1543, was followed by more than one hundred such academies by 1608, bringing about the revival of the Neo-Confucian group while at the same time promoting education in rural areas. Among the academies was the Tosan Sŏwŏn of Yi Hwang (T'oegye). An important movement which the founders of these academies launched in the late sixteenth century was that of *hyang'yak*, or the "village code" movement. Embodying the four objectives for the promotion of mutual encouragement of morality, mutual supervision of wrongdoing, mutual decorum in social relations, and mutual succor in time of disaster or hardship, they enhanced the solidarity among the Neo-Confucian *literati* and between them and the local inhabitants.

The Rise of Factional Strife. Once the memories of the *literati* purges faded away, intellectual conflict and power struggles between conservative orthodox Confucians and the doctrinary Neo-Confucian scholars, coupled with personal rivalries among the high government officials who represented their own regional interests, brought about a long period of factional strife beginning in 1575.

This unfortunate chapter in the history of the Yi dynasty was opened by two officials—Shim Ŭi-gyŏm and Kim Hyo-wŏn. Shim lived in the western ward of Seoul, hence his followers were called the Western Men. Kim's residence was in the eastern ward of Seoul, and his followers were called the Eastern Men. Most of the Eastern Men were the followers of Yi Hwang, who had emphasized the importance of the principle governing nature and human nature called *i*; whereas most of the Western Men were the followers of Yi I, who emphasized the importance of the energizing element called *ki*. As factional strife grew, many private academies became involved in it, throwing the whole academic community into serious disarray.

The victory of the Eastern Men faction in this power struggle restored an uneasy peace in the world of politics. However, the Eastern Men faction was split into the Northern Men and the Southern Men groups, while the Western Men faction was divided into the Old Doctrine and the Young Doctrine groups, bringing a long period of political chaos created by the men of "Four Colors," meaning the four factions. Eventually, the Old Doctrine faction gained primacy in the late eighteenth century, but this did not restore political stability.

Rebellions. As the ruling class was embroiled in a power struggle, the national defense system deteriorated as the system of the Stabilizer Granaries, which was established to maintain the price level of grain, became inoperative when surplus grain dwindled. The system of the Charitable Granaries too became less beneficial to the peasants when users (those who received grain loans during the spring hunger season) were required to pay a ten percent user's fee, increasing the burden on the poverty-stricken peasants. As a result, many peasants left their villages, becoming wanderers or "fire-field" people who burned mountain slopes and grew food for sustenance. Yet others became bandits.

In such a situation, in 1562 a bandit leader called Lim Kŏ-jŏng (Yim Kkŏk-chŏng) in Hwanghae Province brought about the first serious peasant rebellion of the Yi period, killing a large number of people and destroying many towns and villages. Soon after this, a rebel named Chŏng Yŏ-rip in Chŏlla Province was planning to overthrow the government, but the plot was discovered in 1589 and he was executed. Then in 1624, an official named Yi Kwal brought about a rebellion. Yi had helped King Injo to succeed to the throne which King Kwanghaegun vacated in 1623 under the pressure of the Western Men. Yi became disgruntled when he discovered that the reward he was given for his contribution was that of a lower level. Thus, he raised a rebel force in P'yŏng'an Province and marched to Seoul, forcing the king to flee to the southern town of Kongju. His rebellion was crushed by royal troops, but the political situation remained unstable.

Foreign Invasions. Between 1592 and 1636 Korea suffered

two foreign invasions while witnessing the unending factional strife. The first disastrous foreign invasion came
when Korea refused the passage of Japanese troops to go
to conquer China. In 1592, a large number of Japanese
troops under Toyotomi Hideyoshi invaded the southern
coasts of Korea and moved inland. With the great naval
victory of the Korean admiral Yi Sun-shin in the Battle of
the Hansan Sea using his newly invented iron-clad and
heavily armed "turtle boats," together with the rise of the
people of all walks of life against the invaders, a stalemate developed as the occu-
pied territories were recovered.

*"Turtle boat" in the
Battle of the Hansan Sea.*

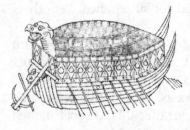

In 1597, the Japanese
launched a second invasion
when truce talks broke
down. But well-prepared Korean troops, along with Chinese troops which arrived to
assist the Koreans, prevented
the occupation of most of
Korea by the Japanese while Admiral Yi won another
victory at sea. With the death of Toyotomi Hideyoshi, Japanese troops withdrew from Korea in 1598.

The seven-year war of the Japanese left deep scars in
Korea. Enormous property damage had been inflicted by
the Japanese. The size of taxable land shrank from 1.7
million *kyŏl* to 540,000 *kyŏl*. Many palaces, including
the Kyŏngbok Palace in Seoul and numerous historic
structures, were destroyed, farms were laid to ruin, and
tens of thousands of people were killed. The population
was decreased as over 200,000 skilled workers, particularly ceramic workers, were taken captive to Japan,
destroying Korea's ceramic industry. As a result, a Korean
hatred of the Japanese began to take deep roots. A *shijo*

poet, Pak Il-lo, described the state of affairs as follows.

> *Higher than mountains*
> *The bones piled up in the fields.*
> *Vast cities and great towns*
> *Became the burrows of wolves and foxes.*

Before Korea could recover from the severe wounds inflicted on her by the Japanese, factional strife revived as Korea encountered the threats of the Jurchens (Manchus), who established the state of Later Chin (late renamed Ch'ung) in Manchuria and forced Korea to adopt an anti-Ming, pro-Manchu policy. When the new Korean king abandoned his predecessor's pro-Manchu policy in 1624 and adopted a pro-Ming policy, the Manchus increased their threats to Korea. It was at this juncture that the aforementioned rebellion of Yi Kwal occurred, with Seoul being occupied. The rebels were defeated, but Korea encountered a second foreign invasion in 1627 as Manchu troops penetrated as far south as Hwanghae Province, forcing the Yi court to seek peace by accepting the role of younger brother to Later Chin.

When Korea refused to acknowledge the sovereignty of the empire of Later Chin (now renamed Ch'ing), the Manchus launched their second invasion in 1636, subjugating Korea and making it a vassal to the Ch'ing dynasty, which became the ruling dynasty in China in 1644. Although the second Manchu war was a short one, it also left deep scars in Korea, this time in the northern part. Farm properties were destroyed and tens of thousands of people were taken away to Manchuria as captives. A tremendous amount of gold, silver, grain and other products were sent to the Ch'ing court as tribute. Kim Sang-hŏn, a scholar who was taken hostage to the Manchu court, left the following departing *shijo*:

> *Fare thee well, Mt. Samgak,*
> *We shall meet again, Han River,*
> *I leave the mountain and rivers of my homeland.*
> *In these uncertain times;*
> *Who could tell when I shall return?*

When, between 1654 and 1658, the Manchus clashed with the Russians in the Amur (Black Dragon) River region, the Korean government sent a squadron of riflemen to assist the Manchus. In 1712, negotiations carried out between Korea and China set new boundaries between the two nations. With this, Korea abandoned its territorial claims in southern Manchuria.

Reform Advocates and New Trends

In 1628, a Dutch ship was wrecked near Cheju Island and its crew who were rescued were kept in Korea to help in making weapons. This group was joined by the crew of another Dutch ship, *Sparrow Hawk*, which was wrecked near Cheju Island in 1653. Its crew were likewise kept as hostages at weaponeries.

The Korean government could have treated them well and secured their assistance in obtaining information regarding the Western world, importing some of its technology and promoting Western Learning as the Japanese had done earlier. Instead, the Korean government imprisoned these men, forcing them to work as slave laborers and displaying absolutely no interest in learning anything from the West. While some died in Korea and during the Manchu wars, Hendrik Hamel, the cargo master of the *Sparrow Hawk* and some of his companions, eventually escaped from Korea to Nagasaki, Japan. In 1668, after Hamel had returned to Holland, he wrote a book introducing Korea to the West.

Be that as it may, there were reform-minded kings and scholars who advocated strengthening the nation and making some change for that purpose. At the same time, new economic, social, and cultural trends developed from the late seventeenth century on.

Self-awakening and the Reform Movement. After suffering devastating foreign invasions and encountering domestic upheavals, the Korean government carried out some reform measures. King Sukchong, who reigned 1674-1720, reorganized the military, establishing five new army garrisons in the capital area and a military training command. He also revamped provincial garrisons. He established the Office of Embankment Works and initiated various projects, digging ponds and constructing reservoirs for irrigation purposes. He also coined new money, called *sangp'yŏng t'ongbo*, and brought about commercial development. However, he witnessed the revival of malicious factional strife which resulted in the death of many scholar-officials, including Song Shi-yŏl. The minimal economic recovery which had been achieved after the 1630s was negated. To make matters worse, the population grew from five million in 1668 to 6.8 million in 1717, making the shortage of food progressively worse. In 1671 alone, some 300,000 people were reported to have died of starvation.

Sangp'yŏng t'ongbo.

Facing these problems, a group of reform-minded scholars emerged in the seventeenth century, preaching what became known as "Practical Learning"(*Shirhak*). Among them were Yi Su-gwang (Chibong, 1563-1628), Yu Hyŏng-wŏn (Pan'gye, 1622-73), Yi Ik (Sŏngho, 1681-1763) and Yu Su-wŏn (1696-1755). Yi Su-gwang in his *Topical Discourses*, Yu Hyŏng-wŏn in his *Memoirs of Pan'gye*, Yi Ik in his *Discourses of Sŏngho* and *Record of Concerns for the Underprivileged*, and Yu Su-wŏn in his *Idle Jotting* examined and criticized the Yi dynasty's political condition, the land system and taxation, and the prevailing social maladies, proposing many changes. These *Shirhak* scholars were critical of the "empty talks" of theoretically oriented, doctrinary Neo-Confucian scholars. They insisted that all ideas and practices should be judged on their utilitarian merits. Their main concern was the improvement of the welfare of the nation and people. Meanwhile, Han Paek-kyŏm (1562-1615) wrote the *Treatise on the Geography of Korea* and Pak Se-dang (1629-1703) authored the *Manual of Farming*.

Those *Shirhak* scholars who emerged in the eighteenth century were extremely active in promoting various new ideas as they contributed toward the development of academic interests in various fields. They advocated a clean break with tradition and the discovery of new ways for the solution of national problems and social and economic ills. A revolutionary idea that they introduced was that the king could not exist without the people, but the people could exist without the king. Some of them who advocated what is known as "Northern Learning" were particularly concerned with economic and social reconstruction, expressing extremely critical views on existing social patterns and economic systems. Many of them traveled to Peking, China, witnessing the various changes taking place there. Upon their return to Korea, they wrote their memoirs in which they preached Korea's need to change. Among them were Hong Tae-yong (1731-83), who wrote *Peking Diary*, and Pak Chi-wŏn (1737-1805), who authored *Jehol Diary*. Meanwhile, Pak Che-ga (1750-?) wrote a book entitled *Discourses on Northern Learning*, in which he strongly criticized the traditionalism of Koreans.

These scholars and those who came after them stimulated the rise of a new interest in the study of Korea's history, geography, and culture, and at the same time produced a large number of books concerning politics, economy, and social matters. Among the historical writings were an encyclopedia of Korean studies entitled *Reference Compilation of Documents on Korea*, published in 1770, *Annotated Account of Korean History*, *Comprehensive Record of Successive Reigns*, which dealt with the history of the Yi kings up to Yŏngjo, and two books entitled *History of Korea*.

Many geographical studies were also published. Among them were *Studies on Historical Geography of Korea* and *Studies on Our Land*. The writing of such books as *Ecological Guide to Korea*, *Studies on Routes and Roads*, and *Studies on Mountains and Rivers* reflected the wide range of academic interests of the *Shirhak* scholars. The production of *Map of Korea* by Chŏng Sang-gi (1678-1752) was an important accomplishment. Studies on the Korean language were also advanced when *Explication of Korean Phonology* and *Treatise on Korean Scripts* were published.

Chŏng Yak-yong (Tasan, 1762-1830) was a prolific scholar who was converted to Catholicism. As one of the leading *Shirhak* scholars, he authored many books and essays on politics, economy, education, and other matters. Among his works were: *Admonitions on Governing the People*, *Treatise on Farmland*, *Design for*

Good Government, and *Toward a New Jurisprudence,* which dealt with political and economic matters. He also wrote *Studies on Our Land,* as well as *Catalog of Fishes of the Chasan Island* and *Comprehensive Treatise on Smallpox,* reflecting his varied interests.

Among other books which *Shirhak* scholars and others authored was *Biography of Renowned Korean Generals.* Following the publication of a book entitled *Farming in Korea,* and as the cultivation of sweet potatoes increased, three books dealing with the growing of sweet potatoes were published.

Following the publication of *Supplement to the National Code* during the reign of Yŏngjo, *Supplement to the Five Rites of State* was published. After this, two military books entitled the *Revised Illustrated Manual of Military Training and Tactics* and the *Comprehensive Manual of Martial Arts* were published. During the reign of Chŏngjo, the *Reference Compilation of Documents on Korea,* the *Comprehensive National Code,* the *Exemplar of Documents and Letters of State,* the *Documents on Foreign Relations,* the *Records of the Ministry of Taxation,* and the *Records of the Ministry of Punishment* were published.

Reform Kings. In 1724, Yŏngjo who reigned 1724-76, was enthroned, and he stabilized the political situation, reduced factional disputes, and improved economic conditions. Under the policy of "equal opportunity," he brought able scholars into the government regardless of their factional affiliations, and despite the crisis created by the Rebellion of Yi In-jwa in 1728, he enacted the Uniform Land Tax Law. Under this law, about one percent of the harvest from each *kyŏl* was payable by the peasants as land tax in cotton cloth or in coins, as well as in grain. With this, the tribute tax law, which had been burdensome to the peasants, was abolished. In order to administer the new law, the Agency to Bestow Benevolence was established.

In 1750 the Equalized Tax Law was enacted, reducing the payment of the cloth tax from two bolts to one as new taxes on fishing tools and vessels, trading vessels, and salt were added. As before, the *yangban* were exempt from paying these taxes. At the same time, in order to check the abuses of power by governors and other local magistrates, the system of king's secret inspectors was instituted.

These reform measures enabled the peasant to have more food as the new laws stimulated the growth of cottage industry and commercial activity. At this juncture, organized merchant groups emerged, promoting commerce. Among these were merchants in Seoul called *Kyŏngsang*, merchants in Kaegyŏng who were called *Songsang*, and those merchants called *Mansang* in Korea's northern border towns who were engaged in trade in Manchuria. Meanwhile, the Peddlers Guild of local pack and back peddlers was formed as other guilds and mutual aid financial institutions were established throughout the country.

King Chŏngjo, who succeeded Yŏngjo in 1776, instituted a benevolent relief program for the poor, banished shamans from the court, and continued reform measures that his predecessor had initiated. He established a royal institute called the Kyujanggak, encouraging the development of scholarship. The freeing of government slaves in 1801, except those who worked at government weapons and Chinaware manufacturing places, stimulated the rise of the artisan class and the increase of craft industry, as these former slaves with various skills became free artisans, and worked at paper, iron goods, and brassware manufacturing places. The recovery of the ceramic industry was slow in coming. However, the potters restored ruined kilns and began to produce a growing amount of white porcelain along with brown wares.

The Development of Popular Culture

As the Confucian oriented political and social order lost its legitimacy and prestige, a popular culture promoted by some disillusioned Confucian *literati* as well as common people developed from the late seventeenth century, enriching the cultural life of the Koreans.

Popular Literature. In the late fourteenth century, Kim Shi-sŭp had written a strange story entitled *New Stories of the Golden Turtle*, patterned after the strange tales of China. It was the first tale written with Korea as its background.

A significant cultural development was the writing of novels and tales in Korean. Kim Man-jung was the first one to do so when he published a popular novel entitled *Dream of Cloud Nine* in 1689 for the non-*yangban* readers. After this, Hŏ Kyun, another *yangban* scholar of the early seventeenth century, enriched the field when he published the *Tale of Hong Kil-tong*, a novel in which he exposed social injustices. In 1757, a *Shirhak* scholar, Pak Chi-wŏn, wrote the *Tale of Yangban*, ridiculing the *yangban*. Following this more non-*yangban* oriented novels and tales appeared for popular consumption. Among these works, which reflected the social and economic realities of the commoners and other lower-class people and described the manners and customs of the time, were the *Tale of Ch'unhyang*, the *Tale of Shim Ch'ŏng*, the *Tale of Changhwa and Hongnyŏn*, and the

Tale of Hŭngbu. Among historical novels published were the *Story of Lim Kyŏng-ŏp* and *The War Diary of 1592.*

The Rise of New Painters. To be sure, traditional painting and calligraphy continued to flourish in the hands of "literati painters" in the seventeenth century and after. Among them was the renowned calligrapher and painter Kim Chŏng-hŭi (Ch'usa, 1786-1856), who was also an accomplished epigrapher, and Chang Sŭng-ŏp (1843-97), whose painting, "Plum Blossom Red on White" won high praise.

However, influenced by *Shirhak* scholars, who promoted the new intellectual trends and Korean studies, painters such as Chŏng Sŏn (1676-1759) produced Korean landscape paintings such as "The Diamond Mountains" and "Storm Lifting Over Inwang Mountain,"

One of Ch'usa Kim Chŏng-hŭi's calligraphic works.

discarding the Chinese-style painting of idealized landscape, and bringing realism into native landscape painting.

At the same time, genre painters emerged and produced works depicting scenes from the ordinary, everyday events of both the *yangban* and the common people. Among these painters were Kim Hong-do, Shin Yun-bok, and Kim Tŭk-shin of the late eighteenth and early nineteenth centuries. Whereas Kim Hong-do specialized in painting various activities of the common people—drawing dancers, house-builders, teachers and pupils, travelers, wrestlers, and others in action. Shin Yun-bok painted contemporary customs, portraits of female entertainers (*kisaeng*), or the "gentlemen" at social gatherings. One of Kim Tŭk-shin's masterpieces was a delightful painting entitled "Breaking of the Calm."

Meanwhile, new painters who displayed an individualistic style emerged in the seventeenth and eighteenth centuries. Although Kang Hŭi-an had already introduced a new style of painting in the fifteenth century, men who were influenced by the Chiejiang branch of the Southern Sung school of painting emerged, promoting what is called the *Chŏlp'a* style in Korea. These painters produced a highly individualistic style of painting which used a minimum number of bold brush strokes, creating an impression and mood rather than describing scenery. Kim Myŏng-guk's "Dharma," "Moon Viewing by the Rock," and "Homeward Bound in the Snow," Han Shi-gak's "P'odae"(spirit of good omen), Yi Myŏng-uk's "Chat Between a Fisherman and a Woodcutter" and Shim Sa-jŏng's "Goblin playing with a Toad" are masterpieces which display originality, simplicity, spontaneity and liveliness.

The Development of Folk Culture. While the disenchanted Confucian scholars produced new literature and art, the common people, whose antagonism toward the *yangban* culture had grown, promoted a popular culture which enriched the otherwise dreary life of the masses.

Folk painting that developed in the middle of the late Yi period was a significant aspect of the growing folk culture. It encompassed a broad range of subjects, depicting real life and beliefs as well as fantasy. Some of the folk paintings had Buddhist, Taoist, and shamanist overstones, while others depicted the agony of the masses.

A key characteristic of this type of painting was its coloring, which traced back to the "Five Elements of Thought" of shamanism, which viewed the world in terms of the harmony and juxtaposition of five colors—red, white, yellow, blue, and black. Most folk paintings reflected folk beliefs which were expressed in folklore, and the paintings were often used to attract good spirits or fend off evil ones. The symbols of longevity were popular subjects: the sun, water, rocks, pine trees, bamboo, and the herb of eternal youth. Folk painters also produced decorative art work, the subjects of their paintings being such objects as furniture, penholders, reading tables and books, as well as birds and animals.

Folk musicians and dancers popularized old as well as new songs and dances. Folk songs, called *t'aryŏng*, became ever popular while farmers' music, called *nong'ak*, was performed on various occasions by amateur musicians dressed in colorful costumes. Meanwhile, professional folk musicians popularized operatic recital of old and new tales, developing the art of *p'ansori*. Traveling troupes of entertainers, called *kwangdae* or *namsadang*, provided popular entertainment similar to what the Western circus, jesters and troubadours had done.

The performance of masked dances such as the Lion Dance, and puppet plays, most of which satirized the *yangban*, became increasingly popular as a form of social protest. Hiding behind masks, the common people revealed their indignation against the ruling class as a whole. The most popularly used musical instruments which folk musicians used were the hourglass-shaped drum called *changgo*, a small hand-held drum called *sogo*, a barrel drum called *puk*, cymbals and gongs, and a high-pitched copper bugle.

Korea in the Early Nineteenth Century

Political and Social Situation. After the death of Chŏngjo, two young kings were enthroned at the ages of eleven and eight, in 1801 and 1834, respectively. During this period what little had been accomplished in the recent past was almost completely undone as the influence of queens and their families grew, bringing on what is known as "power politics (*sedo chŏngch'i*)."

Political, economic, and social conditions deteriorated badly in the early nineteenth century as power politics of queens and their family members became rampant, and a new factional strife developed, creating an extremely unstable political situation. *Sedo chŏngch'i* refers to the monopoly of political power and its abuses by the two families (Kim and Cho) which had provided queens. A large number of the Kim and the Cho clans and their allies occupied key positions in the government and abused their privileges, creating a growing dissatisfaction and disunity among the members of the ruling class. Many offices, particularly those of tax collectors, were bought and sold as many incompetent magistrates were appointed.

At this juncture, a new factional strife revived when the "Party of Principle (*Pyŏkp'a*)" of the Northern Men faction launched its bitter attack against the "Party of Expediency (*Ship'a*)" in order to dislodge the men of the "Party of Expediency," most of whom were the Southern Men who were either Catholics or tolerant toward Catholicism. Whereas the men of the "Party of Expediency" deplored the cruel and punitive action which had been taken by the unforgiving King Yŏngjo, causing the death by starvation of his misbehaving son (Crown Prince Changhŏn), the men of the "Party of Principle" justified the king's act. When Ch'ŏlchong, who reigned 1845-63, took the throne, the anti-Catholic policy was relaxed, but the Kim clan of Andong held power. By 1854, most of the Southern Men who belonged to the "Party of Expediency" had been excluded from power.

Meanwhile, what historians called the "disarray of the three administrations" occurred. The first two refer to mismanagement by local tax collectors, who bought their offices, in handling the collection of the land tax and the military service tax; the third was related to mismanagement of state granaries. The disarray in the land tax system came when local tax collectors added a variety of surcharges and handling fees, and levied a tax on abandoned fields. In addition, they extorted payments from the peasants in order to recover the money they had spent to purchase their office. Moreover, they collected the military service tax (paid in cloth) from the peasants on behalf of family members of the "soldiering order" who had died.

The third disarray refers to mismanagement of the grain loan system. The officials in charge of state granaries collected a ten percent illegal user's fee from the peasants who borrowed grain from the state granaries. In addition, they forced the peasants to borrow more than they needed so as to collect more illegal user's fees. Needless to say, these abuses by local officials added a financial burden on the peasants while promoting their antagonism toward the government. In such a situation, bandit groups such as "fire brigands" and "water brigands" were formed everywhere. As the government was bankrupted and no relief measures were undertaken, the discontent and restlessness of the poverty-stricken masses reached a critical point.

Amid this sad state of affairs, in 1812 Hong Kyŏng-nae's rebellion erupted in P'yŏng'an Province, followed by one on Cheju Island in 1813, and an uprising of a group of bandits in 1816. To make matters worse, the great floods of 1810 and 1811 in the south and that of 1820 which struck the whole country were followed by five others between 1822 and 1832. They reduced the population from 7.5 million in 1807 to 6.7 million in 1832.

In the spring of 1862, a disgruntled ex-official brought about an uprising in Chinju, Kyŏngsang Province, which was followed by ones of Cheju Island and Iksan, Chŏlla Province, plunging the country into chaos.

As political order deteriorated, economic stagnation grew worse, and social conditions grew chaotic, certain changes occurred in the *yangban* system. First of all, the number of fallen *yangban* increased for a variety of reasons. The Japanese and Manchu invasions had already inflicted severe blows on the *yangban* class, destroying their properties and enabling their slaves to flee. It is said that some *yangban* were forced to sell their status to the commoners for economic reasons.

The rigid class structure was beginning to break down. While the "middle people" group, which had the hereditary technical and specialized jobs in the central government, was improving its social position, an increasing number of sons of commoners purchased and moved into lower government services, gaining semi-*yangban* status.

An important aspect of social change was the rise of the number of successful candidates in the higher civil service examination from P'yŏng'an Province, the area which had been mistreated by the central government. Another important social change was the gradual disappearance of slavery. The number of slaves declined from 350,000 in the fifteenth century to less than 200,000 by the seventeenth century due to the Japanese and Manchu wars. The number continued to decrease in the late seventeenth and eighteenth centuries, and the freeing of government slaves in 1801 reduced the numbers even further. Whereas, those slaves who were allowed to serve in the military gained freedom afterwards, many bought their freedom from the fallen *yangban* families, or from the government by paying corvée tax.

A New Religious Movement. In the late eighteenth century, Catholicism, known in Korea as "Western Learning," which was introduced in the seventeenth century, won an increasing number of converts, including some reform-minded scholars. One of the leaders of the Catholic movement was Yi Sŭng-hun (1756-1801), son of a high government official, who had been baptized in Peking. After returning to Korea, Yi founded the first Catholic church in Seoul, winning many converts among young Confucian scholars. Among them were Chŏng Yak-yong and his brother. After a Chinese priest entered Korea secretly in 1795, followed in the 1830s and 1840s by a dozen French priests and a Korean priest, Kim Tae-gŏn, later to become the first Korean saint who had been ordained in Macao, secretly entered Korea. Catholicism grew in particular among the underprivileged commoners, including many mistreated women.

The growing Catholicism was regarded by reactionary, conservative Confucian scholar-officials as "an evil heterodox," and met with their strong reaction. A series of anti-Catholic persecutions began in 1801, producing a growing number of martyrs. Among those who were executed in the early persecutions were the Chinese priest and many women. Father Kim Tae-gŏn himself was among the martyrs of 1846. Despite persecution, the number of converts increased to about 200,000 in the 1850s.

As the government was engaged in anti-Catholic persecution, a Korean named Ch'oe Che-u (1804-64), who had advocated social reform, particularly the equality of men and the sexes, established a new religion called the Eastern Learning, *Tonghak*, preaching among other things, the concept of the unity of man and God. His thesis was that mankind and the Supreme Being are one and the same; therefore one must treat man as a divine being. At the same time, Ch'oe expressed his negative opinion of Catholicism as well as of outmoded Confucian teachings and social institutions.

The founder of the *Tonghak* religion was arrested and executed by the government in 1864 as a heretic, but his religious teaching and social reform movement survived, winning more converts among the oppressed and exploited masses.

6
The Twilight of
the Yi Dynasty, 1860-1910

IN the mid-nineteenth century, the Kingdom of Chosŏn entered the modern age totally unprepared to cope with what it was to bring. Ready or not, Korea was destined to weather the storm at the dawn of the new age. In doing so, the policy makers of Korea, who were tradition bound, unenlightened, and disunited, made numerous errors in dealing with a variety of unfamiliar problems, bringing about not only the demise of the Yi dynasty, but also the tragic end of Korean independence.

Korea on the Eve of the Modern Age

The New King, the Regent, and the Reform. In early 1864, a twelve-year old boy, who was a distant relative of the late king, was enthroned as Kojong. His reign lasted until 1907. Since he was a minor, his father was installed as his regent with the title of Hŭngsŏn Taewŏn'gun. No sooner were the ceremonies for the ascension of Kojong over than the strong-willed Regent launched his resolute reform program aimed at strengthening the monarchy and

Portrait of the Taewŏn'gun (Yi Ha-ŭng, 1820-1898)

the restoration of the former glory of the Yi dynasty.

The first step the Regent took to achieve his objectives was the appointment of new high officials regardless of their factional affiliations or social background. He then took steps to replace the military tax paid in cloth, which had been levied on the commoners, with a household tax payable by all, including the *yangban* families. He set up village granaries, surveyed grain stored in government granaries, and imposed death sentences or banishment on those officials who had enriched themselves by illegal means.

One of the most ambitious projects of the Regent was the restoration of Kyŏngbok Palace, which had been reduced to ruins by the Japanese. In order to do so, he instituted a special land surtax on all landholders, a gate (transport) tax on merchants who transported merchandise in and out of Seoul, minted new money called *tangbaekchŏn*, making one new coin worth a hundred times more than the old copper coins, and solicited "voluntary" donations for the project. The palace reconstruction project that began in 1865 was completed in 1867. However, the methods of raising state revenue and funds for the palace restoration project, together with other reform measures the Regent implemented, brought about a storm of protests, particularly on the part of the *Yangban literati* and merchants. The Regent became extremely unpopular.

To make matters worse, the Regent first banned the restoration or establishment of new private academies and shrines, and then levied the land tax on them from 1868, and closed down in 1871 all but forty-seven private academies, confiscating all the lands they possessed and freeing all their slaves. Such action on the part of the Regent provoked the bitter opposition of conservative Confucians, especially those of the Old Doctrine and the Northern Men factions.

As the world was growing smaller and diplomatic and commercial relations between the Eastern nations and those of the West were expanding, the Regent pursued the policy of isolation in order to prevent Korea from becoming entangled in unfamiliar foreign relations with and contaminated by what he called the "Western barbarians." However, from 1832, Western nations developed an increasing interest in opening Korea for trade. After a British merchant ship visited Korea seeking trade in 1845, a british warship surveyed Korean waters near Cheju Island. Then, in 1846, a French warship making overtures for trade visited Korea, followed by two Russian warships which did likewise in 1854, causing death and injuries among the Koreans.

Meanwhile, the Regent became fully aware of what was transpiring in China in the 1840s and 1850s. Those wars, such as the Opium and the Arrow wars, which China was forced to fight against the British first, and then the combined forces of England and France, made the Regent more determined not to allow Korea to become entangled with the Western powers. As if defying his policy, in 1866 Ernest J. Oppert, a German who was a naturalized U.S. citizen, made two voyages to Korea on American merchant ships, seeking trade. This was at a time when the largest anti-Catholic persecution ever carried out was in progress, producing over 7,000 Korean martyrs. Nine French priests who had secretly entered Korea were among those who were executed.

Korea's Encounter with the Western Powers. While the bloody anti-Catholic persecution was in progress, an American merchant ship, *General Sherman*, sailed up the Taedong River to Pyongyang, believing that it was sailing up the Han River to Seoul. The ship was grounded as the tide went out, and when the crew by their misconduct aroused the indignation of the governor of Pyongyang and the local inhabitants near Yanggak Island the ship was burned and its crew was put to death. This was the Sherman Incident of August 1866.

When the French minister in China learned from a French priest who managed to flee from Korea to China that many French priests were being executed in Korea, he had the commander of the French naval force invade Korea to punish the Koreans, seek an apology, and exact a treaty from Korea. The French Asiatic Squadron of seven warships invaded Korea in September 1866, attacking Kanghwa Island and defense installations along the Han River in preparation for an attack on Seoul itself. The resistance of the Korean military units was such that the French were unable to sail up the Han River, and the invading force left Korea in November, returning to China. Meanwhile, in 1868, Oppert made another voyage to Korea, this time to rob the royal tombs in Ch'ungch'ŏng Province. His party was caught as they engaged in their tomb-robbing ventures, but they managed to flee. One of the tombs which they had violated was no other than that of the father of the Regent himself.

The second "foreign disturbance" came in 1871, when the U.S. government, which had refused to send a joint expedition with the French to Korea in 1866, ordered its minister in China to launch military action against Korea in order to receive an apology from the Korean government for the destruction of the *General Sherman* and exact a treaty from it. As a result, Commodore John

Rodgers, commander of the U.S. Asiatic Squadron was ordered to go to Korea. Arriving in Korea in May 1871 with five warships, the American troops attacked the fortifications on Kanghwa Island and captured one of the main forts after killing all the Korean troops there while losing a small number of Marines. Facing the determined resistance of the Koreans, the U.S. force withdrew from Korean waters and returned to China in early July.

These two wars which the two Western powers forced upon Korea achieved nothing. If anything, these actions only increased the anti-foreign feelings of the people and strengthened the isolation policy of the Korean government. It was at that time that the Regent had ordered the placement of stone monuments in Seoul and throughout the kingdom, warning against the Western threats to the nation. These stone monuments had the government edict incised on them. It said, "Western barbarians invaded our land. Not to fight back is to invite further attacks. Selling out the country in peace negotiations is the greatest danger to be guarded against...." With this the policy of isolation was officially declared.

The National Debate. As early as the late eighteenth century, the *Shirhak* scholar, Pak Che-ga of the Northern Learning, had argued in favor of developing trade relations with Japan and the Western nations as a means to strengthen the nation. Those who shared such an opinion advocated the opening of Korea to the West in the 1830s. Among them was Ch'oe Han-gi, who authored such books as *Descriptions of the Nations of the World.*

When the pressure from the West increased, the latter-day *Shirhak* scholars such as Pak Kyu-su, grandson of the *Shirhak* scholar, Pak Chi-wŏn, a government interpreter O Kyŏng-sŏk, who visited China many times, and a Buddhist monk, Yu Tae-ch'i, demanded the end of

Korea's isolation and the importation of new cultural influences for the betterment of the nation. When the French and American invasions came, these men became ever more convinced that Korea could no longer be content with the status quo and remain "a hermit kingdom."

However, the Regent and even the critics of his reform programs, were determined to keep the doors of Korea closed to the West, preaching what they called *ch'ŏksa*, or "rejection of heterodoxy." Like many Japanese Shinto nationalists at that time, these men regarded the Western people as "barbarians," and the opening of the nation to them would be welcoming their "evil ideas and ways."

Meanwhile, the relationships between the Regent Taewŏn'gun and Queen Min (wife of King Kojong) and Queen Dowager Cho deteriorated. Supported by the critics of the Regent, such as Ch'oe Ik-hyŏn, an isolationist who submitted a memorial denouncing the Regent, they brought about the retirement of the Regent in 1873 when the king reached the age of maturity. With this Queen Min and her relatives in the government gained a power monopoly in alliance with conservatives both in and outside the government.

The Opening of Korea, Early Modernization, and Domestic Politics

New Relations with Japan. It was Japan which used military force to reach its objectives. As early as 1869, the Meiji government of Japan, which had overthrown the Tokugawa Shogunate, requested the establishment of new relations between Korea and Japan as it notified the Korean government regarding the Meiji Restoration. When the Korean government was unwilling to respond favorably to the Japanese request, in 1875 the Japanese government dispatched its warships to Korea. When the Japanese warship, the *Unyō-kan*, illegally entered Korean waters near Inch'ŏn, it was fired upon by the garrison force on Kanghwa Island. Using this incident as a pretext, the Japanese government sent a large squadron of warships to Korea in early 1876, threatening Korea while appeasing those Japanese who had been agitating for a war with Korea since 1869.

Facing an imminent war threat brought about by the Japanese in February 1876, the Korean government, despite the vociferous and vehement opposition of the Regent and others, concluded the Kanghwa Treaty of February 1876, establishing new diplomatic and commercial relations with Japan. Under this, and another supplementary agreement, Japan forced Korea to grant special privileges to Japan, making Korea a subordinate nation to Japan as the Western nations had done to China and Japan earlier. Among these special privileges were low import tariff and extraterritorial rights of the Japanese subjects in Korea.

The Rise of the Progressives. The way in which Japan forced Korea to sign the Kanghwa Treaty and other agreements aroused the nationalistic scholars who subscribed to progressive ideas. These young Confucian scholars, such as Kim Ok-kyun and Pak Yŏng-hyo (brother-in-law of the king) had been influenced by the ideas advanced by latter-day *Shirhak* scholars, and they became convinced that the only way to strengthen the nation and safeguard Korea's national independence was modernization of its political, economic and social systems, as well as its culture by importing those systems and cultures from advanced Western nations. Consequently, there emerged a group of nationalist reform advocates collectively known as *Kaehwadang*, or "the party of the advocates of Progress and Enlightenment."

The progressives were also influenced by a booklet entitled *Korean Strategy*, written by a Chinese diplomat in Japan, who advised the Koreans to maintain a pro-China policy, while cultivating friendly relations with Japan, to open its door to the West, and to import advanced culture and technology. The booklet was given to a Korean envoy who visited Japan in 1880, and upon his return the envoy presented it to the king, causing considerable political controversy. Be that as it may, the Progressives, individually or as a group, advocated the opening of Korea to the West, strengthening of the nation's economy and military, and political, social, and cultural reforms. They were impressed with the ways in which the Japanese were modernizing and strengthening their country.

Modernization and Conservative Reaction. The conclusion of treaties with Japan and the presentation of the aforementioned booklet to the king, along with the growing pressure from the Western powers, provided a strong reaction among the conservatives. One of them even demanded that the envoy who brought the booklet to Korea be punished, initiating a movement which came to be known as "reject lecherous thoughts and repel the barbarians from abroad."

Despite such opposition, in October 1880, the moderates in the government influenced the young king to adopt a momentous decision to establish diplomatic relations with the United States and carry out some reform measures. Early in 1881, the new Office for the Management of State Affairs was established, and in February the king sent his third fact-finding mission to Japan, and a group of students and artisans on a training mission to China. Meanwhile, the king secretly sent a Buddhist monk to Japan to negotiate with the Americans there, and authorized Kim Ok-kyun to travel to Japan to learn more about that the Japanese had done since 1868. Shortly after the third mission to Japan returned to Korea in 1881, a Japanese military officer arrived and established a new military unit called the Special Skills Force, initiating military modernization.

The sending of missions to Japan and the new military program provoked a strong reaction on the part of the conservatives, such as Ch'oe Ik-hyŏn, who submitted an essay entitled "Five Reasons Against the Opening of Korea." In it Ch'oe pointed out that the Japanese were no different from the Western barbarians, and the opening of Korea would allow the evil teachings of foreign religion to enter Korea. Meanwhile, some moderate conservatives advocated the idea to combine "Eastern ethics with Western machines" to strengthen the nation and ward off foreign threats. Similar ideas had been advanced in China and Japan.

The Opening of Korea to the West. The United States, which had failed to settle the issue with Korea by force regarding the Sherman Incident, adopted a peaceful means to open Korea and sought both Chinese and Japanese assistance. While Japan refused to offer its good offices, Li Hung-chang, who was in charge of foreign affairs of the Chinese government and whose secret design was to induce the United States to recognize China's sovereignty over Korea and crush the Japanese notion that Korea was a sovereign and independent nation, offered his good offices to the United States. Thereupon, he advised the Korean king to conclude a treaty with the United States, and as a "plenipotentiary" he negotiated for Korea with an American representative (Commodore Robert W. Shufeldt) at Tientsin, China.

The Treaty of Amity and Commerce (often called

Shufeldt, or Chemulp'o treaty) between the United States and Korea was signed on May 23, 1882 at Chemulp'o (now Inch'ŏn), Korea, ending Korea's isolation policy. Although the United States did not recognize Korea as China's dependency in the treaty, it was an unequal treaty whereby the United States secured many special privileges such as low tariff rates and extraterritorial rights for its citizens in Korea while none of these were extended to the Koreans in America. After this, Korea concluded similar treaties with England and Russia in 1883, followed by those with Russia and Italy in 1884, France in 1886, and other Western nations afterwards. Needless to say, the signing of these treaties antagonized the conservatives, including the ex-Regent who had already attempted in 1881 to replace Kojong with his other son.

Domestic Upheaval and Foreign Rivalry

The Imo Military Insurrection. In July 1882, the soldiers of the old military units in Seoul, who were resentful of preferential treatment given to the troops of the Special Skills Force, and who had not been paid for a year, carried out a riot in Soul. Taking advantage of the situation, the ex-Regent Taewŏn'gun turned the riot into an insurrection in alliance with its leaders. During the insurrection, the Japanese military instructor was killed, and when the rebel soldiers and mob attacked the Japanese legation, the Japanese minister had the legation buliding burned down and fled to Japan via Inch'on. Queen Min escaped certain death by fleeing the palace in disguise, but one of her relatives, who was a high official, was killed and many supporters of the Mins were also put to death. After taking over the palace, the ex-Regent with the consent of the king, took charge of the government.

No sooner had he taken over the government than the ex-Regent dismantled the Special Skills Force, restoring the former Five Army Garrison system, and abolished the Office for the Management of State Affairs, nullifying the initial reform measures implemented by the government.

Discovering what had happened in Seoul, and alarmed by Japan's dispatch of troops to Korea, Li Hung-chang, with the consent of the Korean envoys in Tientsin, sent some 4,500 Chinese troops to Korea to restore law and order in Seoul and achieve what he failed to achieve earlier, namely the reassertion of China's sovereignty over Korea. Arriving in Korea in August, the Chinese commander had the Taewŏn'gun arrested and taken to China. The insurrectionists were subjugated, and Queen Min returned from her hiding place in the countryside to Seoul, restoring her control over the government. Meanwhile, the Japanese forced the Korean government to sign a treaty on August 10, 1882, pay 550,000 *yen* indemnity for lives and property of the Japanese lost during the insurrection, and permit the stationing of a company of Japanese troops to guard the Japanese legation in Seoul.

After accomplishing its initial objectives, the Chinese government dispatched a highranking official to Korea as the Chief Commissioner of Diplomatic and Commercial Affairs, in order to establish direct Chinese control over Korea. At the same time, a new trade agreement was signed between Korea and China, granting the Chinese special privileges, and the Chinese government sent its agent, a German named Paul Georg von Moellendorff, to Korea as head of the Korean Maritime Customs Service and adviser to the Korean foreign office. A Chinese commander, Yüan Shih-k'ai, took control over the Korean Army.

The Coup d'État of the Progressives. Despite the growing chinese control in Korea, the moderate reform advocates in the Korean government were able to bring about some positive actions. In January 1883, the Office of the Management of State Affairs was reinstated as the Foreign Office, and the Office for the Management of Internal Affairs was renamed the Office for the Management of National and Military Affairs. In September 1883, the government established an English language school in Seoul to train interpreters under American instructors.

As the Korean Maritime Customs Service went into operation, the king sent a good-will mission to Japan in October 1882 and secured a 170,000 *yen* loan from a Japanese bank to finance reform projects, and in july 1883, he sent a good-will mission which included several Progressives to the United States. It was in 1882 when the good-will mission went to Japan that its chief delegate, Pak Yŏng-hyo, hurriedly created the Korean national flag, which is currently the national flag of South Korea.

After the good-will mission returned from Japan, a group of students were sent to Japan to receive modern military education as well as other training at the Japanese military academy and at Keio University, and

Two leading Progressives:
Kim Ok-kyun (left) and Sŏ
Kwang-bŏm (right).

when American wheat seed and cattle arrived following the visit of the good-will mission to the United States, the king established an experimental farm called "American Farm." Meanwhile, in October 1883, Pak Yŏng-hyo and other Progressives published the first modern gazette named *Hansŏng Sunbo* with the assistance of the Japanese. The *Hangsŏng Sunbo* was a thrice-monthly gazette published by the newly created Office of Culture and Information of the Seoul city government when Pak Yŏng-hyo was mayor. At the same time, Kim Ok-kyun and other Progressives were given minor positions in the government.

However, the power struggle between the conservatives, represented by Queen Min and her nephew Min Yŏng-ik, and the Progressives grew intense in 1883. Whereas the Progressives wished to bring about rapid modernization and establish complete independence of Korea with the help of Japan and the United States, the conservatives were reluctant to do so while maintaining a pro-Chinese stand. Meanwhile, personal animosities between Min Yŏng-ik on one hand and Pak Yŏng-hyo on the other grew extremely bitter as the Progressives became more nationalistic (anti-Chinese) and increasingly aggressive in terms of national strengthening and modernization. The fall of Vietnam to France when the French defeated China in a war in the 1883-1884 period made them only more impatient. They were convinced that Chinese domination over Korea would eventually lead to the fall of Korea to a foreign power as in the case of Vietnam. In such a situation, the Progressives were resolved to take drastic action. To do so, they sought the assistance of the Japanese government, and although the latter was reluctant the Progressives were able to receive a promise of military cooperation from the Japanese minister in Seoul. With his assurance, they decided to strike a blow against the pro-Chinese reactionaries and conservatives before they did so against them.

On the eve of December 4, 1884, the Progressives carried out a *coup,* assassinating several key top government officials and severely wounding Min Yŏng-ik. The Japanese soldiers and Korean troops who sided with the Progressives quickly surrounded the palace, and the Progressives persuaded the king and the queen to approve their actions and establish a new Council of State in the hands of the Progressives and others who shared their views and concerns. This event is known as the *Kapshin Chŏngbyŏn* in Korean history.

In the early morning of December 5, the new State Council emerged and a fourteen-item reform program was proclaimed. In their proclamation, which was preserved in Kim Ok-kyun's *Journal of 1884,* which he wrote in exile in Japan, they demanded the release and return of the Taewŏn'gun from China and the end of the tributary relationship with China. Among the reform measures which it included were: abolition of ruling class privileges and establishment of equal rights for all, appointment of men of talents in the government regardless of social origins, the revision of the land tax laws and the routing out of the extortionate practices of the petty officials, punishment of those notorious officials whose evil and venal acts had brought the nation to its present state of affairs, cancelation of all outstanding grain loan debts owed by the peasants to the government, the abolition of all superfluous government agencies, and adoption of a new method for the establishment of a national policy.

All seemed well for the Progressives. But it was not. While they were busy setting up a new government, on December 6, the Chinese military commander, Yüan Shih-k'ai, in collusion with reactionary Korean generals, took counter-measures. The royal palace quickly fell into their hands, over a hundred Progressives were killed, and the king was taken into Chinese custody. The Japanese minister fled to Japan, reluctantly taking a half dozen surviving Progressives, including Kim Ok-kyun and Pak Yŏng-hyo, with him. With this, the opportunity to bring about rapid modernization was lost.

Following the fall of the Progressives, the Chinese tightened their control over Korea, putting Queen Min and her relatives in charge of the government. In January 1885, the Japanese government forced the Korean government to sign an agreement whereby Korea agreed to pay a large sum of money as indemnity for the lives lost and property destroyed, and punish those who were "responsible" for those deeds.

China and Japan were on the verge of war. But, neither side was ready to go to war at that time, and in April 1885 the representatives of Japan and China met in Tientsin to sign an agreement regarding Korea. They agreed to withdraw all troops from Korea, except the legation guards, not to send troops to Korea except to protect lives and properties of their nationals in the event of rebellion or a mass uprising, and when either side did so, it would inform the other party.

Modern Development. Despite these turbulent events, modernization of the country moved ahead. First of all modern education developed. After a modern school established by a Korean emerged in Wŏnsan in 1883, two mission schools for boys were established in 1885 by American missionaries, followed by the establishment of the first school for girls by an American woman missionary in 1886. This girls' school eventually became the prestigious college (later university) for women named Ewha. A dozen other primary and secondary mission

The first school for girls in Korea. (Ewha School in 1886).

schools for boys and girls were established after 1886. The significant fact was that these schools were for the children of the commoners who had absolutely no educational opportunity before. Meanwhile, in July 1886, the government established a palace school named Yukyŏng Kong'wŏn to provide modern education to sons of high *yangban* families.

Protestantism was introduced by Dr. Horace N. Allen, an American medical missionary who arrived in 1884. After his arrival, many more Protestant missionaries from Canada, England, and the United States, along with Catholic priests and nuns from Europe arrived, winning an ever increasing number of converts. The first modern medical clinic was established in 1885 by Dr. Allen. The popularity of Christianity which was regarded as modern civilization grew, attracting more converts.

With the growth of Christianity, a new culture evolved. The singing of Christian hymns and other Western songs became widespread as the reading of the Bible increased literacy among both men and women of the commoner class. In fact, the tune of a Scottish melody, *Auld Lang Syne*, became the tune of the new patriotic song whose lyrics were written by a Korean patriot, Yun Ch'i-ho. The introduction of the organ and other Western musical instruments brought about rapid development of modern music. The contribution which Christianity and foreign missionaries made toward cultural modernization was enormous as a large number of new Korean leaders emerged as the graduates of those mission schools.

Modern journalism also emerged. Although the thrice-monthly, *Hansŏng Sunbo*, which the Progressives had published, was abolished in 1885, in 1886 the government published a new newspaper named *Hansŏng Chubo* (The Seoul Weekly), using both Korean and Chinese until it was abolished by the Chinese in 1888. After that, there was no Korean newspaper until 1896 although several Japanese newspapers emerged in Korea in 1893 and 1894. Meanwhile, Yu Kil-chun, who returned to Korea after studying at an academy in the United States in 1885, too late to participate in the December coup of 1884, published in 1889 his book entitled *Observations in the West*, advocating rapid modernization of Korea.

Military modernization also took place in 1883 as the government established the Bureau of Military Study and Training while sending a group of young students to Japan to study military and other subjects at Japanese schools. Modern weapons were imported from the United States and Japan, and a military factory was established. An American general and two officers were employed in 1888 to train the Korean military leaders at the newly established military school.

Although economic and social modernization lagged far behind, the establishment of the Korean Maritime Customs Service in 1883, and the emergence of two Korean commerical firms in that year, coupled with the coining of new currency, the employment of a German in 1884 to promote modern agriculture, and the establishment of an experimental farm signified certain economic change.

The establishment of telegraph lines between Korea and China in 1883 and 1885 facilitated modern communication as the installation of gas lamps in the palace brought about unmistakable signs of modernization.

The Uprising of the Tonghaks and Peasants. The Koreans were greatly angered and perturbed when the Anglo-Russian rivalry in the Far East led to the British occupation of a group of small Korean islands, collectively called Kŏmundo, off the western south coast in 1885 without permission of or pre-warnings to the Korean government. The British strategy was to harass the Russian ship transportation to and from Vladivostok, which was located at the southern tip of the Maritime Province which the Russians had taken over from China in 1860.

Efforts made by both Korean and Chinese governments brought about the withdrawal of the British naval forces from Kŏmun Island in 1887 and removal of Russian threats to occupy Korean territory. It was at this juncture that proposals were made without any result by a German and a Japanese for the neutralization of Korea.

The Koreans were also disturbed by the growing Sino-Japanese rivalry on Korean political and economic fronts. On the political front, they were engaged in a legal dispute regarding the sovereignty of Korea which China refused to recognize but which Japan insisted upon. As China refused to recognize Korea's sovereignty, the Chinese commander, Yüan Shih-k'ai, in Korea, claimed that he was China's "viceroy" in Korea, while Li Hung-chang who was Director of Foreign Affairs in the Chinese government acted as if he were a Korean king.

On the economic front, both China and Japan were competing for Korean markets. Ever since the conclusion of the Korean-Japanese treaties in 1876 and 1877, and the opening of Korean ports to the Japanese, the Chinese who had monopolized Korea's foreign trade began to lose ground as the Japanese increased their exports to Korea. Japanese economic penetration not only eroded Korea's village economy, but also increased Korea's imports. In 1893, Korea imported 3.8 million *yen*'s worth of goods, (1.9 million from China and 1.9 million from Japan) while its exports amounted only to 1.7 million *yen* (1.5 million to Japan and 134,645 *yen* to China). Korea was in a serious internal and external situation.

These domestic and foreign issues, the growing Christianity, the declining village economy, and certain government mismanagement led to the development of the strong anti-government and anti-foreign sentiments of the conservative Confucian *literati* as well as those of the *Tonghak* believers. The *Tonghak* believers had been seeking the legitimacy of their religion, exoneration of Ch'oe Che-u, the founder of the *Tonghak* sect, who was executed in 1864, and the prevention of the spread of foreign religion. At the same time, they were antagonized by illegal taxes which the local officials collected from the peasants.

In 1892, the *Tonghak* believers held a large gathering, demanding the exoneration of Ch'oe Che-u and an end to suppression of their sect, and sent a petition to Seoul. Their demands were rejected, but the government pledged to order the local officials to stop persecution of *Tonghak* believers. Not satisfied with this, they held another large assembly in April 1893, resolving to engage in an open struggle with the government.

To make matters worse, the tyrannical magistrate of Kobu county, Chŏlla Province extorted in 1894 large amounts of money from the peasants by illegal means, and refused to pay the peasants who worked for the government, provoking an uprising of both the *Tonghak* believers and the peasants. When the peasants in the Kobu area joined the *Tonghak* force under the leadership of Chŏn Pong-jun, and began their armed struggle against the government in April 1894, the peasants and *Tonghak* believers in Ch'ungch'ŏng Province also rose in armed struggle, bringing what is known as the *Tonghak* Uprising. To be sure, the major contingents of the *Tonghak* Uprising, which is often called the *Tonghak* rebellion, a peasants war, or even a peasant revolution, were the *Tonghak* believers themselves, but when Chŏn raised the rebel armies they were joined by a large number of peasants, as well as fallen *yangban* and many illegitimate sons of the *yangban* who had been socially discriminated against. Thus Chŏn galvanized many discontented groups into the largest armed uprising in Korean history. An important aspect of this historical event was that the uprising which began as a domestic reform movement became an anti-Japanese war when the government force and that of the Japanese launched a joint campaign against the rebels in late 1894.

As the rebels rose, the *Tonghak* leaders issued a proclamation which stated that "the people are the root of the nation...The whole nation is...united in their determination to raise the righteous standard of revolt, and to pledge their lives to sustain the state and provide for the livelihood of the people." A four-point manifesto issued by the *Tonghak* leaders included an item which stated that "Japanese barbarians" must be driven out. Thus, although the *Tonghak* Uprising was that of a socially mistreated, economically exploited peasant class heavily burdened with taxes and other levies, and religiously persecuted people, it was also a nationalistic uprising against foreign power.

The Critical Decade

The period between 1894 and 1904 was a critical decade for Korea. It was during this time that the war between China and Japan was fought in and around Korea, and the war between Japan and Russia began at the end of the period.

The Sino-Japanese War and Its Impact. When the *Tonghak* Uprising became an open rebellion, the weak Korean government asked for Chinese help. Meanwhile, a truce was reached between the *Tonghak* rebels and the government after the fall of Chŏnju, the capital of the North Chŏlla Province, and as the government agreed to prevent the officials and *yangban* from draining the blood of the peasants by their illegal extortions, the rebels withdrew from Chŏnju. After this, local directorates consisting of the fallen *yangban* and the *Tonghak* leaders were set up, and the Headquarters Directorate under Chŏn issued a twelve-point reform program, which included: (1) elimination of the chronic mistrust between *Tonghak* believers and the government, (2) punishment of corrupt officials, (3) control of improper conduct of the *yangban*, (4) burning of all documents pertaining to slaves, (5) banning of collection of all arbitrary and irregular taxes, (6) "severe punishment" of those who collaborated with the Japanese, (7) cancellation of all outstanding debts, and (8) distribution of land.

The Chinese government whose aim was to strengthen its control over Korea sent an army of 3,000 soldiers and a naval force to Korea, violating the agreement which it had signed with the Japanese in April 1885. The Chinese force arrived in Korea in June 1894.

Meanwhile, the Japanese government concluded that it now had a legitimate cause to fight a war with China, and the time was right. Consequently, it sent an army of 8,000 troops and a naval force to Korea. The Japanese force arrived only a short time after the arrival of the Chinese force.

Efforts made by the Korean government to bring about withdrawal of both Chinese and Japanese troops failed. As the war clouds hung over Seoul, the Taewŏn'gun, who had been released by the Chinese and was allowed to return to Korea in 1885, attempted to dethrone the king and install another of his sons as king in collaboration with the Chinese commander in Pyongyang.

The Sino-Japanese War began at the end of July 1894. At the commencement of hostilities between China and Japan, the Japanese put Seoul under siege, and forced the Korean government to cancel all existing agreements with China and sign a series of agreements with Japan. With this, the Japanese forced the Korean government to launch a joint military operation against the *Tonghak* rebels as they forced the Korean government to implement a series of reforms.

The Kabo Reform. The reforms that the Korean government carried out between July 1894 and January 1896 are collectively called *Kabo* reform, taking the name from the cycle name of the year in which they began. These reforms were implemented under the leadership of Prime Minister Kim Hong-jip. In December 1894, former members of the party of the Progressives who had fled to Japan in December 1884 were brought back to Korea.

Following the arrival of the Progressives from Japan, a coalition cabinet of Kim Hong-jip and the Progressives was formed. Pak Yŏng-hyo was named home minister while Sŏ Kwang-bŏm became justice minister, and several

Japanese and an American were employed in the government as advisers. At this point, the Deliberative Council was established as a top policy making organ. On January 7, 1895, King Kojong took oath before the Royal Ancestral Shrine in Seoul. His oath, a fourteen-point "Guiding Principles for the Nation" is often called "the fourteen-article charter." In it he pledged that he would establish firm national independence, improve education and technical training, strengthen the military, revise legal codes, and abolish class distinction. Shortly after that, the Council of State was replaced by a modern cabinet which included eight ministries: foreign affairs, home affairs, military affairs, justice, education, finance, agriculture and commerce, and industry. Under the Ministry of Home Affairs, the Metropolitan Police was created and the Bureau of Postal Service was attached to the Ministry of Industry. In April, the administrative districts of the nation were redrawn, and eight provinces were replaced by thirteen provinces by dividing large provinces (P'yŏng' an, Hamgyŏng, Chŏlla, and Kyŏngsang) into north and south. (See Map 9) Meanwhile a new Office of Palace Affairs was established, separating financial matters of the palace from the executive branch, and judicial affairs were modernized by establishing modern courts independent of the executive branch and abolishing torture. A normal school was established in Seoul in April 1895, followed by five modern public primary schools in Seoul at the end of that year. Meanwhile, the traditional civil service examination system was abolished.

In social reform, laws were enacted, abolishing the traditional social structure and slavery, and child marriage was outlawed as remarriage by widows was allowed. In military reform in late 1895, two Capital Guards Battalions and four Regional Garrison Battalions were established, replacing the old military units. Unfortunately,

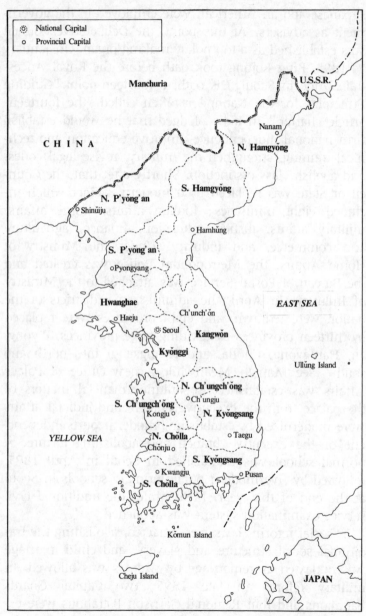

Map 9. NEW ADMINISTRATIVE DISTRICTS 1896–1945

however, the Progressives were once again forced to flee from Korea in July 1895 for their alleged plot to dethrone Kojong, and pro-Russian elements were given cabinet appointments.

Despite some unfortunate events of 1895, which will be discussed in the next section, the spirit of reform was sustained as the king adopted a new reigning era name and issued an ordinance on December 30, 1895 urging others to have their traditional topknots cut-off as he himself cut off his topknot and had a modern haircut. The haircut ordinance aroused a storm of objections from conservative Confucians, as well as many riots. On January 1, 1896, the Gregorian calendar became effective.

Death of Queen Min and the King's Flight to the Russian Legation. The Japanese were successful in defeating the Chinese on land and at sea, and they and the Korean government force crushed the *Tonghak* insurgents by early 1895. Chŏn Pong-jun and other leaders of the insurgents were arrested in January 1895 and were executed or sent into exile. The victorious Japan forced China to sign the peace treaty at Shimonoseki, Japan, in April 1895, collecting a large sum of war indemnity, leasing the Liaotung peninsula from China, taking over Taiwan and its adjacent island, and forcing China to recognize Korea's independence.

However, the influence of the Japanese fell in May 1895 as quickly as it had increased in Korea in 1894 when France and Germany under Russian intimation brought what is called the Triple Intervention on Japan, Forcing Japan to cancel the lease of the Liaotung peninsula from China. Japan, which won the war against China, was unable to reject the demand jointly presented by these three powerful Western nations.

When Japan succumbed to the pressure of the three

Western powers, exposing its weaknesses, a dramatic change took place among the Koreans. While some remained neutral, many became pro-Russian. Among them was Queen Min who sought Russian assistance in removing Japanese domination in Korea while the king himself vacillated.

Witnessing the growing anti-Japanese feelings, the Japanese minister, Miura Gorō, adopted a simplistic solution for Japan's dilemma in Korea, and, in collusion with Japanese expansionists (the so-called *shishi*) who were in Korea, they assassinated Queen Min in her sleeping quarters on the night of October 8, 1895. When the truth about the death of the Korean queen was made known, the Japanese government recalled its minister to Korea as Japanese influence in Korea declined sharply.

The nation was shocked as anti-Japanese sentiment became more intense. Armed Koreans known as the Righteous Armies rose throughout the country, harassing Japanese troops still remaining in Korea. But the king whose palace was surrounded by Japanese troops was helpless. Sensing the tension rising in Seoul, and perhaps anticipating the king's arrival at his legation, the Russian minister brought an additional number of Russian Marines from Inch'ŏn to Seoul, strengthening the security of the Russian legation.

Late on the night of February 11, 1896, pro-Russian Koreans spirited the king and his crown prince out of his palace to the Russian legation. This was followed by a bloody attack against the pro-Japanese cabinet members. Prime Minister Kim Hong-jip and other ministers were killed, while some of them fled to Japan, bringing the sudden collapse of Japanese domination in Korea, and the emergence of a pro-Russian cabinet. The king stayed at the Russian legation until February 1897.

During the year the king stayed in the Russian legation,

the Korean government came under strong Russian influence as many Japanese-sponsored reform programs were abandoned. The king sent a secret envoy to Russia and concluded in 1896 an agreement with the Russian government in which Russia promised both financial and military assistance, however reluctantly it might have done so. Meanwhile, imperialist powers of England, France, Russia and the United States secured numerous concessions from the Korean government with the help of the Russian minister. As these powers gained mining, timber, and fishing concessions, as well as the right to construct railways, Russian advisers and military instructors arrived, arousing strong reaction not only from the Japanese, but also from Korean nationalists.

The Rise of New Nationalists. Witnessing the ominous signs appearing all around, new nationalists arose, advocating the promotion of the spirit of independence and cultural and social reform movement. Among several nationalist organizations of the new reform advocates the most active one was the Independence Club which was founded in July 1896 and whose mentor was a former Progressive, Sŏ Chae-p'il, who had fled to Japan in 1884

Dr. Sŏ Chae-p'il (Philip Jaisohn) and a copy of English edition of The Independent.

and then migrated to the United States, earned an M.D. degree, and became a U.S. citizen with the Anglicized name of Philip Jaisohn.

Dr. Jaisohn returned to Korea in January 1896 "to teach the people and cultivate new leadership" in Korea. After arriving in Korea, he established a Korean-language newspaper named *The Independent* with an English edition in April, and helped the young nationalist reform advocates form the Independence Club, which quickly tore down the gate that symbolized Korea's subservience to China and erected on its former location a stone arch, naming it the Independence Gate. The leaders of the Independence Club turned the Hall of Cherishing China into a lecture hall, preaching nationalism and the spirit of enlightenment. Dr. Jaisohn was appointed to the Privy Council.

The members of the Independence Club and other nationalist organizations were extremely critical of the king's actions taken after February 1896, and they urged the king to return to his palace, abandon his reliance on Russian help which they saw as dangerous to Korea's independence, and adopt progressive domestic and foreign policies so as to restore domestic unity and develop friendly relations with all the nations of the world. They believed that Korea's reliance on Russia would only antagonize Japan, and would bring disastrous consequences to Korea.

While urging the king's departure from the Russian legation, they advised him to make Korea an empire, putting it on equal footing with other empires, and strengthen the nation's ability to maintain its sovereignty and independence while bringing economic, social, and cultural advancement. Their slogan was national independence, cultural enlightenment, and economic and social reconstruction.

The Independence Club sponsored lecture series and public assemblies since its inception, urging the government to adopt reform programs. But the government in the hands of conservatives and reactionaries refused to do so, although the king left the Russian legation and established residence in Tŏksu Palace in February 1897, and elevated himself to Emperor, renaming Korea the Great Han Empire in October. At this juncture, many members of the Independence Club were appointed to the Privy Council.

While the members of the Independence Club preached self-strengthening, Russian financial advisers were withdrawn, the Russo-Korean Bank closed down and the Russian military instructors left Korea. Meanwhile, the Independence Club organized a mass meeting of officials and the citizenry in Seoul (Chongno intersection) in February 1898, pressuring the government to implement the six-item resolution the mass meeting had adopted.

The king was agreeable to adopting most of the proposals made by the mass meeting, but the reactionaries were not, and they mobilized the members of the Peddlers Guild to attack the reform advocates and break up all their meetings. Meanwhile, the Korean government had the U.S. government remove Dr. Jaisohn from Korea, and he and his wife left Korea in May. Moreover, the anti-Independence Club officials in the government brought charges against the members of the Independence Club for their alleged plot to establish a republic, dismissed its members from the Privy Council, and arrested many. With this, the last opportunity for Korea to bring about its own self-regeneration and for the safeguarding of its independence was lost. It seemed to a foreign observer in Seoul at that time that the collapse of the reform sentiment within the Korean government was complete and that the situation was hopeless. After the departure of Dr. Jaisohn, Yun Ch'i-ho continued the pub-lication of *The Independent* for a while with the help of an American missionary, but it was soon abolished. Meanwhile, in 1898 pro-Russian elements attempted to replace Emperor Kojong with his son, or assassinate him, as the Korean government continued to make mining and fishing concessions to foreigners.

It was at this point that Korean students became politicized as new Korean-language daily newspapers and Christian newspapers appeared. A dozen more mission schools and Korean private schools were established. Meanwhile, the first railway constructed by the Japanese began its operation between Seoul and Inch'ŏn in January 1899 as the construction by the Japanese two-trunk rail-way lines between Seoul and Pusan, and Seoul and Shinŭiju was underway. Korea had been modernized, the new patriotic song was sung, but its national survival was hanging in a precarious balance.

The Demise of the Yi Dynasty and Korean Independence

The inept leaders of the Korean government failed to no-tice the signs of the times as war clouds gathered over East Asia. Unprepared, they were unable to prevent mili-tary occupation of the country for the second time in ten years by the Japanese Imperial Army. The gallant struggle of the Koreans was insufficient to prevent the in-crease of Japanese domination first, and then their forced annexation of Korea.

Korea's Loss of Its Sovereignty. Japan and Russia concluded an understanding in April 1896, and another agreement in January 1898 in order to avoid direct confrontation over Korea. However, the Russian lease of the Liaotung peninsula from China in 1898, after forcing Japan in 1895 to cancel its lease of that same region from China in the name of promoting international peace and tranquility in the Far East, aroused both anti-Russian feelings of the Japanese and their fear of Russian expansionism.

Although Russia had no particular territorial designs in Korea, it would not allow Japan to regain the dominant position in that country. Thus, the Russian government rejected various proposals made by the Japanese after 1896, including their proposal to divide Korea into two spheres of influence. The Japanese government even expressed its willingness to recognize Manchuria as a Russian sphere of influence if Russia recognized Korea as a Japanese sphere of influence. This is the so-called *Man-Kan kōkan* scheme of the Japanese.

The occupation of Manchuria by Russian troops in 1901 increased Japanese antagonism. After an international expeditionary force, including a large number of Russian and Japanese troops, crushed the Boxer Uprising in China in 1900, Russia did not withdraw its troops from China as other nations had done. Instead, Russian troops were relocated to Manchuria, joining Russian railway guards who were already there. Moreover, Russia sent more troops into Manchuria after 1901.

While pressuring the Russians to take their troops out of Manchuria, Japan concluded the Anglo-Japanese Alliance in 1902, and secured U.S. support for its designs in Korea. Having the support of England and the United States, the Japanese became bold, delivering an ultimatum to Russia in late 1903. When no satisfactory answer was received, a Japanese naval unit attacked the Russian naval base of Port Arthur on the Liaotung peninsula on February 8, 1904 without declaring war. This was the prelude to the Russo-Japanese War.

While fighting the war, Japanese troops put Korea under their military occupation once again and forced the Korean government to sign a series of agreements. At the same time, in 1904, the Japanese secured from the U.S. President Theodore Roosevelt not only a freehand, but also actual encouragement to establish their control over Korea. Then in July 1905, U.S. Secretary of War William H. Taft met Japanese Prime Minister Katsura Tarō in Tokyo and exchanged their views on Korea and the Philippines. Their views were documented in the *Taft-Katsura Memorandum* in which Taft expressed his opinion, which was later supported by Roosevelt, that Japan's control over Korea was desirable.

Although Japan forced Russia to recognize the independence of Korea in the peace treaty signed between them at Portsmouth in September 1905, ending the war, the Japanese had no intention of permitting the Koreans to enjoy their sovereign rights and independence. The winning of the war against Russia only prompted the Japanese to finalize their aggressive plan for Korea. Some Japanese advocated outright annexation of Korea, but the Japanese government took cautious steps. Thus on November 17, 1905, the Japanese forced the Korean government to conclude a treaty, putting Korea under Japanese protection. However, the Korean emperor refused to approve the treaty.

Struggle for National Survival. Korean patriotism was aroused when the Japanese established the Residency-General, took away Korea's sovereign right to conduct its own foreign affairs, made the Korean government a Japanese puppet in 1905, and abolished its army and took away police and judicial administration in 1907. Some patriots committed suicide while some took up arms against the Japanese, forming the Righteous Armies. Meanwhile, tens of thousands of Koreans emigrated from Korea to the Maritime Province of Russia, Manchuria, and the United States.

Those who remained in Korea formed many reform societies such as the Society for Fostering Leaders, the New People's Society, and the Northwest Educational Association and many other regional education associations, as well as the Association for Women's Education, preaching the gospel of nationalism as they promoted a self-strengthening movement. Scholars published history books and biographies of famous military heroes of the past such as Ŭlchi Mundŏk of Koguryŏ, Kang Kam-ch'an of Koryŏ, and Yi Sun-shin of the late sixteenth century, arousing the spirit of nationalism. When the *Korean Daily News* of Yang Ki-t'ak launched a national debt redemption movement in 1907, patriotic Koreans, including a large number of women, joined the movement raising funds to repay the three million *yen* debt Korea owed to Japan.

Many foreign books such as the *History of the Fall of Poland* and the *History of the Fall of Vietnam* were translated into Korean to arouse the nationalistic concerns of the people, warning of the imminent danger to Korea's survival as an independent nation. While nationalist scholar Chu Shi-gyŏng formed the Society for the Standarization of Korean Writing and wrote books to promote studies on Korean language, others were busily establishing schools to educate young Koreans as a means to strengthen the nation. By 1910, some 2,230 private schools had emerged.

In such a feverish patriotic mood, in 1907 Emperor Kojong sent secret missions to both the U.S. and to The Hague where an international peace conference was held. Kojong's envoys visited these places, but neither the American government, nor the European powers were willing to render any assistance to Korea to regain its sovereignty. Discovering what the emperor had done, the Japanese forced him to abdicate in favor of his son, who took over the throne in 1907 as Sunjong and quickly became a hostage to the Japanese.

While some 17,690 Righteous Army insurgents gave their lives for Korea in over 2,800 armed clashes with Japanese troops between 1907 and 1910, other patriots such as Ch'oe Nam-sŏn, who established a publishing house in 1906, published the first children's magazine named *Sonyŏn* in which he published a poem entitled "From the Sea to Children," introducing a new form of poetry. Advocating the development of a strong self-image among Korean children, he wrote in part:

> *The sea—a soaring mountain—*
> *Lashes and crushes mighty cliffs of rock.*
> *Those flimsy things, what are they to me?*
> *"Know ye my powers?" The sea lashes*
> *Threateningly it breaks, it crushes.*
> *Who has not bowed his head*
> *Before my sovereignty, let him come forth.*
> *Princes of earth, challenge me if you will.*
> *First Emperor, Napoleon, are you my adversary?*
> *Come, come then, compete with me.*

At this juncture, the novelist Yi In-jik published *Tears of Blood* and other novels, while Yi Hae-jo published his novels *Liberty Bell* and others. In March 1908, in San Francisco two Korean students assassinated Durham W. Stevens, an American who had been employed by the Korean government in 1905, but actually worked against Korea as a secret Japanese agent. In October 1908, in Harbin, Manchuria, a Korean patriot, An Chung-gŭn, assassinated Itō Hirobumi, who was regarded as chief architect for Japanese aggressive plans in Korea and served as the first Resident-General from 1905 to 1909. The killing of Itō made Japanese imperialists only more determined to end Korea's existence as a nation.

The final act of the Korean tragedy was played out on August 22, 1910 when the Japanese military commander deployed troops, surrounded the royal palace, and forced Emperor Sunjong to approve the treaty of annexation which had already been signed by his ministers a few days earlier. With this came the end of the Yi dynasty and Korean independence. Ch'oe Nam-sŏn wrote the following poem, reflecting the sullen but unbending mood of the Koreans.

> *We have nothing.*
> *Neither sword nor pistol,*
> *But we do not fear.*
> *Even with an iron rod*
> *They cannot prevail.*
> *We shoulder righteousness*
> *And walk the path without fear.*

7

The Struggle for National Liberation and Restoration, 1910-1945

ALTHOUGH the Treaty of Annexation, dated August 22, 1910, stated that Korea and Japan were united "in order to maintain the peace and stability of Korea, and to promote the prosperity and welfare of Koreans," the Japanese did not make Korea an integral part of the Japanese empire and did not promote the prosperity and welfare of the Koreans. Moreover, contrary to the Imperial Rescript issued by the Meiji Emperor of Japan when the annexation treaty was made public and which stated that the Koreans were to be treated as if they were Japanese subjects and would enjoy rights and privileges under his "benevolent rule," the Koreans received none of these things. Instead, they were put under a harsh, military rule that lasted until August 15, 1945. From 1905, a Japanese military force of a division and a half (16,000 men) were stationed in Seoul and elsewhere in Korea. Then in 1916, two new army divisions were dispatched to Korea with their division headquarters at Pyongyang and Nanam, respectively. (See Map 10)

During this long, painful period for Koreans, the pervasive Japanese colonial rule affected all aspects of

Korean Life, leaving the legacy that would exert a profound influence on post-World War II development in Korea. The Koreans were humiliated and mistreated, and the manpower and natural resources were exploited to benefit Japan. Under such circumstances, Koreans at home and abroad were engaged in a struggle for national liberation, regeneration, and restoration, looking toward the coming of a new dawn of the history of the Korean people.

Early Japanese Colonial Rule

The Japanese Colonial Government and Administrative Districts. When Korea was taken over, the Japanese renamed it Chōsen, called its people *Senjin*, not *Nihonjin* (Japanese), and renamed Seoul Keijō, or capital city. Korea was regarded as a *gaichi*, or "outer land."

The Japanese established the Government-General of Korea as their colonial government in Korea, headed by a Governor-General of Korea, who was appointed by the Japanese emperor and was responsible to him as well as to the Japanese prime minister. The Governor-General was empowered to issue laws and regulations, and to mobilize Japanese troops in Korea and send them to Manchuria. Therefore, all governors-general, except one who was a retired admiral, were army generals on active duty. As if to humiliate the Koreans, the Japanese constructed a massive government-general building in front of the traditional buildings of the Kyŏngbok Palace, removed the Kwanghwa Gate, which was the main entrance to the palace, and established a zoo on the Ch'anggyŏng Palace grounds.

The Governor-General was assisted by the Director-General of Administration, who headed the Secretariat of the

Seoul (Keijō)
Provincial capital

CHINA

U.S.S.R.

Ch'ŏngjin

N. Hamgyŏng

N. P'yŏng'an

Shinŭiju

S. Hamgyŏng

Hamhŭng

S. P'yŏng'an

Pyongyang

Hwanghae

Haeju

Ch'unch'ŏn

EAST SEA

Kangwŏn

Seoul

Kyŏnggi

Ullŭng Island

N. Ch'ungch'ŏng

Ch'ungju

S. Ch'ungch'ŏng

Taejŏn

N. Kyŏngsang

Taegu

YELLOW SEA

N. Chŏlla

Chŏnju

Kwangju

S. Chŏlla

S. Kyŏngsang

Pusan

Kŏmun Island

Cheju Island

JAPAN

Map 10. KOREA UNDER JAPANESE COLONIAL RULE

Government-General. Under it were various bureaus which carried out colonial policy and programs. All directors-general, bureau chiefs, and section chiefs, and more than a half of all clerical positions in the Government-General were Japanese. As late as 1937, 52,270 out of 87,552 officials in the central, municipal and provincial governments, as well as other agencies, were Japanese.

In addition to the Japanese Imperial Army divisions stationed in Korea, the Japanese colonial government had a 40,000-man Japanese gendarmerie and the civil police at its disposal to maintain law and order. The size of the civil police increased from 5,683 men in 1910 to 7,100 in 1912.

A Central Advisory Council was established in September 1910 to assist the Governor-General, and a handful of Koreans who had collaborated with the Japanese were appointed to the sixty-five-member council. All judicial officials (judges and prosecutors) and attorneys were Japanese. A significant fact is that none of these Japanese officials in any branches or levels of the colonial administration spoke or understood Korean.

Korea was divided into thirteen provinces (See Map 10), and Keijō (Seoul) was designated as a special municipality, called *fu* in Japanese. The Mayor of Keijō-fu, and initially all provincial governors were Japanese. At a later period, one or two Koreans were appointed as provincial governors. Some county chiefs were Koreans, and all township heads and village chiefs were Koreans. Needless to say, all police chiefs and superintendents of education were also Japanese.

Cultural and Educational Policy. The early cultural policy of the Japanese was aimed at the destruction of Korean nationalism and racial consciousness. Thus, under the press law of April 1908, which was promulgated during the protectorate period, all Korean newspapers and magazines were abolished and all public assembly was banned. The singing assembly of Korean patriotic songs was outlawed and the display of the Korean national flag was banned. The only newspapers in Korea were those in the Japanese-language published by the Japanese. The suppression of the freedoms of speech, the press, and assembly was such that even a Japanese newspaper reporter of the *Tokyo Nichi Nichi Shimbun* complained.

Many mission or other private schools where Korean nationalism was expressed by teachers or students were closed down, all Korean political and social organizations were disbanded, and religious services were put under police surveillance. At the same time, the possession by Koreans of firearms or other weapons, was disallowed.

Already several hundreds of Koreans had been imprisoned because of speaking out against the Japanese, and then between December 1910 and January 1911 some 700 Korean leaders, many of whom were religious leaders, were arrested on the grounds of an alleged assassination plot against the Governor-General. Of this group, 105 persons were prosecuted and imprisoned, producing the Case of 105 Persons. Between 1910 and 1918, over 200,000 Koreans who had been classified as "undesirable" persons were interned. Among them were many scholars and religious leaders.

The colonial government's education ordinance of August 1911 stated that the purpose of education in Korea was to produce "loyal and obedient" and useful subjects of the Japanese emperor. After that, it adopted a system of four-year primary education, and a four-year secondary school system for boys and a three-year secondary school system for girls. The Japanese policy was not to educate too many Koreans and or train them in scientific and technical fields. Thus, unlike in Japan where a six-year primary education was made compulsory, only a handful of public schools were established. Consequently, in 1919, when the population was about 17 million, only 84,306, or 3.6% of Korean children attended public primary schools, while some 245,000 Korean children were still attending village schools called *sŏdang*. Only five public and seven private secondary schools for boys and two public and four approved private secondary schools for girls existed in Korea as of 1919. Meanwhile, the number of private schools decreased from 1,317 in 1912 to 690 in 1919. There were only two small private liberal arts colleges (Sungshil and Yŏnhŭi) and one private medical college (Severance) for Koreans during this period. All three of these colleges were established by foreign mission boards. In 1918, three public professional schools (law, medical, and mining) established before 1910 were elevated to colleges, but for all practical purposes they were for the Japanese. One public college which was primarily for Koreans was a college of agriculture and forestry. Having been denied educational opportunity in Korea, some 3,471 Koreans went to Japan to attend colleges and universities there between 1910 and 1919.

All school textbooks were published and all school curricula were set up by the Bureau of Education of the Government-General. The study of Japanese language and history was made compulsory at both primary and secondary schools as Japanese was made the official language. However, the Korean language was taught at both levels until 1938, but no Korean history was taught at any school. Most teachers of primary and secondary schools were Japanese.

The Impact of the Early Economic Policy.   In 1910, the Bureau of Land Survey was established, and the Land Survey Ordinance was put into effect immediately. The colonial government had already taken over a large amount of land, including forests, formerly owned by the Yi royal household. The purpose of the land survey was to classify the land according to the size of holdings, establish legal ownership or rights to cultivate farmlands, and make the collection of the land tax more efficient. Under the law, all owners and cultivators were required to prove their legal ownership, or right to cultivate the land. Most of the big landlords were able to prove their ownership, but a large number of small owners and former tenants were unable to prove their rights for one reason or another. All those lands whose ownership could not be proven were taken over by the government. The land survey completed in 1918 led to the government ownership of 21.8 million acres, or 40 percent of farm and forest lands by 1930, and some 270,000 acres of land were turned over to a semi-government organ of Japan called the Oriental Development Company. Other Japanese firms also received land grants later. The Oriental Development Company in turn sold these lands to Japanese farmers who were brought to Korea, increasing the Japanese population in Korea from 171,500 in 1910 to 346,000 in 1920. As a result, while the number of Japanese owner-cultivators increased, the number of Korean tenants likewise increased. Whereas all those who owned more than fifty acres of land were Japanese, most Korean landlords were those who had between two and twenty acres of farmland. Of 2,672,669 Korean farm households in 1918, 66,331 were absentee landlords, or owner cultivators, 535,135 owned some land and rented some, 1.1 million were tenants with less than 2.5 acres of farmland of their own, and 971,203 households were those of pure sharecroppers.

The Government-General promulgated the protective Company Law in December 1910. This law, which required all commercial and industrial firms to have a minimum capital assets and a certain number of Japanese directors and administrative staff, virtually banned the establishment of new Korean firms. For one thing, Koreans would not have Japanese directors or staff in their firms. Moreover, Koreans could not meet the requirement for the minimum amount of capital assets.

As a result, while Japanese firms grew from 109 in 1911 to 262 by 1918, the number of Korean companies increased from 27 in 1911 to a mere 39 during the same period. The number of Japanese-owned factories increased from 185 in 1911 to 650 in 1916 while the number of Korean factories grew from 66 to 416 during the same period; but most of the Korean factories were small, employing less than fifty workers and engaging in light industry. Several new taxes such as tobacco and liquor taxes were added, increasing the tax burden of the people. In order to develop the economy, between 1910 and 1920 many railway projects were completed, increasing the railway mileage from 590 to 890. The major trunk lines were the Seoul-Pusan, the Seoul-Shinŭiju, and the Seoul-Wŏnsan lines.

The March First Movement and Its Aftermath

The March First Movement. Harsh suppression and worsening economic conditions spurred the Koreans at home to launch an independence movement. Many underground patriotic organizations were formed. Among them were the Council of Righteous Soldiers for Independence, the Society for the Restoration of the Korean Nation, the League for the Restoration of National Autonomy, and a women's society named the Pine and Bamboo Society. There also emerged in Korea branches of overseas Korean nationalist societies.

In late 1918, some Koreans learned of American President Woodrow Wilson's "fourteen-points" formula for the reconstruction of world order. They were strongly influenced and encouraged by Wilson's ideas, including the principle of self-determination of people under colonial rule. Riding the world-wide liberal tide, believing that force was now a thing of the past, that an age of reason and peace had arrived, and that Koreans had a right to restore their national independence, certain groups of Koreans launched a national independence movement in 1918, to be known as the March First Movement.

The March First Movement was organized by nationalist scholars and religious leaders in Korea who had been studying various ways to take overt action for Korean independence. In January 1919, at a time when it had become clear that Korean students in Japan were about to take action, the former emperor of Korea, Kojong, died and his funeral was scheduled to be held on March 3. Knowing that a large crowd of mourners would be in Seoul in early March, the national independence leaders decided to have a nation-wide independence march for on March 1. They asked a young scholar, Ch'oe Nam-sŏn, to write a Declaration of Independence, and thirty-three leaders affixed their signatures to it when it was finished. Copies of the Declaration of Independence were then printed and sent to local leaders.

The Declaration of Independence expressed the determination of the Koreans to be independent, pointed out the many wrongdoings of the Japanese, and in the three injunctions attached to it admonished the people to take only peaceful, honorable, and upright actions. The Declaration reads in part as follows:

"We hereby proclaim the independence of Korea and the liberty of the Korean people. We announce this to the nations of the world in order to manifest the principle of the equality of man, and we pass it on to our posterity in order to preserve forever our people's just rights to self-preservation... Behold a new world unfolds before our eyes. The Age of Force is gone and the Age of Peace and Righteousness has arrived. The spirit of moral law and humanity... is about to shed its light of new civilization upon the affairs of mankind... Finding ourselves amid this age of restoration and reconciliation, and riding with the changing tide of the world we neither hesitate, nor fear to complete our task... We must guard our distinctive right to liberty and freedom, and pursue the happiness of a full life... It is our sacred duty to exhibit our indigenous creative energy, and crystalize and achieve our people's spiritual glory in the world filled with spring. For these reasons we have been awakened...."

The three principles that the people were asked to follow were (1) exhibition of the spirit of liberty of the Koreans; (2) demonstration of the Korean people's rightful wishes and desires; and (3) taking orderly and solemn actions "so that our desires and attitudes may be honorable and upright."

On March 1, 1919, tens of thousands of citizens of Seoul poured into the streets and at the Pagoda Park in the center of the city the Declaration of Independence was read as the hitherto forbidden Korean national flags waved in the spring air. The excited crowd poured out of Pagoda Park, joining others in peaceful expression of their national desires, shouting "Long live Korea," and "Long live Korean independence."

Meanwhile, the Japanese police arrested the signers of

the Declaration of Independence and others, and launched their brutal suppression of the masses. In major cities and towns the same thing happened as the movement spread into rural areas. The movement lasted over a month, and over two million people of all ages and both sexes were reported to have taken part in it.

Sometime in the course of the March First Movement, radical elements turned the peaceful movement into a violent one as Japanese gendarmerie and police took brutal actions against the demonstrators, producing heavy casualties. According to Japanese reports, 55 Koreans were killed, 1,409 were injured, and 12,522 were arrested. (However, a Korean nationalist estimated that over 7,500 Koreans were killed, 15,000 were injured, and some 45,000 persons were arrested.) A total of 715 houses were burned down, and 447 church buildings and many Korean schools were destroyed. On the other hand, only six Japanese gendarmes, two policemen, and a civilian were killed, and about 130 Japanese were wounded.

The March First Movement did not restore Korean independence, but it made the whole world know that Koreans were not happy under Japanese rule and that they desired freedom and independence. Along with what the Japanese did to suppress it, the Movement itself discredited the Japanese in the eyes of Western leaders. It even moved conservative Confucians to demand at the end of March the independence of Korea "in accordance with the wishes of heaven." Thus, The March First Movement forced the Japanese to modify their colonial policy in Korea. Meanwhile, hundreds of thousands of Koreans, including many nationalist leaders, began to emigrate from Korea to China and elsewhere.

Realizing that a fundamental policy change was necessary, the Japanese government revised the Organic Regulations of the Government-General of Korea in August, and for the first time, a non-army general, Saitō Makoto (a retired admiral), was appointed as the new governor-general.

Arriving in Seoul in September 1919, Governor-General Saitō was greeted by a Korean nationalist who attempted to assassinate him at the Seoul railway station. Undaunted, he declared that he would pursue a "civilized rule," and began to remove the more objectionable outer trappings of colonial rule while further entrenching Japanese colonial rule. Saitō allowed the publication of some Korean-language newspapers and magazines. However, these papers and magazines were put under strict government censorship and all daily issues and magazines and books published in Korean were ordered to be censored before they were circulated. Often certain sections of the newspapers were blocked out, or the entire daily and monthly issues of the newspapers or magazines were confiscated. Freedom of association was expanded so long as organizations did not challenge the legitimacy of Japanese colonial rule in Korea.

Saitō abolished the control of the Japanese gendarmerie over the civilians, but the Japanese colonial government strengthened the police force, increasing the number of policemen to 15,300 in 1920, and the number of police stations from 151 in 1919 to 251 in 1920, and that of sub-stations from 686 to 2,495 during the same period. The number of policemen steadily increased to 21,800 by 1930. Moreover, in order to tighten their thought control, the government established a "High Section" in the police force, authorizing it to have absolute power over the press and assembly, and check any and all "subversive" thoughts of the Koreans.

Saitō also adopted a plan to establish within four years a primary school in each township, and he promised that more secondary schools for Koreans would be built.

Subsequently, the number of public primary schools increased from 595 in 1920 to 1,330 in 1935. However, only some 439,000 pupils attended these schools over this period. On the other hand, the number of private primary schools continued to shrink from 603 in 1925 to 342 in 1935.

The number of public high schools for boys grew to 15 and that of girls to 9 by 1935, but a total of only 10,000 students could go to these schools. Meanwhile, private secondary schools increased in number, and some 10,133 students were enrolled at 21 private high schools for Korean boys and girls as of 1935. In 1935 only one in 2,200 Korean youth attended secondary schools.

The new Education Ordinance of 1920 allowed the reopening of a mission college (Sungshil), and the establishment of a new mission college for women (Ewha) and a non-sectarian private college (Posŏng). In 1924, a small preparatory division of Keijō Imperial University was opened, and in 1926 the university proper was opened. However, this small university was primarily for Japanese students. When the university proper was opened, only 89 Koreans were admitted while 220 Japanese entered, and there were only 210 Korean students out of a total 538 students enrolled at the university as of 1935. This imbalance remained until the end of Japanese rule.

Governor-General Saitō brought about the revision of the Company Law in April 1920, lessening the requirements for capital assets for Korean firms and removing the requirement to have Japanese as directors or staff. Consequently, the number of Korean companies grew to 363 while the number of Japanese firms increased to 1,237. The number of Korean factories increased, but again most of them were small and were for light industry. Among some major Korean industrial firms were the Kyŏngsŏng Spinning and Weaving Company, the Kyŏnggi

Spinning Company, the Mokp'o Rubber Company, the Kongshin Hosiery Company, the P'yong'an Rubber Company, and the Hwashin Department Store chain. Saitō adopted an ambitious plan to increase the production of rice so as to export more rice to Japan, where skyrocketing rice prices had brought about wide-spread riots in 1918. His goal was to produce 45 million bushels of rice for Korea, and export 25 million bushels to Japan. As a result, the average annual rice production in Korea increased to 72.5 million bushels during the 1922-26 period, and 85 million bushels during the 1932-36 period. However, during the 1922-26 period, 20 million bushels of rice was exported annually and during the 1932-36 period the annual rice export increased to 47.5 million bushels. Thus, rice production in Korea increased by about 40% during the 1922-36 period, but the export of rice to Japan grew by more than eight times, actually increasing the food shortage in Korea. Moreover, as the import of Korean rice drove prices down in Japan, in 1934 the Government-General discarded the plan to increase rice production in Korea.

The Last Phase of Japanese Colonial Rule

The Japanese aggression in Manchuria in September 1931 and in China in July 1937 brought about what the Japanese called the "critical times." It was joined by an even more critical situation when Japan launched the war against the United States in December 1941. Thus, the fifteen-year period from 1931 to the end of World War II was an exceptionally difficult time for the Koreans as the Japanese capitalists continued to ruthlessly exploit the manpower and natural resources of Korea and the Japanese colonial government made desperate efforts to make the Koreans loyal subjects of the Japanese emperor so as to help Japan achieve its imperialistic designs. Korea changed much during this period, but Korean nationalism did not diminish and the desire to be free from Japanese colonialism persisted.

Japanese Rule in the "Critical Times". In July 1931, General Ugaki Kazushige became Governor-General. He tightened political control, especially thought control, as he implemented various economic projects for the "fulfillment of the sacred aims" of the Japanese empire. One of his slogans was "Unity in Spirit and Increase in Production." He urged Koreans to be thrifty and to bring about "self-regeneration," and even attempted to force Koreans to wear multi-colored clothes and abandon their traditional white clothes, which were the ethnic symbol of the Koreans.

Many new sections were added in the Government-General and several associations, such as the Korean Association for the Imperial Rule Assistance, were established. While increasing the acreage of cotton growing areas to 238,000 acres in 1937, Ugaki set aside the Kaema Plateau as a sheep-raising region, and imported several hundred head of sheep from Australia and New Zealand.

When General Minami Jirō succeeded Ugaki in August 1936, he stressed the importance of promoting the spirit of "mutual existence and mutual prosperity," and "unity and harmony" between Japanese and Koreans, bringing reconciliation between them. At the same time, he made it absolutely imperative to promote the "clear understanding of the national polity" of Japan by the Koreans.

After organizing the Korean Association for General National Spiritual Mobilization in 1937, he formed 750,000 units of Save the Nation Labor Corps — mobilizing Koreans for various labor services — and established the Patriotic Day, the Rise Asia Service Day, and a 350,000-unit Patriotic Neighborhood Association whose members watched each other while performing various "patriotic functions" such as collecting monetary donations and scrap iron, and handling rationed goods, such as towels and soap.

In 1939, Minami instituted the forced assimilation of Koreans in the name of *kōminka*, or the "conversion of the Koreans to Imperial Subjects." His real design was to eradicate ethnic identity of the Koreans, and destroy the spirit for restoration of Korean independence. In order to achieve these objectives, in 1938 he had Korean language instruction abolished at all schools, and forced Koreans to adopt Japanese given and surnames, and to memorize and recite the Pledge of Imperial Subjects at all public gatherings. He urged them to attend Shintō ceremonies and show their patriotism and loyalty to the Japanese emperor. Meanwhile, he began to harass Christians, closing down many churches and mission schools, and in 1940 the permit to publish Korean newspapers was revoked.

With the application of the new Japanese Peace Preservation Law of December 1941, the Government-General tightened thought control even more, and any anti-Japanese, anti-war remarks or activities of the Koreans were ruthlessly suppressed. Prisons were filled with Koreans found guilty of such crimes. In such a situation, Korea became a colony under a fascist rule. The outbreak of World War II in 1941 made the situation even worse.

The last two governors-general, General Koiso Kuniaki and his successor General Abe Nobuyuki, continued the policy instituted by Minami. After the application of the Korean Temporary Security Ordinance of December 1941, some 5,600 Koreans were imprisoned as "thought criminals" or "rumor mongers." Meanwhile, the labor mobilization that was initiated by Minami was accelerated, and some 900,000 Korean workers were taken to Japan to work in mines and factories, increasing the number of Koreans in Japan to 1.8 million by 1943.

After allowing the Koreans to "volunteer" in the Japanese Imperial Army, in 1938, 6,500 Korean college students in Japan were mobilized into the Japanese Imperial Army. As only few Koreans actually volunteered to join the Japanese military, in 1943 a general military conscription law was applied to Korea, mobilizing some 214,000 Korean youths in the military. It was at that time when several thousands of Korean women were mobilized as "Comfort Corps" members, and shipped to war zones to provide sexual services to Japanese soldiers. Meanwhile, in 1944 as more Japanese officials were mobilized in the military, Koreans filled those positions vacated by the Japanese, resulting in a rise in the number of Korean officials to about 50% of the 87,552 central, provincial, and municipal government employees. However, 80% of high positions and over 60% of middle positions were still occupied by Japanese. In 1944, there were only two governors who were Korean among thirteen provincial governors.

In 1944, the Student Labor Mobilization Ordinance was promulgated and a half-day school program was put into effect. Under this ordinance, Korean students were mobilized to work at farms, factories, and various construction sites as more Korean farm youths were forcefully taken away to Japan or to heavy industrial plants in Korea, leaving only the aged, women and children in the villages.

The Nationalist Movement at Home and Abroad

New Nationalist and Reform Movements after 1919. After drinking a bitter cup in March 1919, the Koreans became aware of the fact that if they were to survive, maintain their heritage, and improve their conditions, they had to adopt different methods of doing so. As a result, there developed a "New Life Movement" which stressed self-strengthening. A young writer, Yi Kwang-su, said in an article that Korean independence could not be attained by outside help or by pure luck, and if the happiness of the Korean people should depend solely upon political independence, the Koreans either individually or as a nation had to have the ability to carry out a civilized life and decide "whether they should be assimilated, be autonomous, become independent, or carry out a movement of great historical significance." Such a conviction led many nationalists who remained in Korea to promote ethnic nationalism and the movement for self-regeneration, as well as non-violent resistance.

In order to achieve these new aims, the Korean nationalists formed many societies, such as the Self-Production Society and the Korean Women's Association. Many new societies emerged after that, bringing the number of all types of Korean organizations to 5,728 by 1922. The largest group was made up of religious organizations (2,381), followed by secular youth organizations (1,185). Meanwhile, the newly established *Tong'a Ilbo* initiated self-awakening and self-strengthening through cultural enlightenment.

Intellectuals, Writers, and the Press. The Korean intellectuals quickly took advantage of the new policy of Governor-General Saitō. Ch'oe Nam-sŏn, who had been released after serving a prison term for his connections with the March First Movement, resumed his work as the publisher of a magazine for Korean youth called *Ch'ŏng-nyŏn* ("Youth"). Ch'oe, who believed that the cultural history of Korea was of particular significance and value for the people, and that the revival of Korean spiritual strength was urgent, published the *Historical Records of the Three Kingdoms* by Kim Pu-shik of the thirteenth century. But the publication of such a forbidden book lead to the dissolution of his publishing house.

Other nationalist scholars such as Chang Chi-yŏn were convinced that the Korean language must not only be preserved, but also be purified and systematized. For this reason, they organized the Korean Language Research Society in 1921, and published a journal called *Han'gŭl.* It was reorganized as the Korean Linguistic Society in 1931. Meanwhile, in 1924, some twenty-four nationalist scholars formed an academic society, named Chindan Academy, in order to promote studies of Korean literature and history, and published a journal. Unfortunately, however, both of these societies were forced to close in 1943, and many of its leaders were imprisoned.

Whereas some writers gave up their political struggle against the Japanese and promoted Romanticism and Naturalism as literary vehicles, causing the publication of a literary magazine called *White Tide* in 1922, leftist writers formed the Torch Society in 1922, initiating the proletarian literature movement and "the struggle for liberation of the proletarian class." These radical writers revolted against "art for art's sake", and launched a movement for "art of the people." It was this group which was responsible for the establishment of the Korean Federation of Proletarian Artists, commonly known by its French name, which was abbreviated as KAPF.

In 1920, when the new press law was adopted and the publication of Korean newspapers was allowed, three Korean-language daily newspapers appeared. They were the *Chosŏn Ilbo*, the *Tong'a Ilbo*, and the *Shidae Ilbo* (renamed later the *Chung'ang Ilbo*). Following this, many popular magazines such as *Ch'angjo* ("Creation"), *New Light*, *Eastern Light*, *New Women*, and *Light of Korea* appeared. These newspapers and magazines covertly and overtly promoted the national consciousness of Koreans and preached cultural enlightenment while often suffering censorship by the Japanese. For example, the first issue of the *Tong'a Ilbo* stated that its three primary objectives were: (1) fulfillment of its obligation as the self-appointed voice of the Korean people, (2) promotion of democratic ideals and systems, and (3) promotion of culture and the principle of civility.

All these newspapers and magazines provided outlets for poets and writers to publish their work. Many political and social critics, as well as poets who promoted the poetry of oppressed people, made good use of these mass media. However, these newspapers and magazines began to disappear one by one as the Japanese increased their censorship.

The United Front, Students, Farmers and Laborers. Many rightist and leftist societies of men and women which had risen in the early 1920s were engaged in a variety of cultural and social activities, often conflicting with those in the opposite camp. Realizing that the separate, uncoordinated movements of the rightists and the leftists were detrimental to their anti-Japanese popular struggle, the nationalists formed a united front by establishing a society named Shin'ganhoe ("The New Shoot Society") in 1927. Many conservative right-wing nationalists and radical leftists declined to join it, however.

The Shin'ganhoe quickly established some 140 local chapters, increasing its members to 22,000 within a few months, and launched a new mass movement. The number of its branches had grown to 386 and its membership had increased to 76,939 by 1930. Its main objective was to implement practical plans for the "ultimate solution of Korea's political and economic problems" by rejecting the ideology of compromise and opportunism, bringing Japanese colonial rule to an end.

A year after the formation of the Shin'ganhoe, rightist and leftist women got together and organized their united front by establishing a society named Kŭnuhoe (The Society of the Friends of the Rose of Sharon) in March 1928. The Rose of Sharon was (and still is) the Korean national flower. Joining its counterpart, the Kŭnuhoe organized women writers, teachers, students, and workers, and promoting national consciousness among Korean women. The leaders of Kŭnuhoe paid particular attention to the new problems of Korean women factory workers, as well as those in rural areas, and in conjunction with the Korean YWCA, they launched a rural regeneration movement which included the cultural enlightenment of rural women.

Jealous of the growing popularity of these two organizations, the radical leftist (Communists), who had earlier refused to join them, decided to join their ranks and change the character of their movements under the direction given by the Comintern (the third Communist International) in Moscow. In order to do so, they joined these societies, and following the 1928 December Thesis of the Comintern, they attempted to implant their radical revolutionary ideology among the members of the Shin'ganhoe and Kŭnuhoe. They also initiated a new radical farm and labor movement, rejecting what they called the ideology of the "bourgeois-revolutionary movement." At this juncture, many right-wing nationalists left these societies, leaving the leadership in the hands of the radicals.

Meanwhile, the Socialists, who had formed the Saturday and the Tuesday societies in 1923 and 1924, respectively, and the Communists who formed the Korean Communist Party in 1925, made inroads among high school students, organizing cells and reading clubs, and indoctrinating them to a radical revolutionary ideology combined with strong anti-Japanese sentiment and anti-imperialist ideology.

To be sure, Korean students had much to complain about. Their teachers were mediocre and their facilities were inferior compared with those of Japanese schools. While they had to pass an entrance examination to enter secondary schools, all Japanese students were accommodated at schools without this requirement. Koreans were also resentful of the fact that they could not study Korean history. Then, under both right-wing and left-wing influence, Korean students became increasingly anti-Japanese and hostile to those Korean teachers who collaborated with the Japanese. As a result, many school strikes and boycotts were carried out.

In such a situation, the June 10th Independence Demonstration of 1926 came about, taking advantage of the funeral of the last emperor, Sunjong. The funeral ceremony for Sunjong, who had died in April, was scheduled to be held on June 10. Some radical members of the Ch'ŏndogyo (formerly *Tonghak*) were among the planners, but most of the planners were leftists. As the funeral cortege passed through the main streets of Seoul en route to the burial ground, thousands of students carried out anti-Japanese demonstrations, shouting "Long live Korean independence," "Drive out the enemy," or "Down with the imperialists." The handbills which they scattered included many Socialist and Communist slogans. This incident is commonly called the "Second March First Movement."

Following the June 10th demonstrations, students carried out school strikes, demanding the reinstatement of the teaching of Korean history and language. The Kwangju Incident of 1929 was another anti-Japanese, anti-imperialist struggle of Korean students who had been indoctrinated by leftists. It started with bloody fights between Korean and Japanese students on November 2, 1929 in Kwangju, South Chŏlla Province, but turned into a country-wide anti-Japanese school strike with demonstrations in which some 54,000 students of both sexes from 194 schools participated. Such slogans, as "Down with imperialism," "Long live the proletarian revolution," and "Long live Korean independence," chanted by the protesters or printed on leaflets, clearly showed that the leaders of these nation-wide strikes and demonstrations had been indoctrinated and directed by the radicals. The anti-Japanese student movement continued, producing many victims among Korean students. Some 1,640 students were arrested, 582 students were expelled from their schools, and over 2,300 students were placed under indefinite suspension.

The student movement was suppressed by the police, but the students did not give up their nationalist activity. When a Korean-language newspaper, *Chosŏn Ilbo*, sponsored an "Enlightenment and Anti-illiteracy Movement" in 1929 with the slogan, "Knowledge is strength. We must learn in order to survive," Korean students of both sexes from Korea and Japan joined together and went to the villages, teaching the rural children how to read and write while inspiring in them nationalism. When in 1931 another Korean newspaper, *Tong'a Ilbo*, inaugurated an anti-illiteracy movement called "Go among the people," again hundreds of students volunteered as teachers, and went to rural areas, teaching the rural children and adults how to read and write as they encouraged them to develop ethnic consciousness. From 1929 until these movements were banned by the police in 1934, some 5,750 Korean students participated, teaching some 83,000 men, women, and children at 1,323 localities.

Discovering the changing nature of the New Shoot Society and the Society of the Friends of the Rose of Sharon, detecting who were behind the June 10, 1926 and the Kwangju Incident of 1929, and sensing the resurgence of anti-Japanese sentiment in general, the Japanese police cracked down on the two united front organizations. Suppressed by the police, the radical leaders, who had taken over the leadership of these societies, decided to dissolve both in May 1931 and go underground.

Korean workers and peasants, who were influenced by leftist ideology, brought about many violent labor and farm disputes and strikes in the 1920s. There were some 204 labor organizations and 26 tenant organizations as of 1922. Those labor strikes of the 1927-29 period involved 32 local chapters of labor unions. There were some 6,000 labor disputes in 1927, and 5,000 in 1929. The labor strikes of 1928 and 1929 in Wŏnsan, 1930 in Pusan, 1927 and 1934 in Hamhŭng were among the most significant ones of the Korean workers. Korean peasants were also mobilized by the leftists against Korean as well as Japanese landlords as tenant disputes increased in number. They fought losing battles, but such cases as those in 1929 in Taegu and Kohŭng, and 1930 in Tanch'ŏn, clearly reflected the growing influence of the leftists among Korean peasants. After 1937, all farm and labor unions were dissolved and the labor and farm movement as such all but disappeared.

The Nationalist Movement Abroad. While their compatriots at home were engaged in their struggle against the Japanese, the overseas Koreans in China, Manchuria, Siberia, the United States, and even in Japan carried out various nationalist movements.

A nationalist movement had already begun in the Vladivostok area of Siberia and the Chientao (Kando) region in Manchuria where a large number of Koreans had lived around 1910. The first anti-Japanese organization which emerged in Siberia, where some 100,000 Koreans lived, was the Righteous Army of Yi Pŏm-jin. The nationalists in Siberia also established schools for children, and Korean newspapers and magazines. In Manchuria, where some 300,000 Koreans lived, there was a rise in the number of Korean schools, newspapers, and magazines. The first nationalist political organization of Koreans to emerge in Manchuria was the Korean Revolutionary Corps of Pak Ŭn-shik and Yi Tong-hwi, which was established in 1915 by the end of 1919, as the number of Koreans in Siberia swelled to 200,000 and that in Manchuria to 600,000, more anti-Japanese organizations were formed. Korean nationalists there in the Chientao area had already published their Korean Declaration of Independence in February 1918, and carried out demonstrations in March 1919 in conjunction with the March First Movement in Korea. The formation in 1919 of the Army of Korean Independence by Hong Pŏm-do, the Northern Route Army Political Council by Kim Chwa-jin, the Righteous Fighters Corps by Kim Wŏn-bong in the Chientao area, and the Korean People's Socialist Party by Yi Tong-hwi at Khabarovsk, Siberia vastly increased the frequency of armed clashes with Japanese military, who had attempted to crush the Korean nationalists in collusion with the Manchurian warlord Chang Tso-lin.

Some 7,000 armed clashes took place between the Korean freedom fighters belonging to various nationalist organizations and the Japanese, and occasionally some units of Korean armies went across the Tuman River to harass the Japanese in the 1920s. In October 1920 military units of the Army of Korean Independence and that of the Northern Route Army won a major victory against an overwhelming Japanese force at Ch'ingshanli (Ch'ŏngsan-ri in Korean) in Chientao.

Following this disastrous defeat at the hands of the Koreans, the Japanese increased their military strength in eastern Manchuria as they induced the Manchurian warlord to increasingly harass Koreans. As a result, the anti-Japanese activities of the Koreans declined in Manchuria. However, the Koreans formed a united front, forming the Korean National Council in April 1929. Meanwhile, the Korean nationalists who had refused to join the united front formed their own Korean Independence Party in July 1930, just as the radical Communists who had declined to join the united front joined Chinese Communist military units in Manchuria. In any event after September 1931 when the Japanese launched its Manchurian aggression, the anti-Japanese activities of the Koreans in that area steadily declined. Kim Il-sung(Kim Il-sŏng, real name: Kim Sŏng-ju), a Korean military officer in the Chinese Communist Army, eventually fled to Siberia in 1939 with some 300 partisans, becoming a Russian army officer. Meanwhile, some 260,000 Koreans in Siberia were forcefully relocated by Stalin in 1939 to Kazakistan, ending the anti-Japanese movement of the Koreans in Siberia.

Those Korean Nationalists who had fled to China before 1919 were joined by new political refugees from Korea after March 1919, making China the main stage of the

Korean national liberation movement. In April 1919, a group of Korean nationalists who were in Shanghai formed the Provisional Government of Korea and elected Dr. Syngman Rhee, who was in the United States, as its premier (later president). At the same time, they sent Kim Kyu-shik to the Paris Peace Conference to seek the help of Western nations for Korean liberation. When his delegation returned from Paris without any results, it sent Kim Kyu-shik to the United States as head of the Korean Commission in order to seek American assistance in cooperation with Dr. Rhee.

As disputes developed between Dr. Rhee and the leaders of the Provisional Government of Korea in exile in Shanghai regarding the methods of achieving Korean independence, Dr. Rhee resigned the post in 1922, leaving the government in the hands of more radical elements, and he remained in the U.S. until the liberation of Korea. Some moderates such as An Ch'ang-ho attempted to unite the rightists and the leftists for a common purpose, but their efforts bore no fruit. Meanwhile, in January 1932, Kim Ku, founder of the Korean Independence Party, sent a Korean youth to assassinate the Japanese emperor. Then in April 1932 one of Kim Ku's followers threw a bomb in a park in Shanghai where the Japanese were celebrating their emperor's birthday. Kim Ku, who became the new leader of the Provisional Government of Korea, formed the Korean Restoration Army whose soldiers were trained at a military academy of the Chinese Nationalists. Meanwhile, Kim Wŏn-bong came from Manchuria and formed the Korean Volunteer Corps of the Moderate leftists.

When the Japanese launched their war with China in July 1937 and invaded the Shanghai-Nanking areas, both the Korean Provisional Government and the Chinese Nationalist Government fled from Nanking to Hankow, and

*Leaders of the Provisional Government of Korea in
exile. Yi Shi-yŏng in Korean costume, Kim Ku to his
left, Kim Kyu-shik (fourth from the left in front),
Cho So-ang to his left, and Shin Ik-hŭi to Cho's left.*

then eventually to Chungking. It was at this juncture that
the Korean Communists formed their own military units
and joined Mao Tse-tung in Yenan, fighting the Japanese
in northern China. At the same time, the Korean Restoration Army was expanded under the able leadership of
Yi Ch'ŏng-ch'ŏn and Yi Pŏm-sŏk.

When World War II began in 1941, the Korean Provisional Government in Chungking declared war on
Japan, and its military units fought Japanese troops in
collaboration with the Chinese Nationalists in China and
with the British in Burma.

The Korean nationalist movement in the United States
began in February 1909 with the establishment of the
Korean National Association in Hawaii, to where some
7,000 Koreans had emigrated between 1902 and 1906.
One of its leaders, Pak Yong-man, established Korean
military schools in Nebraska and Hawaii shortly after
1910 to train freedom fighters. Dr. Syngman Rhee, who
had been expelled from Korea in 1912 and subsequently
travelled to the United States, became the new leader of

the Korean nationalist movement. In March 1919, Dr. Rhee sent a petition to President Woodrow Wilson, asking him to initiate steps at the Paris Peace Conference to put Korea under the mandate of the League of Nations as a first step toward the eventual restoration of Korean independence. This petition eventually brought about Dr. Rhee's resignation as the president of the Korean Provisional Government in 1922. However, when Kim Kyu-shik arrived in the United States as head of the Korean Commission of the Provisional Government, Dr. Rhee cooperated with him in order to secure American recognition for the Korean Provisional Government in China. Meanwhile, Dr. Philip Jaisohn, who resided in Philadelphia, and An Ch'ang-ho, who had arrived from China, joined Dr. Rhee for the same purpose. Be that as it may, their efforts brought no satisfactory results as the American government paid little attention to the Korean question until 1943.

As regards the Koreans in Japan, it was much more difficult for them to promote their nationalist movement. Nevertheless, Korean students in Tokyo and elsewhere did launch a movement. In January 1919 they organized the Korean Youth Independence Corps, and in February of that year some 600 Korean students met in Tokyo, drafted a Declaration of Korean Independence, and sent it to the Japanese government and Western embassies. At the same time, many of them returned to Korea to incite the Korean students there. Despite many difficulties, they carried out their nationalist activities as late as 1930, calling for the liberation of Korea.

Meanwhile, some Korean Socialists, Communists, and Anarchists in Japan formed underground organizations and published manifestos. Among them was the Black Current Society, which emerged in 1921, and the Wind and Lightning Society, which was formed in 1922. The plot of a Korean anarchist, Pak Yŏl, whose aim was to assassinate the Japanese crown prince was uncovered in 1923, and many radical Koreans were imprisoned. Radical Korean students formed the People's Front for Culture Movement in 1933 disguised as a literary movement, organizing as well theatrical groups. However, their activities were effectively crushed by the Japanese, especially after 1931.

Korea at the End of Japanese Colonial Rule

As the last year of Japanese colonial rule arrived in 1945, none of the twenty-five million Koreans had voting rights. Only one Korean was appointed to the Japanese House of Peers, and only one Korean who resided in Japan was elected in 1944 to the House of Representatives of the Japanese Diet.

Korea had undergone what amounts to a forced march under Japanese colonial rule from 1910 to 1945, and during this period many changes had taken place, making Korea a semi-industrialized, modern colony valuable to the Japanese empire. The most obvious changes included the development of industries and transportation. At the same time, a certain social transformation took place, the population increased, and large cities grew. Culturally and educationally less progress was made due to the deliberate colonial policy not to produce educated Koreans, scientists, or skilled workers.

Light industry that had begun to develop shortly after 1910 continued to flourish as cheap, unskilled labor was abundant. The development of heavy industry was rapid after the establishment in 1926 of hydroelectric and nitrogen fertilizer plants by the Japanese Noguchi firm, and particularly after the Japanese adopted the plan to make

Korea a "logistic base" for their continental expansionism shortly after the outbreak of the Manchurian Incident in 1931. As a result, the production of coal, iron and steel, electricity, and machines and tools expanded as capital investment by such Japanese firms as Mitsui and Mitsubishi grew enormously. The development of heavy industry in the northern parts of Korea was conspicuous.

As industry developed, the number of workers employed in industry grew from 384,951 in 1932 to 1,375,669 in 1943. Of these, 591,494 were in manufacturing industries, 437,752 were in construction, and 346,423 were in mining. As of 1945 all Korean industrial workers received wages that were 40% lower than those of their Japanese counterparts. Meanwhile, industrial production vastly increased as the following table shows:

Industrial Production, 1930-1944 (unit: ton)

	1930	1944
Coal	884,178	7,049,776
Graphite	20,073	102,706
Iron	532,497	3,371,814
Tungsten	12	833

Gold production grew from 5,876 ounces in 1930 to 22,060 ounces in 1940, then dropping to only 598 ounces in 1944. The production of electric power increased from 146,000 kilowatts in 1930 to 1.5 million kilowatts in 1944.

As a result of industrial development in Korea, the Korean economy became diversified with the shift in industrial origins of commodity products. In 1944, the origins of commodity products were: agriculture, 42%; fisheries, 8.0%; forestry, 5.0%; mining, 6.0%; and manufacturing 39%. The development of industry accompanied the expansion of railway mileage to 3,935 in 1944, and the mileage of roads to 19,200. All railways were single-track except the Seoul-Pusan and the Seoul-Shinŭiju lines. All Korean roads were unpaved, and about 65% of them were narrow, rural roads. As new roads and highways were built, harbor facilities of major ports were modernized to facilitate the shipping of goods and raw materials to and from Japan more efficiently. In 1943, the amount of rice produced in Korea was 83.4 million bushels, but, as has been mentioned, some 45% of the harvest was taken away to Japan or to war zones.

One tragic aspect of the Korean farm economy was the growth of tenancy. In 1913, 22.8% of farm households were self-cultivators, but this number dropped to 14.2% in 1944. Meanwhile, the percentage of partial-tenants also dropped from 32.4% in 1913 to 16.8% in 1944, as the percentage of pure tenants increased from 44.8% in 1913 to 59% in 1944. The number of fire-field people, who eked out their living by growing food on slopes by slash and burn techniques, increased rapidly from about 100,000 in 1916 to about 300,000 in 1936, although after the labor mobilization the number dropped sharply to a few hundred.

In 1945, large Japanese firms were in strong control of the Korean economy, but some Korean manufacturing firms managed to survive by producing commodities exclusively for the Koreans. These commodities included clothing materials, rubber shoes, and ceramic ware. A large number of Korean firms were engaged in the food processing industry. Only one Korean department store (Hwashin) and its chains competed against three large Japanese department store chains. There was only one Korean bank among a dozen large banks in Korea as of 1945.

Korean society was much different in 1945 from what it was in 1910. First of all, its population increased from

14.8 million in 1910 to 25.1 million in 1945. The rate of population growth was about 2.6% and the average life span was about 50. With the increase in population and economic development, large cities emerged. Seoul's population increased from a mere 250,000 in 1910 to about 700,000 in 1945. Other large cities were Pusan, Pyongyang, Taegu, Hamhŭng, Wŏnsan, and Inch'ŏn.

An important aspect of social change was the collapse of the *yangban* system. Thus in 1945, most of the leaders of Korea had their social background in the "middle group" or the commoner class of the Yi period. Although the *yangban* system ended, social equality did not develop although a large number of Korean women were educated and became economically and socially active despite the traditional male-oriented social pattern, which was still very much intact, as Confucian principles and social concepts were practiced by the people as a whole. However, child marriage all but disappeared, and although widows were legally free to remarry, most of them did not. Arranged marriages remained as common as before 1910.

There was almost no social contact between the Koreans and the Japanese, and there were very few inter-marriages between them. Some 712,600 Japanese lived in isolation, enjoying unique privileges under the Japanese rule until of 1945.

A modern communication system was operating in Korea after telegraph and telephone systems and a government radio broadcasting network were installed. However, while few Korean homes had telephones, most of them had radio sets as of 1945. The only Korean-language newspaper was that of the government.

Educational opportunity for Korean youth improved somewhat toward the end of Japanese colonial rule. Thus, some 2.1 million Korean children were attending six-year public and private elementary schools in 1945, but this was only 2.2% of all school-age Korean children. Only 73,000, or 13%, of primary school graduates were attending some 151 middle and high schools for boys and girls. The total number of college students in Korea was less than 3,500. This was less than 7% of the middle or high school graduates. In 1944, only about 240 Korean students were enrolled at Keijō Imperial University which had a student population of 600. Many two-year primary schools were established in rural areas, but Korea's illiteracy rate remained over 75% in 1945. According to Japanese reports, only a quarter of all Koreans comprehended Japanese, and only 13% of them spoke Japanese "without difficulty." Refusing to learn the Japanese language was a form of passive resistance.

As political control was tightened and economic exploi-

A Korean father with Western hat and his children with school caps and traditional Korean costumes. Photographed in 1912.

tation accelerated toward the end of Japanese colonial rule, in 1944 Yŏ Un-hyŏng organized the underground Alliance for Korean Independence to sustain the Korean liberation movement.

8

The Liberation, Partition, and Emergence of the Two Korean States, 1945-1950

WITH the Japanese emperor's acceptance on August 15 of the Potsdam ultimatum of the Allies of July 1945, and Japan's surrender to the Allies, Japanese colonial rule in Korea came to an end. However, Korea did not become an independent nation. Instead, it was first occupied by the U.S. and Soviet troops and then became divided into two states.

The Liberation, Partition, and the Allied Occupation

Allied Decisions on Korea.   At Cairo, Egypt, in November 1943, U.S. President Franklin Roosevelt, British Prime Minister Winston Churchill, and China's Chiang Kai-shek held a conference, and on December 1 issued the Cairo Declaration stating that "in due course Korea shall become free and independent." Stalin of the Soviet Union accepted this decision at the Teheran conference of the Allies shortly after the Cairo meeting. When the Koreans learned of this decision, they welcomed it with tremendous enthusiasm, but they paid little or no attention to the phrase "in due course" in the declaration.

The Soviet Union declared war on Japan on August 8, 1945, and its troops poured into northeastern Korea, quickly moving southward and meeting surprisingly little resistance from Japanese troops. At that time, the U.S. forces were fighting Japanese troops on Okinawa, some 600 miles from Korea. It looked as if Soviet troops would occupy the entire Korean peninsula within a short time.

Faced with an unexpected situation, the United States, which did not anticipate such an early Japanese surrender or weak military resistance, proposed in late August to the Soviet Union to divide Korea into two military operational zones along the 38th parallel: the north (48,191 square miles) as the Soviet zone and the south (37,055 square miles) as the American zone. Stalin accepted such a plan immediately, and ordered his troops to stop their advance at the 38th parallel. Thus, the partition of Korea into two "temporary" military operational zones was accomplished. (See Map 11)

When it became clear that the Japanese emperor would announce his acceptance of the July 1945 Potsdam ultimatum of the Allies, Governor-General Abe Nobuyuki solicited the cooperation of Yŏ Un-hyŏng, a moderate left-wing nationalist who had been in prison, to form a Korean political body to maintain law and order after the Japanese surrender to the Allies. Released from prison on August 15, Yŏ organized the Committee for the Preparation of National Reconstruction (CPNR) and its branches were quickly formed throughout Korea. Meanwhile, security units of the CPNR were also established, maintaining law and order.

Most nationalist leaders, many of whom were released from prison, became perturbed when they learned of the

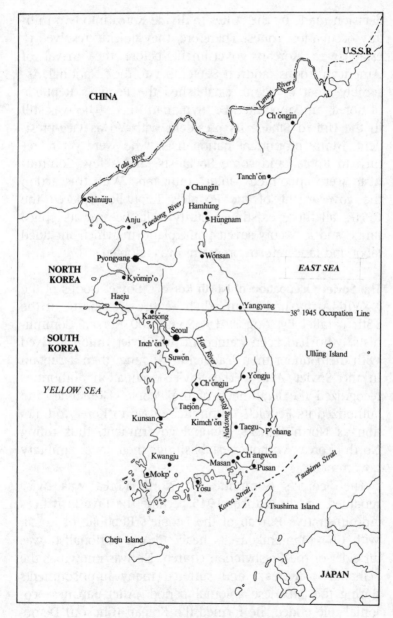

Map 11. PARTITIONED KOREA, 1945

decision made by the Allies to divide Korea into two military occupation zones. Therefore, they quickly resolved to establish a Korean government before the arrival of American troops, and on September 6, the "National Assembly" met in Seoul, established the People's Republic of Korea, and appointed Dr. Syngman Rhee, who was still in the United States, its president with Yŏ as vice-president. Many prominent nationalists, who were yet to return to Korea, and some Socialists, and a few Communists were appointed cabinet ministers. With this action the government of the People's Republic replaced the CPNR, all those existing security units became its police units, and a twenty-seven point platform which included labor and land reform programs was adopted.

The Soviet Occupation of North Korea. Soviet troops of the XXVth Army had occupied the entire area north of the 38th parallel by August 15. Some 300 Korean Communists, who had been trained in the Soviet Union, arrived with them under their leader Kim Il-sung, then a captain in the Soviet Army. The Soviet occupation authorities recognized the legitimacy of the People's Republic, and authorized its People's Committee of North Korea to function as North Korea's regional government, thus ruling North Korea without establishing their own military government.

The People's Committee of North Korea was twice renamed and in October 1945 became the Five Provinces Administrative Bureau of the People's Republic of Korea, with Cho Man-shik as its head. Cho, a nationalist, was an elder of the Presbyterian church. He was known as the "Ghandi of Korea," and suffered many imprisonments during the Japanese colonial period. After Japanese colonial rule ended, he formed the Korean (Chosŏn) Democratic Party of the Christians, nationalists, and intellectuals. Meanwhile, the indigenous Communists reemerged from underground, forming the North Korean Bureau of the Korean Communist Party. The Korean Communist Party was established in Seoul in August 1945.

U.S. Occupation of South Korea. On September 6, a month after Soviet troops invaded Korea, 72,000 U.S. troops of the XXIVth Corps of the Eighth Army arrived in South Korea under its commander, Lt. General John R. Hodge. Entering Seoul, the U.S. occupation authorities accepted the surrender from the Japanese Governor-General, disarmed the Japanese troops, and began the repatriation of all Japanese nationals living in Korea.

Unlike the Soviets, the Americans did not recognize the legitimacy of the People's Republic of Korea and its government, and after outlawing it, they established the United States Army Military Government in Korea (USA MGIK), retained a large number of former Japanese officials and many former Korean officials and policemen who had served under the Japanese, and put South Korea under military rule. The Korean people, who had welcomed American troops as friends and liberators, were bitterly disappointed, and inevitable hostility to the U.S. military rule developed.

In order to soften the Korean antagonism, Gen. Hodge established in October a Korean Advisory Council headed by Dr. Syngman Rhee, a right-wing nationalist who had returned to Korea that month. Meanwhile, Korean nationalist leaders returned to South Korea from the U.S., China, and elsewhere as an ever-increasing number of refugees from the north poured into the south across the 38th parallel.

No American personnel in the American military government, with the exception of a few former missionaries who returned to Korea and were recruited into it, could speak or understand the Korean language. It was therefore necessary for the Americans to employ as interpreters a large number of Koreans who spoke some English and appointed them to various positions within the military government. At this juncture, the Korean Communist Party, which was reconstituted in August 1945 with Pak Hŏn-yŏng as its leader, became active, rivaling the rightist Korean (Han'guk) Democratic Party of the landlords and businessmen, the National Party of the moderate nationalists, and the moderate left-wing Korean Working People's Party of Yŏ Un-hyŏng. Dr. Rhee became the head of the Committee for the Rapid Realization of Independence, which was a coalition of many right-wing political and social organizations. Meanwhile, provincial and district branches of the American military government were set up.

The Moscow Agreement and Its Impact. The Allies which held their meeting in Moscow in December 1945 also dealt with the Korean question. As a result, they agreed to establish a national government of Korea, ending the Allied occupation, and put the new Korean government under a five year trusteeship of the Allies. The American plan to put Korea under a longer period of Allied trusteeship was not approved by the foreign ministers of the Allied nations. Be that as it may, the foreign ministers of the Allies mandated the U.S. and Soviet occupation authorities to form a joint commission and carry out the Moscow Agreement.

The Moscow Agreement of the Allies, which was made public on Christmas Day 1945, aroused the indignation of all Koreans. The agreement was rejected by rightists and leftists alike as they saw it as an insult to the Korean people, and they carried out anti-trusteeship demonstrations day after day as strikes of government employees, shopkeepers, and workers began. On December 30, 1945, in the midst of the political turmoil that developed in connection with the anti-trusteeship plan, Song Chin-u, a prominent right-wing leader of the Korean (Han'guk) Democratic Party was assassinated, marking the beginning of a series of tragic events in South Korea.

North Korea Under Soviet Occupation

Political and Military Development. The Soviet occupation authorities, who established their occupation headquarters in Pyongyang, had no particular plans for Korea except to disarm Japanese troops, accept their surrender, and repatriate all Japanese. However, they began to groom Kim Il-sung, providing him with various types of assistance, and strengthened his power base in cooperation with Koreans who had become Soviet citizens and served in the Soviet Army.

Taking advantage of Russian support, Kim Il-sung destroyed the indigenous Communist leaders one by one, became the First Secretary of the North Korean Bureau of the Korean Communist Party in October, and organized local Communist parties throughout the country, bringing about violent anti-Communist uprisings in Shinŭiju, Hamhŭng, and other places. At the same time, he began to undermine the nationalists.

The Communists, whose number was small, gained their strength when some 22,200 Korean Communists, who had been fighting the Japanese with Communist troops of Mao Tse-tung in northwest China centered around Yenan, arrived in Korea at the end of 1945, becoming the Yenan faction of the Korean Communists. However, at the request of Kim Il-sung, the Soviets allowed these Korean Communists from China to enter

North Korea only after they had been disarmed.

In early January 1946, under Soviet intimation the Communists changed their stand on the trusteeship plan of the Allies, bringing bloody clashes between them and the rightists who were against it. Kim Il-sung, supported by the Soviets, launched his attack against the nationalists as the Soviets put Cho Man-shik and other key nationalists under house arrest, or forced a large number of them to flee to South Korea. After that, Kim's rise to power was rapid as he took over the chairmanship of the Five Provinces Administrative Bureau. At this juncture paramilitary units (Security Units), which were formed in the fall of 1945, were enlarged and were put under the direct control of the North Korean Bureau of the Korean Communist Party. These units were later consolidated into the Korean People's Army.

After crushing the nationalists in February 1946, Kim Il-sung reorganized the Five Provinces Administrative Bureau into the North Korean Provisional People's Committee with himself as its chairman, and in August he brought about the merger of the North Korean Bureau of the Korean Communist Party and the New People's Party of the Yenan faction into the North Korean Workers' Party (NKWP) of 366,000 members. The name of the Communist party in the south had been changed to the South Korean Workers' Party in 1946. By August 1947, the membership of the NKWP had increased to 680,000.

In February 1947, the General Congress of North Korean Provisional People's Committee met and established the North Korean People's Assembly of 237 members, and it in turn established the People's Committee, replacing the North Korean Provisional People's Committee. Kim Il-sung was named its chairman. Thus, as vice-chairman of the North Korean Workers' Party and chairman of the People's Committee, Kim Il-sung increased his power.

Economic and Social Change. In the spring of 1946, the Communists took action to Sovietize North Korea. In March, under the Law on Land Reform, they carried out a sweeping land reform, distributing to 724,522 farm households, free of charge, some 2.4 million acres of farmlands which had been confiscated from the Japanese and Korean landlords and organizations. At the same time, all commercial, financial, and industrial institutions and facilities were nationalized under the Law Concerning the Nationalization of Industry, Railroads, Transportation, Communication, and Banks, dated August 10, 1946. While tax payment was abolished, farmers who received land distribution were obligated to turn over to the state 25% of the harvest while office and factory workers were obligated to perform certain labor duties for the state. After that, grain production increased from 1.9 million tons in 1946 to 2.7 million tons in 1949.

All private businesses disappeared as the government became the sole employer and distributor of goods. Meanwhile, farmers' and labor unions were formed, and all office workers were obligated to join respective unions.

Due to the departure of Japanese engineers and skilled workers, plus the shortage of raw materials and parts, factories and other industrial facilities were virtually shut down. Only small light industrial plants and hydroelectric plants continued to operate. Meanwhile, the Soviets dismantled many industrial facilities, which the Japanese had installed, and transported them to the Soviet Union. Among them was the nitrogen fertilizer plant at Hŭngnam, near Hamhŭng which had supplied all chemical fertilizer needs in Korea.

Meanwhile, in 1946 the Communists established various social organizations. Among them were the Korean

Young Pioneers of children between the ages of 9 and 13, the Communist Youth League for young men and women between the ages of 14 and 30, and the North Korean Democratic Women's League of all women between the ages of 30 and 50. Equality of the sexes was proclaimed under the law of July 30, 1946, which guaranteed equal rights to women. With this, the traditional role of women changed dramatically as they became part of the work force.

Cultural and Educational Change. The Communists brought about cultural and educational change in order to promote Socialism. Their aim was "to arm youth with Communist ideology," and prepare them to be "the builders of a developed Socialism and Communism." All private schools were abolished and all previous six-year primary schools became five-year schools under the Education Law of December 1946. Public three-year middle and three-year high schools were established along with the Kim Il-sung University and a few colleges in 1947. The Communists closed down all churches and most of the Buddhist temples, and took away freedom of religion, speech, and the press. In September 1946, the Party organ, *Rodong Shinmun*, was made the sole national newspaper, publishing solely in the Korean writing system as North Korea abandoned the use of Chinese characters. Meanwhile, they replaced all traditional songs with revolutionary songs.

South Korea Under American Military Rule

Political and Military Development. Facing the increasing anti-trusteeship movement of the Koreans, as well as the growing influence of the Communists who brought about sabotage and labor strikes, Gen. Hodge carried out the Koreanization of American military rule. Thus, in February 1946, a 25-member Democratic Council of Representatives of South Korea was established with Dr. Rhee as its chairman. Unfortunately, Gen. Hodge and Dr. Rhee did not enjoy a cordial relationship as Dr. Rhee, because of his staunch anti-trusteeship policy, failed to cooperate with Gen. Hodge. Moreover, the Democratic Council, which was dominated by the right-wing conservatives, failed to provide necessary cooperation to the American military government. Meanwhile, the Communists and Socialists organized the Korean Democratic National Front in order to counter various American plans. At this juncture, the number of political parties and social organizations with various political ideologies grew to 350, creating a chaotic political situation. The two dominant rightist parties were the Korean (Han'guk) Democratic Party and the National Party, and the two major left-wing parties were the Working People's Party of Yŏ Un-hyŏng, and Pak Hŏn-yŏng's Korean Communist Party, which changed its name to the South Korean Workers' Party in 1946.

In order to prepare the Koreans for their own national security, in January 1946 the American military government established the 25,000-man Constabulary and 2,500-man Coast Guard, giving them military training with equipment confiscated from the Japanese. The Constabulary had only small arms, and the Coast Guard had only small training crafts. Some former Korean officers who had been in the Japanese Imperial Army joined these military units, and when an officers' training school was established by the Americans some of them enrolled at the school.

After encountering difficulties with the Soviets following the convening of the U.S.-U.S.S.R. Joint Commission (see next section), in November 1946 the American occu-

pation authorities established the consultative South
Korean Interim Legislative Assembly (SKILA), which
superseded the Democratic Council. Half of the 90-mem-
ber SKILA was appointed by Gen. Hodge and the other
half was elected through indirect elections. Many of its
appointed members (27) were those of the moderate
rightist party of Kim Kyu-shik and the moderate leftist
party of Yŏ Un-hyŏng. Kim and Yŏ had formed in
October, 1946, the Coalition Committee of the Rightists
and the Leftists, and called for an early reconvening of
the Joint Commission, approved plans for free distribution of farmlands, called for punishment of former
pro-Japanese and for release of political prisoners, and
declared its support of freedom of speech and association.
Gen. Hodge's design was to promote the strength of the
Coalition Committee which supported the trusteeship plan
of the Allies while diminishing the strength of the conservative right-wing groups and suppressing Communist
agitation. However, some 38 elected members of the
SKILA were of those conservative, rightist groups.

Meanwhile, as the South Korean Workers' Party instigated labor unrest and strikes while circulating counterfeit
money it had printed, the American military government
cracked down on the Communists in late 1946, forcing
many of their leaders, including Pak Hŏn-yŏng, to flee to
North Korea. However, the members of the South Korean
Workers' Party went underground, continuing their subversive activities.

The Koreanization of the American military government moved forward when, in August 1946, Gen. Hodge
requested the Military Governor to turn over the operation
of the various departments to Koreans, leaving American
personnel in advisory capacities only. This step was followed by the establishment of the South Korean Interim
Government (SKIG) in May 1947, with a moderate

nationalist An Chae-hong, an ally of Kim Kyu-shik, as Civil Administrator. However, while the SKILA had no independent legislative power as such, the SKIG was given no decision-making power. The American military governor and Gen. Hodge reserved their veto power over both organizations.

In the heat of the political controversy surrounding the trusteeship issue, as well as conflict between the extreme rightist and extreme leftist groups, in July 1947 Yŏ Un-hyŏng was assassinated by a right-wing policeman, and in December 1947, Chang Tŏk-su, another key leader of the Korean (Han'guk) Democratic Party, was assassinated by a leftist. These bloody events were followed by the outbreak of a Communist-inspired and led rebellion on Cheju Island in April 1948.

Economic and Social Conditions. Like the North Korean economy, the South Korean economy suffered when Japanese engineers, technicians, and skilled workers were repatriated to Japan. Some factories of the Japanese were taken over by Koreans and continued to operate, but due to the shortage of raw materials and parts, the number of factories in operation steadily decreased. Then, the decrease of power supply from the north worsened the situation, for some 95% of South Korea's electric power needs had been met by the supply from the north up until 1945. In 1945, some 250 streetcars were in operation in Seoul, but by 1947 the number of streetcars running in Seoul declined to 87 due to the shortage of power and parts. When machines broke down, they could not be repaired because of the lack of trained machinists and technicians, as a result of the deliberate Japanese policy not to train Koreans in scientific and technical fields. Finally, when the supply of electric power was completely cut off in early 1948, South Korea's economy collapsed as nearly all

factories were shut down, increasing the number of unemployed persons to three million, or 7.5% of the population in 1948.

Although no land reform was carried out by the
American military government, it did confiscate Japanese
properties and they were turned over to a newly established New Korea Company. The New Korea Company,
which took over farmlands and other properties which
had been owned by the Japanese, sold some 687,000
acres of farmlands to 588,000 tenant households, or 25%
of the farm population in South Korea. Meanwhile, other
former Japanese properties such as small factories and
shops, as well as houses, were sold, creating many new
Korean entrepreneurs and home owners.

The food production suffered when the supply of
chemical fertilizer from the north stopped in 1945. Only
when U.S. economic aid began and chemical fertilizers
were imported did food production begin to grow, increasing the amount of grain production from 45.7
million bushels in 1947 to 58.6 million bushels in 1948.
However, it was not adequate to feed the ever increasing
population.

The shortage of commodities, including medicine,
food, and fuel (firewood and coal) brought about rapid
growth of inflationary trends. The wholesale price index
(1947 = 100) grew from 143 in December 1947 to 185 in
August 1948. The price of 32 pounds of polished rice in
August 1945 was 220 *won*, but it jumped to 1,000 *won*
in May 1947 and to 1,400 *won* in May 1948. The price
of wheat flour was 130 *won* per 48.5 pounds in August
1945, but it increased to 2,250 *won* in May 1947. A pair
of rubber shoes was sold for 40 *won* in 1945, but the cost
increased to 210 *won* in May 1948. Silk cloth was sold
for 170 *won* per yard in August 1945, but in May 1948
the price of a yard of silk cloth was 3,900 *won*. The

shortage of commodities, including food, brought about
the rise of black markets.

The rapid increase of the population worsened the
economic situation. The population of South Korea in
August 1945 was about 15 million, and it had reached
17.3 million by September 1946, 20 million in 1947, and
then 21 million in 1948. This was in part due to the influx of refugees from the north along with Koreans who
were repatriated from China and Japan. The population
in Seoul jumped from about 700,000 in August 1945 to
1.5 million in the spring of 1948.

In 1946, a Western observer reported that the "situation
is getting worse. There is rampant inflation. Consumer
goods and coal are virtually nonexistent. Food distribution
is inequitable.... Transportation equipment is breaking
down. Unemployment is rising to dangerous propor-
tions.... Hunger is rapidly spreading and will presently result in starvation in many areas by mid summer." Only
relief goods and food provided by the United Nations
agencies and the U.S. government prevented mass starvation and epidemics.

The rapid increase of the population created a serious
housing shortage, and the overcrowded cities witnessed
the decline of social morality and increase in crimes. To
make matters worse, hoodlums and mafia groups
emerged, creating serious economic and social problems.

Cultural and Educational Development. While pursuing
democratic principles, the American military government
did not tamper with Korean culture, but left the Koreans
free to revive their traditional culture. Under freedom of
thought, speech, and the press Korean newspapers and
magazines reemerged. Many societies and institutions
were formed to promote traditional art, while religious
freedom brought about the rapid growth of Christianity

which had been repressed during the last phase of Japanese colonial rule.

Schools were reopened, but the shortage of teachers and funds, together with chaotic political and social conditions, hampered educational development. Moreover, many school buildings were used by the occupation troops, worsening the shortage of classrooms. However, after the steps taken by the National Committee on Educational Planning, which was established in March 1946, educational opportunities slowly increased as all private colleges were reopened. Keijō Imperial University was reorganized as Seoul National University, despite the shortage of professors.

In September 1946, the American educational system of 6-3-3-4 was put into effect and new textbooks were published. Despite many problems, the number of primary school pupils increased from 1.4 million in September 1945 to 2.7 million in the spring of 1948. The most significant aspects of educational change was the removal of military education and political indoctrination of the Japanese period, which were replaced by democratic concepts and methods. Needless to say, instructional programs in Korean language and history were restored. Due to classroom shortage, all primary schools had two shifts, and in 1948 the Teacher Training Center was established in order to train more teachers.

Secondary education also grew as more private schools were established, the number of schools increasing from 253 in 1945 to 415 in 1947 with an enrollment increase from 62,000 in 1945 to 277,447 in 1947. In the field of higher education, the establishment of more national and provincial colleges, along with private higher educational institutions, constituted the most significant development. The number of college students increased from 7,819 in 1945 to 20,545 in 1947. However, the quality of higher education remained low because of the shortage of well-trained professors and the lack of library and laboratory facilities.

The Emergence of the Two Korean States

The U.S.–U.S.S.R. Joint Commission. Despite vehement opposition of a vast majority of the Koreans to the trusteeship plan of the Allies, the two occupation authorities formed the Joint Commission in January 1946, and convened regular meetings in March in order to implement the Moscow Agreement.

Some non-political agreements were reached between the two parties. They included guidelines for transportation and travel between the two zones, exchange of mail, radio frequencies, and supply of North Korean electric power. However, they could not agree on one most important matter, namely to whom the invitations should be issued to participate in discussions leading to the establishment of the Korean government. Such consultation with Korean "democratic" political parties, social groups, and individuals had been mandated by the Moscow Agreement of the Allies.

The American and Soviet representatives in the Joint Commission reached a stalemate when the Soviets refused to invite any individual or organization which opposed the Moscow Agreement to participate in the deliberations of the Joint Commission. The Soviets regarded these organizations and individuals "undemocratic." The groups which rejected the Moscow Agreement (trusteeship plan) included all rightist organizations of Dr. Syngman Rhee, Kim Ku and others, except the moderate National Party of Kim Kyu-shik and An Chae-hong. Giving in to the Russian argument would have meant American concession to the creation of the Korean government mostly in the hands of the Communists and Socialists and a few moderate nationalists. In the end, in May 1946, the Joint Commission adjourned.

Gen. Hodge, who was successful in bringing the conservative nationalists to pledge not to obstruct the work of the Joint Commission, requested the Soviets for the reconvening of the Joint Commission meeting. As a result, the two sides met in May 1947, but the selection of Korean leaders and groups for participation in the Joint Commission meetings again created an impasse. By this time, the Cold War between the U.S. and the Soviet Union had begun, and it became apparent that the Soviets were in the process of establishing a socialist nation in North Korea. Moreover, the Russian head delegate, Gen. Terenti F. Shtykov, made it known that the Soviet Union was "interested in establishing in Korea a provisional democratic government which would be loyal to the Soviet Union." In such a situation, the Joint Commission ended its meeting in August. With this, all communications and traffic across the 38th parallel ceased, and supply of fuel and electricity was cut off.

The U.N. Intervention. Realizing that the implementation of the Moscow Agreement, or settling the Korean question with the Soviets was an impossibility, the American government called for a conference of foreign ministers of the Allies, only to meet with opposition from the Soviet Union. Consequently, in September 1947 the U.S. government submitted the Korean question to the United Nations. Despite the strong objection of the Soviet delegation at the U.N., the General Assembly voted in September to take up the Korean question, and after adopting a resolution on Korea in November, the U.N. General Assembly formed the United Nations Temporary

Commission on Korea (UNTCOK), and sent it to Korea to establish a Korean government and end the Allied occupation.

The U.N. decision was welcomed by South Korea, but North Korea refused to allow the UNTCOK even to visit North Korea. Facing a dilemma, the UNTCOK decided, in consultation with the First Committee of the General Assembly, to have a general election in the south where two-thirds of the Korean population resided. The UNTCOK regarded it legitimate to allow two-thirds of the Korean population to determine their future and establish a government of all Korea.

When the UNTCOK made its decision to establish a Korean government without North Korean participation, many nationalists and moderate leftists became concerned over the possibility that the temporary partition of Korea might become a permanent division. For this reason, Kim Kyu-shik, Kim Ku, and others advocated solving the Korean question by Koreans themselves, and proposed joint efforts with the North Korean leaders. In response, Kim Il-sung invited them to come to Pyongyang to find solutions for the Korean problem.

In April 1948, a group of South Korean leaders made a journey to Pyongyang, and, after a series of meetings with the North Korean counterparts, they arrived at the following five principles: (1) rejection of any form of dictatorship; (2) rejection of monopolistic capitalism; (3) establishment of a united central government through a general election of the entire nation; (4) disallowance of any military base to any foreign power; and (5) early withdrawal of all foreign troops from Korea. After receiving a pledge from Kim Il-sung that he would not establish a separate government in the north, they returned to Seoul. However, they were betrayed by Kim Il-sung, who went ahead and brought about the adoption of a constitution for all Korea by the North Korean Supreme People's Assembly on May 1 without participation of any South Koreans.

The Establishment of the Two Korean States. In spite of Communist terrorism, preparations for the elections were carried out after Gen. Hodge announced on March 1, 1948 that general elections would be held in South Korea (population 21.5 million) on May 10 under U.N. sponsorship and supervision. By April 9, the last day of registration, 7.8 million eligible voters, or 79.9% of the population above the age of 21, had registered, and 842 candidates, including 17 women, ran for the National (Constituent) Assembly.

On May 10, 1948, 7.7 million or 95.5% of registered voters, cast their ballots in the first democratic elections in which universal adult suffrage had been exercised in Korean history. Only on Cheju Island, where a Communist-inspired and led rebellion was in progress, was the election delayed. Despite Communist sabotage and violence (44 persons, including several candidates were killed) 198 members of the 300-seat National (Constituent) Assembly were elected for a two-year term of office. One hundred seats were left vacant to be filled by the North Korean people, and two were to be elected from Cheju Island upon the subjugation of the rebellion.

The National (Constituent) Assembly met May 31, 1948, elected Dr. Rhee as its chairman, and adopted the constitution in June. Following this, it named the nation the Republic of Korea (ROK), and elected Dr. Rhee president of the republic. On August 15, 1948, the Republic of Korea and its government were inaugurated as President Rhee took the oath of office, ending the U.S. occupation of South Korea. The United States and other democratic nations extended their recognition of the Republic of

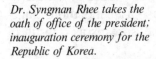

*Dr. Syngman Rhee takes the
oath of office of the president;
inauguration ceremony for the
Republic of Korea.*

Korea immediately, and in December the United Nations
General Assembly recognized the government of the Republic of Korea as the "only lawful government" in Korea.
Following this, the U.N. General Assembly established
the U.N. Commission on Korea, replacing the UNTCOK,
in order to assist in the development of the new nation.

After their failure in July 1948 to reconvene the conference of the representatives of the north and the south, the
Communists in North Korea (population 8 million) carried out elections on August 25, and established the 572-
member Korean Supreme People's Assembly. The North
Korean Communists claimed that some "8.7 million
voters participated" in the "secret elections" conducted in
the south, and elected 360 South Korean representatives

to the Korean Supreme People's Assembly.

The Korean Supreme People's Assembly met from September 3, 1948 in Pyongyang, ratified the constitution of the Democratic People's Republic of Korea (DPRK) and elected Kim Il-sung premier. On September 9, 1948 the DPRK was officially declared into being, and the Soviet Union and its satellite nations promptly recognized it.

Thus, during the months of August and September, 1948, the Korean people witnessed the emergence of the two Korean states, each claiming to be the legitimate one. The temporary military demarcation line (38th parallel) now became the boundary between the two Korean states of one nation, as a new "iron curtain" came down across the Korean peninsula. The die was cast, and more tragedies were yet to be visited upon the Koreans as a result of the division of the country.

The Two Koreas in the Early Stages

Immediately following the establishment of the two separate states, both North and South Korea went ahead to strengthen their respective government's control and national defense, develop economies, reconstruct the social system, and promote education and culture with diametrically opposing ideologies and interests. The only common goal between them was the reunification of their divided motherland.

EARLY ASPECTS OF NORTH KOREAN DEVELOPMENT

After inaugurating the Democratic People's Republic of Korea (DPRK), commonly called North Korea, the Communists carried out many ambitious schemes and programs to build a Socialist state with completely alien ideology, systems and way of life. At the same time, they implemented various schemes to bring about the destruction of South Korea and reunification of the country.

The State and the Ruling Organs. Although the constitution of the DPRK claimed that the entire Korean peninsula was its national territory, its area to the north of the 38th parallel was 48,191 square miles, a little more than half of the peninsula, and the total population was a mere 8 million, or about one third of the total Korean population. It included North and South P'yŏng'an, North and South Hamgyŏng, and Hwanghae provinces, and the northern part of Kangwŏn Province. (See Map 12) Each province was divided into counties, each county into workers' districts or towns and villages. Pyongyang was designated as "the capital of Korea."

North Korea is mostly mountainous, especially the eastern part. Some river basins and small but fertile plains are found in the western region. The Province of Hwanghae was especially endowed with rich farmlands. Of 6.4 million acres of farmlands in North Korea, 1.1 million acres were paddy fields and 5.3 million acres were dry fields. In addition to Pyongyang, the large cities were Hamhŭng, Wŏnsan, Ch'ŏngjin, Shinŭiju, and Sŏngjin (later renamed Kimch'aek).

The three ruling organs of North Korea were the Supreme People's Assembly (SPA), the Central People's Committee and its executive arm called State Administrative Council, and the Korean Workers' Party (KWP). Theoretically, the SPA, which was established in August 1948, is the supreme organ of the state. However, it did not exercise the supreme power of the state and it had no legislative power as such. Its main functions had been to meet quadrennially to hear the reports of the Central People's Committee, approve the national budget and per-

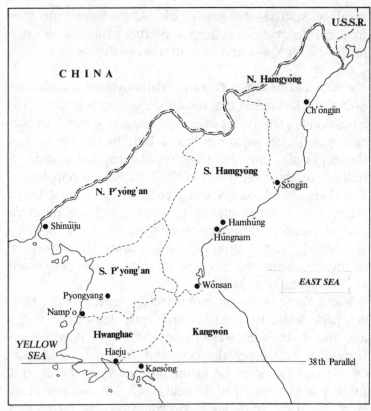

Map 12. NORTH KOREA, 1948-53

sonnel appointments submitted by the Central People's Committee, and other proposals submitted by it. Up until 1957, it had 572 deputies, but only 212 of them met since 360 of them who were supposedly elected in South Korea "to represent" its people did not attend. Up to 1972, the chairman of its Standing Committee represented the state as its head. Each deputy represented 50,000 constituents up until 1962.

The Central People's Committee has been primarily a policy-making and supervisory body of the government under the guidance of the KWP. All its fifteen (17 in

1990) members were elected by the SPA. The State Administrative Council, the executive arm of the Central People's Committee, has been headed by the premier assisted by a varying number (10 in 1990) of deputy-premiers. The State Administrative Council consisted of a varying number of commissions and ministries. Each province, city, county, workers' district, and village had its own people's committee as a supervisory body over the respective local government unit.

In reality, the supreme organ of North Korea has been the Korean Workers' Party (KWP), which emerged when the North Korean Workers' Party and the South Korean Workers' Party were united into one body in 1949. This Party of some 800,000 members was the only political party which enjoyed the monopoly of political power in 1948 as all non-Communist organizations such as the Korean (Chosŏn) Democratic Party of the nationalists, the Fraternal Youth Party of the Ch'ŏndogyo (formerly *Tonghak* sect), the Korean Federation of Christians and the Korean Federation of Buddhists had been taken over by the Communists in 1946. The Party membership had grown to 1.2 million by 1950.

There was no legislative assembly as such in North Korea. All laws and regulations originated in the Party. The key committees of the KWP have been the Central, the Military, and the Control committees. The center of power of the Party resided in the Political Bureau (Politburo) of the Central Committee. Although the Party Congress was to meet every five years, it has been called infrequently.

The People's Army is another powerful organ of the state. Kim Il-sung, then premier and chairman of the KWP, said that the People's Army was the armed forces of the KWP, and it "guards and protects...the course of revolution proposed by the Party." Created in February

1948 with some 20,000 members of the Security Units, it quickly grew in size, and by 1950 it had increased to 24 infantry divisions of 135,000 troops, four mixed brigades of 2,500 men and a tank brigade of 8,000 men which had a large number of Russian-built tanks of various sizes. The Air Force of 2,300 men had over 210 Soviet-built military aircraft, and the Navy of 15,270 men had over 34 naval ships. These units of the People's Army were well equipped with weapons provided by the Soviet Union, and they were well trained by over 2,500 Soviet military advisers and instructors who remained in north Korea, and were assigned to each unit of the armed forces. The People's Army already had a large number of experienced Communist soldiers who returned to Korea either from the Soviet Union or from China. Among them were many Koreans with Soviet citizenship. Kim Il-sung said that the People's Army troops were trained for "the war to liberate the southern half (South Korea) of the Republic."

In addition to the People's Army and the internal security force (police), the KWP mobilized such politically oriented social organizations as the Korean Young Pioneers, the Communist Youth League (later renamed the Socialists Youth League), and the Korean Democratic Women's League, as well as labor and farmers' and other unions in order to strengthen the structure of the monolithic society. The Party indoctrinated the members of these organizations to make the "liberation of the southern half of the Republic" their supreme goal and to be loyal to Kim Il-sung and the Party.

SOUTH KOREA BEFORE THE KOREAN WAR

The history of the Republic of Korea, commonly called South Korea, began in a turbulent domestic and international environment, and the many tragic events that took place in the Korean peninsula shaped the particular character of the South Korean society as it is today. The original aims of building a democratic country were soon frustrated due to many unfortunate circumstances and heritages among which the major ones were the traditional bureaucratism, the lack of experience in self-rule, and the Korean War.

The State, Government, and Defense Structure. Although the constitution of the Republic of Korea stated that its national territory included the entire Korean peninsula and its adjacent islands, the size of the country, 37,055 square miles to the south of the 38th parallel, was a little smaller than North Korea, with population in 1948 of 21.5 million. South Korea was slightly larger than Scotland, or the state of Indiana. The eastern half is a rugged mountainous region while the western half has low hills, river basins, and coastal plains.

When the republic was established, there were nine provinces: Kyŏnggi, Kangwŏn, North and South Ch'ungch'ŏng, North and South Chŏlla, North and South Kyŏngsang, and Cheju. Also within its national boundary was the extreme southern region of Hwanghae Province. (See Map 13) Each province was divided into counties, each county into townships, and each township into towns and villages. The city of Seoul, which was designated as the capital of the nation, and Pusan were given a special city status and were directly administered by the central government. Other large cities were Taegu, Taejŏn, Kwangju, and Inch'ŏn.

The constitution promulgated in July 1948 established the framework of the government for democratic rule. Under the principle of the separation of power, it established the executive, legislative, and judicial branches of the government. It guaranteed the rights of citizens, equality before the law, freedom of speech, the press, religion, and association. Property rights, equality of the sexes, and other rights of the citizens of a democratic state were also guaranteed.

The legislative power was vested in the unicameral National (Constituent) Assembly whose members were elected for a two-year term by universal, equal, direct, and secret vote. Each assemblyman represented 100,000 constituents. The National Assembly was given, in addition to legislative authority, the power to institute impeachment proceedings against the president, vice-presi-

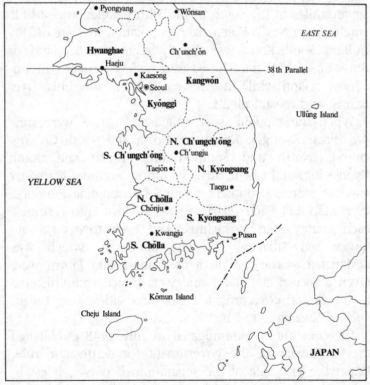

Map 13. SOUTH KOREA, 1948-53

dent, members of the State Affairs Council (cabinet), judges, and other public officials designated by law. In May 1950, the new National Assembly, whose members were elected for a four-year term, was established, replacing the Constituent Assembly which had emerged in July 1948.

The president, who was elected by a two-thirds majority vote of the National Assembly for a four-year tenure, received broad power under the constitution. He was empowered to appoint the prime minister with the approval of the National Assembly, and members of the State Affairs Council, as well as justices of the Supreme Court and judges of the high courts. The president was also given power to propose emergency measures restricting freedom of speech, assembly and the press under certain circumstances. The vice-presidency was a ceremonial post.

The cabinet was called the State Affairs Council, which was an executive arm of the president and whose members were appointed by the president. It was headed by a premier, and in the beginning, it included four offices and ten ministries. While cabinet ministerial posts were filled by political appointees, administrative and judicial bureaucrats were selected through the civil service examination system patterned after that of Japan. The system was revised in 1961 and 1963.

Several unfortunate events which took place immediately after the establishment of the republic made the political situation far worse. Two months after the birth of the republic, a Communist-inspired military insurrection broke out in the Yŏsu-Sunch'ŏn area in South Chŏlla Province, followed by that of Taegu in November. Democratic aspirations suffered as the government became increasingly autocratic with the passage of the National Security Law in November 1948 in the wake of aforementioned rebellions.

The relationship between the president and the National Assembly steadily deteriorated because of the latter's election of the vice-president, who was a close ally of Kim Ku, a bitter critic of the president, and its refusal to approve Rhee's choice of a man as premier. In June 1949 in the midst of political rivalry between the president and the National Assembly, Kim Ku was assassinated, and in October some sixteen members of the National Assembly were arrested for their alleged collaboration with the Communists.

The national defense forces, which were under the control of the Minister of Defense, consisted of the Army and the Navy as of November 1948. In April 1949, the Marine Corps was created, followed by the establishment of the Air Force in October. The national defense forces consisted of about 53,000 men at the time when the withdrawal of U.S. troops from South Korea was completed in July 1949. Some 500 American military advisers remained in South Korea to provide guidance for the strengthening of national defense. The Army had only small arms and no tanks; the Navy and the Marine Corps had only small, light craft, and the Air Force had only 22 planes all of which were trainers. The Military English School, which the American military government had established to train officers, was renamed in 1948 as the Officers Candidate School, and it eventually became the Korean Military Academy.

The Military Service Law of August 1949 established a compulsory system, and all able-bodied men above the age of 20, except those who were only sons or household heads, were subjected to conscription and active duty of two years in the Army and three years in the Navy. College students of draft age were given deferments. By July 1950, the total number of officers and troops in South

Korean defense forces had grown to 67,559.

Thus the Korean people, separated into two nations under opposing ideologies and systems, struggled to develop their economy and construct a new society. However, despite their yearning for peaceful unification, they witnessed the growing tension between the North and South and the military buildup on opposite sides of the 38th parallel as their respective leaders agitated for reunification.

9
The Korean War, 1950-1953

THE Communists made the "liberation of the southern half of the Republic (South Korea)" their supreme goal in the "Korean Revolution." Like the constitution of South Korea, the North Korean constitution had declared that the entire Korean peninsula was within its own national territory.

Prelude

From September 1948, the North Korean Communist had instigated many uprisings and labor strikes in South Korea as they advocated the reunification of the country. They had already succeeded in instigating a rebellion on Cheju Island in April 1948, and then in October they brought about a military insurrection in the Yŏsu-Sunch'ŏn area in South Chŏlla Province through their agents in the military units stationed in Yŏsu. This insurrection took place when the troops in Yŏsu were ordered to go to Cheju to subjugate the rebellion there. A series of border clashes across the 38th parallel occurred frequently beginning in May 1949, and at other places in South Korea the Communists were engaged in guerrilla warfare in the fall of 1949. However, all these uprisings and rebellions were crushed by South Korean troops by the end of 1949.

Realizing that these Communist-led uprisings and rebellions would not bring down the South Korean government, Kim Il-sung made two secret visits to Moscow in 1949, concluding economic and military agreements with the Soviet Union. Various Russian and Chinese sources indicate that Kim discussed his plan to invade South Korea with Stalin at that time, and when Mao Tse-tung of China visited Moscow in 1949, Stalin and Mao also discussed Kim's plan.

Encouraged by the statement made by U.S. Secretary of State Dean Acheson in January 1950 in which he excluded South Korea from the U.S. "defense perimeter" in the Far East, the North Korean Communists decided to launch a war to unify Korea by force. In early 1950, soon after this decision was made, Kim Il-sung went to Moscow, and sought Stalin's approval for the North Korean invasion of South Korea, receiving Stalin's final approval after his return to Pyongyang. After receiving this approval, Kim notified Mao Tse-tung regarding his invasion plan.

Once Kim Il-sung's plan was approved, the Soviet Union replaced all its military advisers in North Korea with combat-experienced high-ranking officers, and quickly sent more tanks and other weapons to North Korea. On the arrival of new military advisers, invasion plans were drawn up by the Soviets and Russian-born Korean officers in the Soviet Army, and the completed battle plans were given to Kim Il-sung in late May. Battle-ready military units were then deployed along the 38th parallel, and by June 22 two command headquarters had been set up. The first battle order written in Russian and Korean was issued to division commanders on June 24.

The Northern Aggression

In the early morning of Sunday, June 25, 1950, North Korean troops opened fire and, spearheaded by Russian-built tanks, went across the 38th parallel. The devastating Korean War had begun. The 56,000 North Korean troops penetrated into South Korea from all points along the 38th parallel at a surprising speed without meeting much resistance from South Korean troops. Just three days later, on June 28, Seoul was captured and the South Korean government was forced to flee south.

Taken by surprise, the American government hastily sent some troops from Japan to Korea to stop the North Korean advance, but by mid-July the first units of U.S. troops had been completely annihilated by the North Koreans near Taejŏn. Meanwhile, the U.S. asked the U.N. Security Council to condemn North Korea and form a U.N. force to be dispatched to Korea to aid the south.

After condemning North Korea as an aggressor, the Security Council asked U.N. member nations to provide troops. Sixteen nations responded to this call and the U.N. Forces were formed with U.S. General Douglas MacArthur as its Commander. The South Korean government also put its armed forces under the U.N. Command.

North Korean tanks roar in Seoul.

U.N. members which provided military assistance for Korea were as follows:

> Ground Forces: Australia, Belgium, Canada, Colombia, Cuba, Ethiopia, France, Greece, Luxembourg, the Netherlands, New Zealand, the Philippines, Thailand, Turkey, the United Kingdom, and the United States.
>
> Naval Forces: Australia, Canada, Colombia, France, New Zealand, Thailand, the United Kingdom, and the United States.
>
> Air Force: Australia, Canada, the Union of South Africa, the United Kingdom, and the United States.
>
> Medical: Denmark, India, Italy, Norway, Sweden, the United Kingdom, and the United States.

Other U.N. members which provided other assistance were Costa Rica and Panama. Military assistance by Nationalist China, Costa Rica, El Salvador, and Panama was deferred.

The North Korean Communists had made three major miscalculations when they launched the war. The first of these was that the U.S. would not intervene, let alone the U.N. The second of these was that if they took over Seoul the South Korean government would surrender and the war would be over. The third was that some "500,000" underground members of the South Korean Workers' Party would bring about the insurrection of the people all over the country and overthrow the South Korean government in collaboration with the invading troops. It is now clear that the third miscalculation was based on a proposal to invade the south made by Pak Hŏn-yŏng, former head of the South Korean Workers' Party who had fled to the north and become deputy-premier and foreign minister in September 1948.

It is now known that the North Koreans had no plan to extend the war to every part of South Korea. Therefore, after taking over Seoul, which in view of its proximity to the North Korean border was a relatively easy target, they waited for the surrender of the South Korean government and mass uprisings all over South Korea. When neither happened, they debated for three days on what to do next, and on July 1 Kim Il-sung ordered his troops to push southward.

The North Korean forces took over Taejŏn on July 20, forcing the South Korean government to move still further south, and more than two-thirds of South Korean territory fell into the hands of the aggressors. Kim Il-sung ordered his troops to take over the Pusan perimeter by August 15 as South Korean and U.S. troops took their last stand in that small area east of the Naktong River. (See Map 14) Meanwhile, U.N. forces began to arrive in Korea.

On September 15, when the U.N. Forces had been sufficiently strengthened, Gen. MacArthur successfully carried out an amphibious landing at Inch'ŏn, trapping North Korean troops in the south. At the same time, U.N. troops launched an offensive from the Pusan perimeter, and headed north. Seoul was recovered on September 28, and in early October U.N. troops crossed the 38th parallel in pursuit of fleeing North Korean troops under the authority of both the U.S. government and the U.N. At this juncture, Kim Il-sung sent envoys to Peking, seeking military assistance from China.

China's Entry into the War

Some time after the U.N. counterattack began, the Chinese Communist leaders had heated debates regarding the wisdom of dispatching Chinese Liberation Army troops to Korea. When Premier Chou En-lai and others opposed such a reckless move and a decision could not be reached, Mao sent Chou to Moscow, seeking Stalin's advice. Stalin, after stating that the Soviet Union was not ready to fight a war in Asia, encouraged China to provide military assistance to North Korea. Thereupon, Chou asked for Russian military protection for China as he agreed to commit Chinese troops in the Korean War. Honoring his commitment, Stalin sent an air division, an artillery division, and combat battalions to the Sino-Korean border. It was this air division which, using its bases in the Manchurian sanctuary, was engaged in air battles against the U.N. Forces.

Mao Tse-tung had already mobilized troops of the Chinese People's Liberation Army and sent them to Manchuria. As the U.N. Forces captured Pyongyang on October 20 and moved up toward the Yalu River, many North Korean Communist leaders and troops fled into Manchuria. The war seemed to be almost over, and Gen. MacArthur said that American boys would be home by Christmas. In the meantime, by October 18, the Chinese Communists had already decided to dispatch troops to Korea.

Sometime in mid-October, 250,000 "volunteers" of the Chinese People's Liberation Army joined the North Koreans in the war, and an "entirely new war" began. Some 1.5 million more Chinese troops fought in the war, forcing U.N. troops to retreat to the south. Seoul was retaken by the Communists in early January 1951. Battered Seoul changed hands for the fourth time, on March 14, when allied forces recovered it.

The Armistice

The U.N. Forces were able to halt two large Communist attacks in the late spring of 1951, and a stalemate developed as bloody fighting continued in the eastern war zone and air attacks by U.N. air units were intensified over North Korea. At this juncture, the U.S. government began secret talks with the Chinese, but the latter's proposal for a simultaneous withdrawal of the U.N. Force and Chinese troops from Korea created a roadblock in the negotiations. At this point, the Chinese brought charges against the United States for alleged germ warfare.

In June 1951, the deadlock was broken when the Soviet Union proposed a plan for a ceasefire. As a result, in late June truce talks began first in Kaesŏng, a South Korean city which had been taken over by the Communists, and then at a small hamlet named Panmunjom. (See Map 14) The two most difficult issues to settle were the location of the truce (military demarcation) line and the repatriation of prisoners-of-war. The truce talks dragged on until July 1953 while fighting continued on the eastern front.

Meanwhile, President Rhee, who did not wish to see the fighting end before North Korea had been completely destroyed, released in mid-June 1953 some 27,000 North Korean prisoners-of-war who did not wish to be repatriated. This action taken by Rhee without any previous consultation with, or authorization of, the U.N. Command caused a serious threat to the truce negotiations. However, the U.S. government persuaded Rhee not to obstruct the peace talks by promising a mutual defense treaty between the United States and South Korea.

The death of Stalin in March 1953, and the failure to make any advance into the south in the spring offensive

*The signing of the
Korean armistice.*

led the North Koreans and the Chinese to negotiate more
seriously with U.N. representatives. Consequently, on July
27, 1953 the Korean armistice was signed. With this,
some 82,000 Communist prisoners-of-war, including
6,700 Chinese, were repatriated while 50,000, including
14,700 Chinese who chose not to go back to their country
were freed. At this juncture, the sixteen U.N. member
nations which had sent troops to Korea issued a declaration that they would fight again if North Korea renewed
its war against the south.

With the signing of the truce, a 150-mile-long zig-
zagging truce (military demarcation) line was established,
and on each side of the line a mile-and-a-half wide
demilitarized zone (DMZ) was set up. At the same time,
Panmunjom, where the truce was signed, was designated
as a neutral zone where the Neutral Nations Armistice
Supervisory Commission established its headquarters.
With the armistice, North Korea lost a sizeable amount of
land in the east while gaining a small but fertile
rice-growing area in the west, including the city of
Kaesŏng. (See Map 14)

Among other things, the armistice provided that three
months after the agreement was signed and became effective a political conference of both sides should be held to
settle the question of the withdrawal of all foreign troops

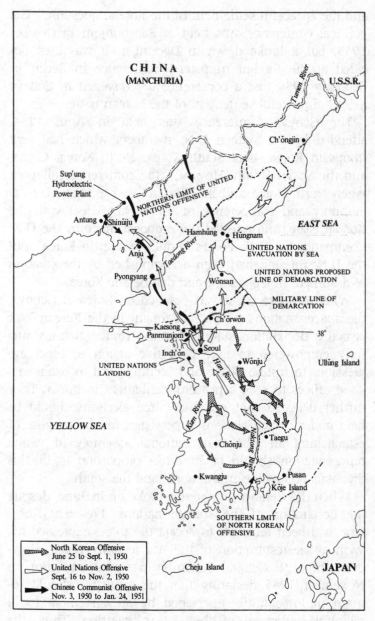

Map 14. THE KOREAN WAR

and the "peaceful settlement of the Korean question." The political conference was held at Panmunjom in October 1953, but it broke down in December. It was then decided at the foreign ministers' conference in Berlin in February 1954 that a conference be convened in Geneva to seek a peaceful settlement of the Korean issue.

The Geneva Conference was held in April 1954, attended by the sixteen U.N. members which had sent troops to Korea, plus South Korea, North Korea, China, and the Soviet Union. However, the conference collapsed when North Korea and its allies refused to recognize the authority and competence of the U.N. to deal with the Korean issue, and rejected the proposal made by the U.N. Command that U.N. Forces should remain in Korea until the U.N. mission had been accomplished by the creation of a unified, independent, and democratic Korea.

When no agreement was reached on Korea at Geneva, the sixteen nations which had fought in the Korean War issued a declaration stating that the United Nations was fully empowered to take collective action to repel aggression, to restore peace and security, and to extend its good offices to seek a peaceful settlement in Korea. They further declared that genuinely free elections should be held under United Nations supervision for the purpose of establishing an all-Korean national assembly in which representation should be in direct proportion to the indigenous population in the north and the south.

When the Geneva Conference broke up in June, despite the declaration of the sixteen nations, President Rhee, who had been reluctant to accept the truce, expressed his wish to see resumption of the war to unify Korea. However, the U.N. General Assembly passed a resolution in November 1955 declaring that the armistice should remain in force until superseded by an agreement for a peaceful settlement of the Korean question. Thus, the question of reunification was postponed *sine die*.

The Korean War caused an enormous loss of human life as well as property damage: 157,500 American casualties, including 33,625 dead; 14,000 casualties (3,188 deaths) of other U.N. troops; and 225,784 South Korean soldiers killed, 717,073 wounded, and 43,572 missing. Some 244,663 South Korean civilians were killed, over 229,000 were wounded, and 387,744 were listed as missing. Included in this number were some 128,936 South Koreans massacred by the Communists during the latter's occupation of South Korea, and another 84,523 who were taken captive to North Korea. The war produced an estimated 100,000 orphans and over 300,000 war-widows in South Korea alone. The capital city of Seoul was completely destroyed and several other major cities suffered similar destruction. The reality of this devastating war would soon become apparent to the Americans at home as plane loads of orphan babies and young children adopted by American families later began to arrive in the United States.

The casualties on the part of North Korean troops were 294,151 dead, 229,849 wounded, and 91,206 missing. North Korean civilian casualties were 406,000 dead, 1,594,000 wounded, and 680,000 missing. In addition, 184,128 Chinese troops were killed, 711,872 were wounded, and 21,836 were listed as missing. Most of North Korea's major cities, including Pyongyang, and industrial plants, hydroelectric power facilities, and rail transportation systems were either destroyed or badly damaged. Over 1.5 million North Koreans were reported to have fled to the south during the war, creating a refugee problem on a scale that could not have been anticipated.

The war that the North Koreans launched to unify the country by force failed to achieve its goal. It only caused tremendous human suffering and property loss as it created bitter animosities between the people in the south and those in the north. It left behind a legacy which was detrimental to later efforts to bring about the reunification of the divided land.

10

Postwar North Korea, 1953-

THE Democratic People's Republic of Korea (North Korea), whose certain destruction was prevented by Chinese military intervention, faced numerous problems after 1953. In addition to economic and social reconstruction, the four most urgent tasks for Kim Il-sung were the consolidation of his rule, the re-building of the Party, economic recovery, and the strengthening of the military.

Despite seemingly insurmountable obstacles, the North Korean leaders, with the assistance given by the Soviet Union, China, and other Socialist countries, rebuilt their political base and brought about economic development as they transformed North Korea into a highly regimented Socialist state.

Political and Military Development

The political structure of North Korea remained the same, but the number of provinces was increased by creation of two new provinces of Chagang and Yanggang, the division of Hwanghae province into north and south, and expansion of Kangwŏn Province so as to include the city of Wŏnsan in South Hamgyŏng Province as its provincial capital, making a total of nine provinces, the same as in South Korea. (See Map 15) Following this, Ch'ŏngjin and Hamhŭng were elevated to the status of special cities, while Kaesŏng and Namp'o were designated as special municipal districts.

When the first postwar elections for the SPA were held in August 1957, 215 deputies were elected. In the beginning, each deputy represented 50,000 constituents, but from 1962 each deputy represented 30,000 constituents, increasing the number of deputies. In December 1972, the SPA adopted a new "Socialist" constitution, creating the offices of president and vice-presidents, and elected Kim Il-sung as president. At the same time, the new constitution lowered the voting age from eighteen to seventeen and named Pyongyang the capital of the state. With the increase of population, the number of deputies grew to 687 when the elections for the 9th SPA were held in April 1990.

The rebuilding of the KWP was gradually achieved. During the war, the Party membership dropped to less than 600,000 from over one million. However, the accelerated recruitment process brought about the increase of Party membership to 1.6 million in 1971, and a little over 2.5 million in 1989, making North Korea's communist party the largest one in the world per capita. The population of North Korea in 1989 was 21.4 million.

In 1989, a five-member Standing Committee of the 15-member Political Bureau of the 145-member Central Committee of the KWP was established as the highest policy-making body of the nation with Kim Il-sung as its chairman. His son, Kim Jŏng-il, who had been groomed as his father's successor, was elected a member of this powerful committee, as well as a member of the Military Committee of which Kim Il-sung was also chairman.

The most significant political development was the

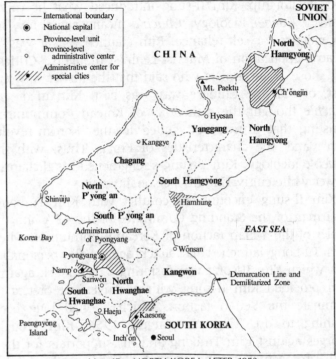

Map 15. NORTH KOREA AFTER 1953

strengthening of Kim Il-sung's dictatorship. Kim had already purged some generals, including Mu Chŏng, in December 1950 for their failure to take over South Korea. Immediately after the war, instead of blaming his own errors, Kim brought various charges against Deputy-premier and Foreign Minister Pak Hŏn-yŏng and other former leaders of the South Korean Workers' Party. Pak was specifically charged as an "American spy" and others were accused of a plotting to overthrow Kim's rule. Following this, Kim purged a large number of Pak's followers, and in December 1955 the execution of Pak himself was announced.

In 1955, as a means to establish his personality cult

and dictatorship, Kim Il-sung introduced what he called *chuch'e* (*juche*) ideology. *Chuch'e* means autonomy, independence, or self-reliance. Kim claimed that it was "a creative application of Marxist-Leninist thoughts." Criticizing those Communists who said that the Soviet way was best, or that the Chinese way was best, Kim made his *chuch'e* thought the orthodoxy of Korean Communism, insisting that it was best suited for the "Korean revolution" and the characteristics of Korea. Thus, with the *chuch'e* ideology, Kim Il-sung strengthened his dictatorial power while cultivating his personality cult.

Kim Il-sung encountered conflict with Kim Tu-bong, chairman of the Standing Committee of the SPA and the leader of the Yenan faction of Korean Communists, when Kim Tu-bong launched his attack against the personality cult which Kim Il-sung was fostering. Such attack against him provided Kim Il-sung with a convenient pretext to eliminate the Yenan faction, which he had long been wishing to do. Thus, in August 1956, Kim brought charges against Kim Tu-bong and his supporters for their anti-Party activities, and purged a large number of his critics, including a deputy-premier, thereby creating discord with the Soviet Union and China. At this juncture, a large number of top Communist leaders fled either to the Soviet Union or China. Following the fall of the Yenan faction, Kim also purged several army generals. It was reported that between 1956 and 1958, some 5,500 anti-Party individuals were arrested and sent to "re-education centers," some 2,500 were executed, and about 60% of Party and government workers were replaced because of their untrustworthiness. Thus, in 1961, Kim Il-sung was able to state that "the anti-Party factional elements and their evil ideological influence" had been extirpated, and "the historic task of achieving the complete unity of the Korean Communist movement" was completed.

In 1966, Kim Il-sung abolished the post of vice-chairmanship of the Party, increasing the power of its chairmanship which he occupied, and in 1972 when the new constitution was adopted, the *chuch'e* ideology was declared the "guiding principle of the Republic." At the same time, Kim Il-sung became the president of the republic while keeping the Party's chairmanship, which was renamed secretary-general. Meanwhile, he had groomed his younger brother to be his successor in the 1960s, but in the mid-1970s he changed his mind, instead designating as his successor his son Kim Jŏng-il.

Military Buildup. The reconstruction of the military was also pushed ahead with the adoption of a compulsory military service system in 1957. The new military conscription law required all able-bodied males between the ages of 18 and 20, and all draftees to serve on active duty for five or six years.

The number of troops of the People's Army grew to 678,000 between the years 1957 and 1979 and then to 990,000 in 1990. Currently, there are 16 army corps, 49 divisions, and 65 brigades, and they are equipped with 3,600 tanks, 2,300 armored vehicles, and 9,400 artilleries. In 1990, the number of sailors in the Navy increased to 45,000 and the Air Force to 80,000. The Navy is reported to have 429 combat ships, 24 submarines, and 237 other craft and the Air Force 840 fighter planes, 480 support planes, and 280 combat helicopters.

In addition to the regular military force, North Korea has 6.8 million men in the reserve, and a two-million-men militia (established in 1959), consisting of men up to the age of 60 and women up to the age of 40, who receive compulsory military training and participate in annual and occasional military maneuvers to be ready to engage in combat at any given time. From 1970, all students above the middle school level were organized into Red Youth Guards and given basic military training. Meanwhile, in 1966 the process for the fortification of the entire nation began as more military airfields were constructed and large tunnels were dug to store air and naval crafts. Some time after that, the North Koreans began to dig several tunnels under the demilitarized zone across the truce line for the purpose of using them as secret invasion routes into South Korea. These tunnels were discovered in 1974, 1975, and 1978. According to recent information, North Korea not only produced a large number of Scud B missiles after 1987, but also established Scud launching pads along the truce line.

Economic and Social Development

Economic recovery and development was not only the most urgent, but also a difficult task for the North Korean government after the war. It was estimated that about 80% of North Korea's productive capacity was destroyed by the war and many industrial plants and hydroelectric dams were either destroyed or badly damaged. The production of electric power dropped to one million kwh, coal production dropped to 708,000 tons, and cement to 27,000 tons in 1953. The grain production decreased to less than 1 million tons in the same year. The population also declined to about 7.5 million.

Economic Development. In order to reconstruct the economy, the North Korean regime carried out various plans with assistance from the Soviet Union and other Socialist countries: one three-year plan (1954-56), one five-year plan (1957-61), one six-year plan (1971-76), and two seven-year plans (1961-67 and 1978-84). The three-year plan of 1954-56 was designed for postwar recovery, whereas the subsequent plans were aimed at industrial expansion, particulary in heavy industry. The first seven-year plan of 1961-67 was completed in ten years, ending in 1970, and the first six-year plan of 1971-76 ended in 1977 for a variety of problems, including the shortage of funds and materials. In 1985, the third seven-year plan began.

Under the tightly controlled economic system, systematic state planning, a total mobilization of manpower, and financial and other assistance given by the Soviet Union and other Socialist countries, North Korea's economic recovery and development was rapid up to the middle of the 1960s. Thus, the gross national product (GNP) increased from $320 million in 1953 to $3.6 billion in 1967 and per capita income increased from $41 in 1953 to $218 in 1967. During this period, the share of agriculture in the GNP declined from 59.1% to 19.3% while the share of industry increased from 23.2% to 62.3%.

After 1967, with the decrease of Soviet aid, coupled with the growing bureaucratism, economic growth slowed down. However, the GNP reached $13.6 billion by 1982 with per capita income of $736 in that year. In 1989, North Korea's GNP reached the $21.1 billion mark with per capita GNP of $987. The annual average GNP growth rate up to 1988 was 3.0% but it dropped to 2.4% in 1989. A Soviet scholar reported in 1990 that North Korea's GNP in 1989 was actually $19.5 billion with per capita GNP of $400.

In order to increase production, Kim Il-sung gave much "on-the-spot" guidance, inaugurating several new programs. The first of these was the "Flying Horse" Movement that began in 1958. In this movement, some one million workers were mobilized and formed into "Flying

Horse Work Teams," and they were assigned to various projects to lead the local workers. All farms were organized into 3,843 co-operative farms in 1958, ending private ownership of farmlands, and they were ordered to follow the "Ch'ŏngsan-ri Method," which Kim Il-sung outlined at a model co-operative farm at Ch'ŏngsan-ri, near Pyongyang in 1960. It was aimed at increasing the enthusiasm and technical skills of lower level Party workers assigned to co-operative farms, as well as farmers, dismantling the bureaucratism and "commanderism" of the Party workers. For the industrial workers, Kim Il-sung introduced the so-called "Taean Method" at a factory located at Taean near Pyongyang in December 1960. This method was said to be a counterpart of the "Ch'ŏngsan-ri Method," aimed at promoting collective leadership of the Party committee and the workers at each plant. In February 1973, three revolutions (thoughts, technology and culture) were initiated in order to promote economic growth. With this, some 60,000 selected young Party cadres were organized into "Three Revolutions Small Units" and they were sent to farms and factories to force farmers and workers to work harder.

Under the state planning, which gave priority to the development of heavy industry, North Korea achieved impressive results in industrial growth. The annual average growth rate of industry during the 1957-61 period was 36.6%, but then it dropped to 12.8% from the mid-1960s, and in the 1970s and 1980s it further decreased. Be that as it may, between 1954 and 1979 the production of electric power grew to 40 million kwh, coal production to 65 million tons, cement to 8.8 million tons, and chemical fertilizer to 4.5 million tons in 1979. After 1979, North Korea stopped publication of detailed reports on economic growth, and accurate assessment of economic development after that year is difficult. However, it was reported that in 1989 North Korea produced 55.5 million kwh of electricity, 85 million tons of coal, 7 million tons of steel, 13.5 million tons of cement and 5.6 million tons of chemical fertilizer. Meanwhile, between 1953 and 1979 the number of industrial workers increased from 524,000 to 1.5 million. Because of emphasis given to the development of heavy industry, the development of light industry lagged far behind, creating a severe shortage of daily commodities and lowering living standards. All non-basic commodities such as soap, towels, shoes and clothing were rationed, and the price of non-rationed goods such as pens, radio sets, and bicycles were too high for average workers to afford.

The task to achieve self-sufficiency in the food supply was a monumental one for North Korea. Although there are rice-growing areas in the west, North Korea had cultivated mostly millet and potatoes, depending heavily on the supply of rice from the south prior to 1945. After the Korean War, the eastern regions became corn growing areas, as the Hwangju and Sariwŏn areas remained a fruit growing region with apples being the main crop.

In order to increase rice production, North Korea carried out ambitious reclamation projects, converting tidal flat regions and low hills into food growing areas. Farm houses were relocated on the hillsides from the paddy fields to increase the rice-growing acreage. The manufacturing of chemical fertilizer began in 1956, with the reconstruction of the chemical fertilizer plant at Hŭngnam.

Although North Korean reports were unreliable, the North Korean government announced that the amount of grain produced increased from 2.3 million tons in 1954 to 9 million in 1979. Other independent sources estimated that the actual amount of grain production in North Korea in 1979 was no more than 4.9 million tons. Of this, 2.4 million tons were rice and the remainder,

corn. In 1989, North Korea's actual amount of grain production was about 4.9 million tons, due to the drought
and floods of the previous four years. Of this, 2.2 million
tons were rice and 2.7 million tons were corn. Thus the
severity of the food shortage continued as the population
steadily increased from about 7.5 million in 1954 to 21.4
million in 1989.

The chronic shortage of grain forced North Korea to
purchase a large amount of food from the Soviet Union
and China. In the 1970–76 period alone, it spent $112
million to purchase grain from abroad. In such a situation, food was rationed to individuals according to their
age and the type of work they performed: industrial
workers received more, whereas the aged and children
received less. Of the rationed grain, 25% was rice and
75% was corn.

Commerce as such did not exist in North Korea, and all
the stores were government-operated. No private businesses, including restaurants, were allowed. All apartments
and farm houses were government owned, and rents were
unbelievably low; a monthly rent for an average worker's
apartment with a bedroom, a kitchen, and a bathroom was
$2.50 per month, plus utilities (about $4). However, wages
for workers were also low. The average wage of a factory
worker was about $90 per month as of 1989, and that of
medical doctors and college professors was about $185 per
month in 1989.

Taxation, "a relic of the old societies," according to the
North Korean leaders, was abolished, but the people with
income were "encouraged" to make donations to the
government for a variety of purposes, and save as much as
possible "for financial assistance to be given to the South
Koreans" later.

The farmers in co-operative farms turned over their
products to the government and received a certain share

of the harvest, as well as monetary payment for the grains and other items they produced. All farmers were bound to the collective farm as all factory workers were bound to their factory, and only after receiving permission from the government could they change their profession. But getting such permission was almost impossible.

The most troublesome economic problem of North Korea was its chronic trade deficit. Spending some 35% of its national budget annually for the military, and having little to export, North Korea's debts to the Socialist countries, which were its main trading partners, steadily increased. For example, in 1975 its exports were $400 million compared to its imports of $1,075 million. After North Korea established trade relations with Japan and a few other non-Socialist countries in 1970 (South Korea and the U.S. had no normal trade relations with North Korea as of 1990), the situation became worse and by 1989 its imports had grown to $2.5 billion while its exports amounted to only $1,559 million. Consequently, in 1979 North Korea became the first Communist country to default on its foreign debt, and as a result, Western credits were severely curtailed. In 1979, North Korea concluded an agreement with Japan, rescheduling the repayment of past debt over ten years, starting in 1980, but in 1983, again unable to make the semi-annual payment, North Korea approached Japan for postponement of payment on debt principal, and signed another agreement with Japan, postponing its payment of debt until 1986. However, North Korea was unable to keep its promise in 1986.

In 1984, North Korea initiated joint ventures with some capitalist countries. At the same time, "private business" was parsimoniously allowed, but visitors in 1989 reported seeing no private stores or businesses as such.

Economic conditions have deteriorated in recent years.

According to Japanese sources, North Korea's foreign trade declined by 10% in 1989, and the situation could not be improved because of unpaid debts and the conversion by Socialist countries to hard currency. In 1989, North Korea's exports at $1.6 billion was 6.6% lower than the previous year, and its imports at $2.5 billion was also 12.1% lower. Its exports to China fell by 20.7% to $185 million and its imports rose by 9.3% to $377 million. North Korea's trade deficit in 1989 was $900 million, and its foreign debt in 1989 was estimated at $6.8 billion with its indebtedness to the Soviet Union as of November at $3.6 billion, and to Japan at about $330 million.

The drastic reduction of Soviet economic aid, coupled with its demand for payments by North Korea for goods it purchased from the Soviet Union in hard currency, increased the economic hardship of North Korea. At the same time, the reduction of oil and grain sales by both China and the Soviet Union to North Korea after 1987 created a serious economic situation. Various reports published in 1989 and 1990 indicated that the unprecedented food and gasoline shortage brought about dangerous political and social repercussions in North Korea.

The Society. The Communists turned North Korea into a closed, tightly organized, and highly regimented society with a Spartan life style. Its slogans such as austerity, uniformity, and conformity reflected the way of life of the people. The constitution stated that "the rights and duties of citizens (were) based on the collectivist principle of one for all and all for one." Although it was to be a classless society, a new elite, privileged class of high-ranking Party officials emerged there.

Although the constitution stated also that "the state effectively guarantees genuine democratic rights and freedom... to all citizens," the people were given no freedom of speech, association, religion, publication, residence, travel, or profession. However, all citizens above the age of seventeen received voting rights under the constitution of 1972. Having no freedom to travel or change their jobs or residence, the North Korean people were required to obtain travel permits for internal travel (no ordinary citizens could travel abroad), and secure permission to change jobs or location of their residence within a village or town, or to another place.

Only a handful of selected foreigners from the Free World were allowed to visit North Korea for a particular purpose up to 1980. After that time, more foreign visitors from the Free World were allowed to enter North Korea. However, the number remained small up to 1988 and only those who were selected were allowed to travel to selected localities within North Korea.

Everyone was required to belong to at least one social organization except the elderly: children up to the age of 13 joined the Young Korean Pioneers, the young men and women between the ages of 14 and 30 the Socialist Working Youth League, and all women between the ages of 30 and 50 belonged to the Korean Democratic Women's League. All those organizations were regarded as "honor bodyguards and death-defying fighters" and "defenders of the Party," and they were expected to carry out the orders of Kim Il-sung on behalf of the "Korean revolution."

All farmers were organized into farmers' unions, and all office and factory workers were organized into their respective unions. Various professional people such as doctors, nurses, teachers, writers, musicians, artists, actors, and film-makers belonged to their respective professional unions. Together with the military, these social organizations and unions became effective instruments of the Party, championing the *chuch'e* ideology and

Statue of Ch'ŏllima ("Flying Horse"). Under this symbol the people were subjected under slave labor.

participating in the "Flying Horse" Movement of the 1950s and 1960s, the Movement for the Three Revolutions—thoughts, technology, and culture—of the 1970s, and the Movement for the Creation of Speed of the 1980s for the production of more goods and food.

Sexual equality was enforced as traditional human relationships were discarded. At the same time, traditional social customs were abolished, and all traditional seasonal holidays were replaced by new national holidays, including such holidays as that of the birthdays of Kim Il-sung and his son, Kim Chŏng-il. The historic kinship system was also abolished, and friendship was replaced by the comradeship of the revolutionaries.

The North Korean Communists regarded the traditional family system as a feudalistic legacy. The new home, said Kim Il-sung, must be "a laboratory for promoting the revolutionary theories of Socialism." As a result, patriarchal authority lost its legitimacy and all children were taught to regard Kim Il-sung as "the father of the people." At the same time, child-rearing was taken over by the state, and all children three months old to age five were nurtured at state-run nurseries and kindergartens under the 1976 Law on the Rearing and Education of Children. In 1981 some 60,000 such nurseries and kindergartens were established to accommodate some 3.5 million children. Under such a system, the children were indoctrinated during formative years with *chuch'e* ideology to be loyal to Kim Il-sung and become a "Socialist Man."

The Party outlawed prostitution and extra-marital sexual activity as it abolished concubinage. It also set the legal marriage age of men to 30 and women to 27. Wedding ceremonies were simplified as were also the funeral rites which had traditionally been elaborate and costly. The traditional ancestor-worship practices were not outlawed, but people were discouraged from continuing this age-old custom.

For economic development, North Korea's railway mileage was increased to 2,680 miles by 1989. Most of this is single-track, while some are electrified. The two new railway lines constructed after 1954 were the southern line which links Sariwŏn with Wŏnsan via Sep'o, and the northern line between Kanggye and Hyesan. Of some 12,000 miles of roads, only 292 miles are modern highways. Only public transportation has been available for most people as the ownership of private automobiles was virtually impossible.

North Korea's social engineering involved urbanization and rural reconstruction. New streets and workers' apartments were constructed, and electrification was carried out. Meanwhile, names of several cities were changed. For example, such industrial cities as Sŏngjin in North Hamgyŏng Province became Kimch'aek, Chinnamp'o in South P'yŏng'an Province was renamed Namp'o, and Kyŏmip'o, a steel town in North Hwanghae Province was renamed Songnim. The two cities of Hamhŭng and Hŭngnam were incorporated into one large industrial center.

The most spectacular urban transformation took place in Pyongyang, the city which was completely destroyed by the war. The new city planning implemented widened and paved streets, and electric bus lines were installed. The re-routed tributaries of the Taedong and Pot'ong rivers into the city became modern canals along which government buildings, cultural halls, and parks were built. On the hillside, the massive Museum of the Korean Revolution and the Children's Palace were built. Apartments for office and factory workers were constructed in and around the city, changing the ancient city into a modern metropolis.

The rural reconstruction, in addition to relocation of farm houses from paddy fields to hillside to expand the rice-growing acreage, involved construction of new roads, new houses for the farmers along with nurseries, kinder-gartens, schools and people's cultural halls, and electricity reached every village. The most spectacular rural trans-formation took place at the previously mentioned hamlet of Ch'ŏngsan-ri, which became a model cooperative farm district.

The North Korean government encouraged population growth up to mid-1960s, but after that it was discouraged due to food shortages. To achieve this end, it set a legal minimum marriage age and encouraged the couples to have only two or less children. As a result, the annual population growth rate of 3.5% had dropped to 2.5% by 1980, and it further dropped to 1.67% by 1989. The North Korean population of about 7.5 million in 1953 had grown to 18.5 million by 1982, and in 1990 it reached the 23 million mark. About 60% of the population was concentrated in the western coastal regions.

Cultural and Educational Change

North Korea's philosophy of education and the content and form of culture became revolutionized in character. Article 36 of the 1972 constitution stated that the state "builds a true people's revolutionary culture which serves the socialist working people," and Article 39 in the same constitution stated that "the state implements the principles of socialist pedagogy, and brings up the rising generation to be steadfast revolutionaries who fight for society and the people, to be man of a new Communist type...."

Educational System and Practices. The North Koreans insisted that "only when we eliminated vestiges of the old ideas remaining in the minds of the people, educated them with the ideology of Communism, and constantly

North Korean school children studying Kim Il-sung's thoughts.

exalt class consciousness and the revolutionary spirit...
can we allow them to express their conscious zeal and
creative power." In 1958, Kim Il-sung stated the following six educational objectives: (1) to educate the people to
know the superiority of socialism and communism over
capitalism, (2) to promote the people's realization that a
better future would and could be built through human
efforts, (3) to eradicate individualism and selfishness, (4)
to promote socialist patriotism and proletarian inter-
nationalism, (5) to cultivate the spirit of love for work,
and (6) to teach the people the revolutionary ideology of
uninterrupted revolution and cultural reform for progress.

According to such philosophy and purpose, new school
systems and pedagogy were established. In 1954, the new
4-3-3-4 school system replaced the previous 5-3-3-4 system, and in 1958 the four-year compulsory primary education system was implemented. After replacing the
three-year senior middle school system in 1959 with a
two-year technical schools and two-year senior technical
schools in 1960 a nine-year compulsory education system
(primary school through technical schools) was adopted.
In the period between 1960 and 1972, however, the 4-5-4
system was adopted. In 1973, the middle school became
a four-year school, making the length of the secondary
school six years and in 1975 an eleven-year universal,
compulsory educational program, including a one-year
preschool program, was launched. All schools in North
Korea were free.

In addition to the nation's top educational institution of
Kim Il-sung University, many technical and specialized
universities and colleges were established throughout the
country. Most of them were state institutions, but some
provincial colleges were also established. Only selected
graduates of secondary schools were privileged to attend
these higher educational institutions. Meanwhile, many

"factory colleges" were established after 1960, educating the working youth at their place of work, and village schools were established to teach the people how to read and write, bringing the literacy rate of the people up to above 90% by 1989.

In 1988, there were some 4,700 primary schools, 4,100 middle schools, 600 senior technical schools, and 168 colleges and universities. The nation's highest academic institutions, in addition to universities, were the Academy of Science and the Academy of Social Science. Many other academies of specialized economic fields and research institutes were also created after 1960.

Culture and Revolution. A socialist culture maintained and controlled by the Party emerged in North Korea. The primary aim of the Party was to make all forms of literature and arts reflect socialist realism, or partisan allegiance. As a result, the idea of "art for art's sake" was discarded altogether, and the Party emphasized the elimination of old thoughts and the old culture.

Regarding religion as "the enemy of science and progress," the Party abolished all established religions, and forced all clergymen and monks to join the labor force. All church buildings were torn down, and all but a few historic Buddhist temples were preserved. Only after 1984 did the North Korean government allow the people to hold religious meetings, but no proselytizing was permitted. According to some sources made available in 1989, there are about 10,000 known Christians and 10,000 known Buddhists, and some 500 homes were used for Christian meetings. However, only some fifty government certified individuals were reported to conduct religious services. Most "church" goers were reported to be those over age 50.

All North Korean newspapers and magazines have been

published either by the Korean Workers' Party, or by the government and its agencies, and no foreign newspapers or magazines have been sold in North Korea. The major newspapers were *The Workers' Daily* (*Rodong Shinmun*) and an English-language paper, *The Pyongyang Times.* The Foreign Language Publishing House in Pyongyang, which is the state-owned and operated agency, is the sole publisher of foreign language books.

All television and radio broadcasting systems were state operated, and the broadcasting frequencies were strictly controlled by the Party. No foreign television or radio broadcasting was permitted to be viewed or listened to, and no foreign movies were shown, except those from the Soviet Union and China.

After discarding traditional folk and other songs and dances, the Communists nurtured revolutionary songs and dances, and those songs which glorified and praised the accomplishments of "Great Leader Kim Il-sung" and his relatives. A number of songs were dedicated to his "heroic deeds," and several musical plays and motion pictures were produced to glorify him, his partisan fighters, Party cadres, and heroes of the People's Army. Of some 300 North Korean songs, 80% were in praise of Kim Il-sung. They even changed the names of certain flowers to "Kim Il-sung flower" and "Kim Jŏng-il flower."

Traditional painting and literature were likewise dis-carded, and only those which aroused the revolutionary spirit and socialist consciousness were allowed to be produced. Thus, all North Korean paintings, novels, and stories were related to the revolutionary activities of Kim Il-sung, his partisan fighters, Party cadres, and People's Army troops before and during the Korean War. Needless to say, no foreign songs or plays, were imported, except those inspired by revolutionary activities of the Soviets and the Chinese.

North Korea discarded the use of Chinese characters and published all printed materials in Korean script only. Under the rule of Kim Il-sung and the Korean Workers' Party, the northern half of Korea became a Korean state with radically different political, social and economic systems and culture from those of the south. At the same time, Kim Il-sung established a seemingly solid foundation of the Kim dynasty. With various means and excuses, many men and women, including the former members of the Partisan group of the Manchurian days who had loyally served Kim Il-sung, have been killed or forced to flee from North Korea. By 1980, many of them had died of natural causes, leaving Kim Il-sung to rule the country as his personal domain rather than a Socialist "democratic people's republic," betraying the hopes of those Communists who died for the cause.

As of 1990, Kim Il-sung, his son Kim Jŏng-il, along with other relatives, exercise firm control over the nation. Kim Il-sung is currently the president of the nation (reelected in 1990) and chairman of the National Defense Council, the Secretary-General of the Korean Workers' Party and chairman of its 5-man Standing Committee and chairman of its 15-man Political Bureau, as well as chairman of the Central People's Committee, and a member of the ruling group of the Supreme People's Assembly. Kim Jŏng-il, his father's heir apparent, is the First Vice-chairman of the National Defense Council, a member of the Standing Committee of the Political Bureau, a member of the ruling group of the Supreme People's Assembly, and one of the secretaries of the Party. Kim Il-sung's wife, Kim Chŏng-ae, is chairman of the Korean Democratic Women's League and a member of the Supreme People's Assembly.

Vice-president Pak Sŏng-ch'ŏl, son-in-law of the late former vice-president Kang Yang-uk, who was a cousin of

a maternal grandfather of Kim Il-sung, is also a member
of the Central People's Committee. Hŏ Tam, late husband
of a cousin of Kim Il-sung, who had been foreign minister for a long time, was chairman of the Foreign Relations
Committee of the Supreme People's Assembly. Another
relative, Kim Chung-lin is one of twelve secretaries of the
Party. Although Gen. O Chin-u, an old comrade of Kim
Il-sung of the Partisan days who supported Kim Jŏng-il,
was removed from the Central People's Committee in
June 1990, he retained the post of defense minister, and
membership in the 5-man Standing Committee of the
Political Bureau, as well as the membership in the Supreme People's Assembly.

Although there have been rumors of military coups and
assassination attempts made against Kim Il-sung and Kim
Jŏng-il in recent years, North Korea has maintained its
political stability under one-party rule of the Korean
Workers' Party and Kim Il-sung's despotic power,
solidifying the foundation for the succession of power
from Kim Il-sung to Kim Jŏng-il.

The granting of the rank of marshal to Kim Jŏng-il in
August 1991 and then his taking the place of his father
as Supreme Commander of North Korea's armed forces in
December led many to speculate that Kim Il-sung would
step down and his son would succeed his father as Secretary-General of the KWP and President of the DPRK in
the spring of 1992. But such changes did not take place
as North Korea celebrated the junior Kim's 50th birthday
in February and the senior Kim's 80th birthday in April
1992. Be that as it may, these changes solidified Kim
Jŏng-il's position as heir apparent while strengthening his
control over the state. Meanwhile, the reappearance in
August 1993 of Kim Il-sung's brother on the political
scene after some 17 years of absence (he was purged in
1974), and his election as a regular member of the

Politburo of the Central Committee of the KWP along with his appointment as Vice President of the state, seemed to have restored the family unity of Kim Il-sung and strengthened the foundation of the Kim dynasty.

North Korea's economic situation continued to deteriorate after the fall of 1990 of the Soviet Union which had been its primary benefactor for many decades. North Korea's GNP growth was 2.4% in 1989, but it fell to -3.7% in 1990. -5.2% in 1991, and -7.6% in 1992. Its GNP in 1992 was a mere $23.3 billion with per capita GNP of $1,000. Its grain production dropped from 4.8 million tons in 1990 to 3.9 million in 1993, increasing the shortage of grain supply to two million tons. Its volume of foreign trade declined from $4.64 billion in 1990 to $2.72 billion in 1991 with a trade deficit of $700 million. Foreign debts grew from $7.86 billion in 1990 to $9.28 billion in 1991. Such a state of economy led the KWP in December 1993 to admit its failure to achieve the goals of the third 7-year plan of 1987-93.

North Korea Today

North Korea is at a critical juncture in its history as the winds of democracy have swept across Eastern Europe, two Germanys were united, and the Cold War era came to an end following the collapse of the Soviet Union in 1990.

Although the world has changed, North Korea has remained unchanged. It is still ruled by a single political party under a dictatorial leader, and it is still a closed, isolated country. Its society is still highly regimented, its people enjoy no freedoms as they are indoctrinated by the propaganda of their leaders. It is estimated that some 125,000 political dissidents and individuals suspected of being disloyal to Kim Il-sung and Kim Jŏng-il have been detained at ten concentration camps. Its leaders are still vainly hoping to bring about the overthrow of the South Korean government either by subversive means or by force. North Korea is a country which has one of the largest armed forces (990,000 regular troops) in the world. Its population is 23 million and growing.

Despite the rapidly changing world order and the collapse of Communist systems, the North Korean leaders show no signs of modifying their systems and they seek no peaceful means to bring about a mutually beneficial relationship between the north and the south. The North Korean leaders have been indoctrinating the people since 1987 with a new slogan which says, "we live by our own way," clinging desperately to an ideology and system which is no longer viable, thereby refusing to recognize the signs of the times.

With a bankrupt economy, North Korea created an international crisis by disallowing the International Atomic Energy Agency to conduct its full investigation of unclear facilities in North Korea, despite its signing the Nuclear Non-proliferation Treaty in 1985. Moreover, North Korea refused to implement the two important agreements which it concluded with South Korea in December 1991 and February 1992. The first one was the Agreement on Reconcilliation, Nonaggression, and Exchanges and Cooperation, and the second was the Agreement on a Nuclear-Free Korean Peninsula.

To make matters worse, North Korea announced in March 1993 its intention to withdraw from the NPT, creating bitter disputes with South Korea, the United States, and the IAEA. The intense negotiations conducted by the United States and South Korea with North Korea produced no satisfactory results as of March 1994 as tension mounted in the Korean peninsula.

11
South Korea, Political History After 1953

THE Republic of Korea (South Korea), whose national existence was preserved by the military assistance of the U.N. Forces, faced many problems of national reconstruction. Among these the most difficult one was the realization of democratic aspirations.

The political history of South Korea, whose territory was slightly increased as a result of the establishment of a new boundary line between the north and the south (see Map 16), has been that of the struggle for democracy. This struggle has been carried out by the people of South Korea during the span of thirty five years following the end of the Korean War, which includes seven periods: the First Republic, which ended in 1960; the Second Republic of 1960-61; the military junta rule of 1961-63; the Third Republic of 1963-72; the Fourth Republic of 1972-79; the interim period of 1979-81; the Fifth Republic of 1981-88; the Sixth Republic of 1988-93. The last period was succeeded by that of the Seventh Republic, which began in February 1993.

The First Republic After the War

After WWII, unlike their compatriots in the north, the South Korean people enjoyed various freedoms and rights, including religious freedom. However, in speech, assembly, and the press, their rights were restricted under the National Security Law of 1948. Although they could speak freely, form social associations, and publish newspapers and magazines, they could not freely criticize the government or its policies, organize socialist or communist societies, or publish any which could be interpreted as seditious materials or which praised or aided the Communists. The restrictions imposed on the press caused particular problems that lasted up to 1988.

Although President Syngman Rhee received a doctoral degree in political science from Princeton University, was well acquainted with American democratic principles, and his speeches with democratic rhetoric, his personality traits and behavior were more like those of the autocratic monarchs of the Yi dynasty. Thus, instead of acting as an elected president of a democratic republic, he fostered an imperial presidency with indisputable and unchallengeable monarchical sovereignty. In such a way he undermined the system which was established to promote democracy, provoking opposition both in and outside of the National Assembly.

As the relationship between the president and the National Assembly steadily deteriorated, President Rhee sought the support of the police and the army, marking the beginning of the politicization of these two arms of national security. All top positions on the police force and high-ranking military positions were filled by Rhee's political appointees.

During the Korean War, the president became more

autocratic. Realizing that the new National Assembly elected in May 1950 would not reelect him, in July, after promulgating martial laws, President Rhee and the Liberal Party forced his opponents in the National Assembly to pass a constitutional amendment, instituting a direct, popular election of the president and the vice-president. Dr. Rhee was reelected in 1952 by the majority of votes cast by rural voters who had benefitted from the land reform carried out in 1949. Following this, Dr. Rhee's autocratic rule was strengthened while his Liberal Party became increasingly corrupt and abusive.

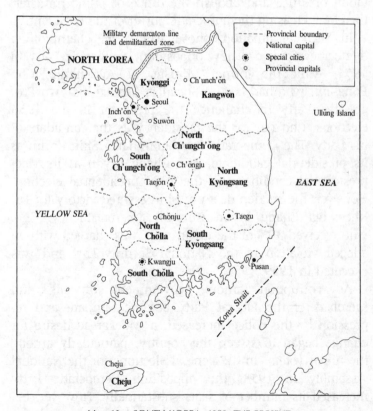

Map 16. SOUTH KOREA, 1953-THE PRESENT

In August 1953, a month after the signing of the Korean armistice, the government returned to Seoul from Pusan, and in October the Mutual Defense Treaty between the Republic of Korea and the United States was concluded. However, critical attitudes of the American government toward President Rhee began to surface, and the voice of opposition at home grew louder.

Believing that he alone could lead the nation, in November 1954 President Rhee had members of his party in the National Assembly amend the constitution to exempt the incumbent president from the two-term limitation of office and abolish the office of prime minister, thereby increasing the autocratic power of the president.

In such a situation, those who were championing democracy formed a new opposition Democratic Party in 1955, while the former Minister of Agriculture, Cho Pong-am, who had been a Socialist, formed his own Progressive Party to challenge the president in the 1956 elections. Cho ran for the presidency as the candidate of his party. The Democratic Party nominated Shin Ik-hŭi as its presidential candidate, and Chang Myŏn as its vice-presidential candidate for the 1956 presidential election. However, the sudden death of Shin assured victory for Dr. Rhee, but Chang Myŏn won the vice-presidency. Cho, who received 30% of the urban vote, was charged with an alleged violation of the National Security Law and was executed in 1959.

As corruption among government officials and members of the Liberal Party became rampant and repression by the police increased, a widespread desire for change began to sweep the country, particularly among the urban voters. In the general elections for the National Assembly in 1958, the opposition Democratic Party increased its number of seats substantially. However, being aware of the danger of losing its absolute control, the

Liberal Party-dominated National Assembly repealed the Local Autonomy Law and passed a new National Security Law, promulgated in December 1958, so as to strengthen the government's control.

In the fourth presidential election, held in March 1960, Dr. Rhee and Yi Ki-bung ran as the presidential and vice-presidential candidates of the Liberal Party, respectively. Three weeks before the election, the Democratic Party's presidential candidate, Cho Pyŏng-ok, died while receiving medical treatment in the United States, once again assuring the election of Dr. Rhee. However, the election of Yi was uncertain. As a result, the ruling Party resorted to corrupt and fraudulent means to elect Yi, who defeated Chang Myŏn, the vice-presidential candidate of the Democratic Party, by a large margin.

While the incumbent vice-president, Chang, resigned in protest over the March election, popular reaction against the autocratic President Rhee, his corrupt and nepotic administration, and the Liberal Party, which employed various illegal means to strengthen government control in collusion with the police, exploded immediately after the March election. Fierce student riots erupted throughout the country, particularly in the Pusan-Masan area, producing casualties among students and culminating in the Student Uprising of April 1960.

When the student uprising took place in Seoul on April 19, many college professors and citizens joined them, clashing with the police. Martial law was declared, and troops were mobilized when the police became powerless to control the situation. The mobilized troops, however, chose to remain neutral, refusing to take any actions against the demonstrators, who were demanding the resignation of the president and his cabinet, the nullification of the March 15 election results, and fundamental political reform to foster democracy, as well as the removal of corrupt policemen and profiteers from the government. Meanwhile, the pressure increased from the United States for President Rhee's resignation. In the end, on April 26, President Rhee tendered his resignation, followed by the resignation of the cabinet members. Thus, the First Republic, which began on a note of great hope, collapsed in a violent uprising.

The First Republic not only frustrated the people's desires for democracy, but it achieved little in foreign affairs. To be sure, it established diplomatic relations with some 23 Free World nations, but it was unable to settle issues with Japan, although talks were held between the two governments. In addition to Dr. Rhee's strong anti-Japanese sentiment and attitudes, the issues related to South Korea's demand for a large sum as reparation from Japan, and the establishment of the Rhee Line, formerly the MacArthur Line, that divided the sea between Korea

Students clash with the police, April 19, 1960.

and Japan, prevented the two nations from establishing diplomatic and commercial relations.

The Second Republic, August 1960–May 1961

On April 27, the hastily convened National Assembly appointed Foreign Minister Hŏ Chŏng as the head of a caretaker government with the hope that a clean, just, and democratic government could be established.

In mid-June, the National Assembly adopted constitutional amendments, establishing an upper house, called the House of Councillors, in the National Assembly, restoring the office or prime minister, abolishing the post of vice-president, and reducing the power of the president. When members of the House of Councillors were elected for a six-year term of office in July, the members of the House of Representatives (lower house) were also elected for a four-year term of office.

The newly established National Assembly elected Yun Po-sŏn as president and Chang Myŏn as prime minister, and the Second Republic emerged in August. At this juncture, the cabinet became responsible to the National Assembly, the president became a ceremonial head of state, and the power of the legislative assembly vastly increased. With this change, it was hoped that the establishment of a parliamentary democracy and the restoration of human and civil rights would become a reality. The Second Republic re-established local autonomy, and local governors were elected and local assemblies were established in December 1960.

However, the Second Republic was handicapped from the start. It had no mandate from the people and both President Yun and Prime Minister Chang lacked fortitude and political skills, although both of them being from the

Democratic Party desired the fostering of democracy. The Chang administration was indecisive in dealing with former leaders of the Rhee regime, and seemed too tolerant toward left-wing radicals. It was unable to cope effectively with the ideological and social cleavage between political and social groups, and failed to gain the confidence of the people as it brought about no visible economic improvement.

The ruling Democratic Party itself was badly split and it had no suitable solutions to economic and social problems. Meanwhile, new student demonstrations erupted as the influence of the Communists among them grew. In October, they invaded the National Assembly and demanded "revolutionary legislation" imposing stiffer penalties for the ousted officials of the First Republic. Under pressure, on December 30, the National Assembly adopted the "Law Concerning the Restriction of the Civil Rights of Those Who Committed Anti-democratic Acts" prior to April 1960.

Agitation by students for direct negotiation with North Korean students, aimed at reunification of the country, created extreme anxiety and turmoil as their activity increased the danger to national security. Meanwhile, there were many violent campus riots by the students against their school administrators and professors who had collaborated with the Rhee administration. As the shortage of food increased and the number of jobless people grew, the crime rate rose. Such a chaotic state of the nation set the stage for the military revolution that was to follow.

The Military Rule, May 1961–December 1963

As some had suspected, on May 16, 1961, a military revolution, led by a small group of young, disgruntled Army officers headed by Major General Park Chung-hee, took place. Two days later, the Second Republic had been overthrown. The Military Revolutionary Committee(MRC), which emerged on May 16, proclaimed that their aims were to protect the country from Communist threats, remove corrupt and inefficient military leaders, de-politicize the military, and reconstruct the nation's political, economic and social systems, thereby establishing a clean government and social justice.

The MRC took over the government, declared martial law, dissolved the National Assembly, abolished local autonomy, forbade all political activity, banned student demonstrations, and imposed press censorship. It persuaded President Yun to remain in office, and it also persuaded Army Chief of Staff, Gen. Chang To-yŏng, who did not participate in the planning of the revolution, to become chairman of the MRC and lead the revolution. Shortly after this, the MRC issued its Six Pledges, which included one that promised the restoration of a civilian rule, and on May 19, acting as a legislative body, it adopted the Law Concerning Extraordinary Measures for National Reconstruction. In late May, the MRC was renamed the Supreme Council for National Reconstruction (SCNR), making it the highest administrative organ of the nation, and a new executive branch (cabinet) headed by the chairman of the SCNR, and a new judicial branch were established.

The revolutionaries created new institutions and adopted new laws to tighten government control over subversives and anti-state protestors. Thus, in June 1961, the Korean Central Intelligence Agency (KCIA) was established, and on July 3 the Anti-Communism Law was promulgated. The purpose of this law was "to strengthen the anti-Communist posture, which is the first goal of the national reconstruction effort; to block the activities of Communist organizations which tend to jeopardize the safety of the State; and to secure the safety of the State and freedom of the people." The law designated Communist organizations as "anti-State organizations," and any persons praising, encouraging, or co-operating with anti-state organizations or their constituent members were subject to punishment by penal servitude.

When Gen. Chang was removed from the chairmanship of the SCNR in June 1961, Gen. Park became its chairman, and announced that political activity would be permitted in early 1963 to pave the way for the restoration of a civilian government. In November 1961, Gen. Park visited the United States and made peace with the American government.

In March 1962, the SCNR promulgated the Political Activities Purification Law, and established the Political Activists Purification Committee. This law was aimed at the elimination of "old politicians" from politics, and some 4,743 "old politicians," who were accused of committing various political crimes in the past were put on the blacklist. Eventually, some 3,633 were purged, banning them from politics until August 1968. In a bitter political controversy surrounding this law and the purging of such a large number of former politicians, in March 1962 President Yun resigned, and Gen. Park became Acting-President.

While implementing various strong measures to purify the political arena, punish political criminals, restore social order, control economic decline and arrest black-marketeers and hoodlums, the SCNR revised the constitution, and the amended version was approved in late December in a national referendum. Meanwhile, the Political Party Law was promulgated on December 30, 1962, reviving the political activities of those who had not been

Gen. Park, chairman of the SCNR, meets President John F. Kennedy at the White House, November 1961.

purged.

In January 1963, as stability returned, the ban against political activity was removed, and new political parties emerged. The leading ones among them were the Democratic Republican Party (DRP) of the revolutionaries with Gen. Park as its head; and the Civil Rule Party of the former president, Yun Po-sŏn.

Gen. Park, who retired from the Army and ran for the four-year-term presidency as the candidate of the DRP, defeated former president Yun by a narrow margin in the presidential election held in October 1963. In the general election for a new National Assembly (once again unicameral), the DRP won a majority. With the inauguration of President Park on December 17, the Third Republic emerged.

The Third Republic, December 1963-December 1972

The government of the Third Republic faced many internal problems. The wholesale price index in Seoul rose (1960 = 100) to 149.3 in 1963 as the population increased to 27 million. The GNP was a meager $26 billion with a per capita income of $98.

Being a thoroughly military man, President Park was primarily interested in establishing stability, economic development, and strengthening national defense. Like many of his contemporaries, he was not familiar with democratic principles or a democratic way of life. Furthermore, it was his belief that the democratic way would not only bring about slow economic progress, but also social disunity and a weakening of national defense. The democracy he spoke of was not Western liberal democracy, but a "guided" or "limited" democracy, restricting civil liberties and freedoms of speech and press for the sake of the greater good of the society as a whole. Thus, he spoke of "Korean democracy." On the other hand, he was familiar with the bureaucratism and military leadership of Japan of the Meiji period(1868-1912) which, under strong government leadership, brought about economic modernization and military development under its guiding ideology called *ishin*, or "revitalization and renewal." Therefore, he considered that a short-term "strong rule" was not only unavoidable, in view of the prevailing national conditions, but would also be beneficial for national development.

It was his conviction that if the principle of "guided democracy" was applied to suit the Korean situation under the strong and positive leadership of the government, his weak and backward country could be transformed into a developed and strong nation. Such a philosophy led him to exercise strong power first, and then launch the *Yushin* ("revitalizing reform") movement at the end of the Third Republic in order to bring about the "rejuvenation of the people and the society."

Being primarily concerned with national security and anxious to develop the national economy while promoting social cohesion, the government saw fit to invoke emergency measures frequently whenever domestic tranquility was broken. In March 1964, large student demonstrations broke out in Seoul, protesting against the negotiations with Japan to establish normal relations between the two countries, and in June the government declared its first emergency in the Seoul area. In August 1964, the National Assembly enacted the Law Concerning the Security of Educational Institutions and the Law Concerning Press Ethics, and tightened its control over the campus activities of the students as well over the press. Meanwhile, the Central Intelligence Agency arrested some forty persons in August, charging them with violation of the National Security Law, thus setting a pattern of political control by the Korean CIA.

Despite violent opposition, the government signed the normalization treaty with Japan in June 1965, established new diplomatic and commercial relations, and secured a large loan. The National Assembly, controlled by the ruling Democratic Republican Party, passed a bill, without the participation of the opposition lawmakers, authorizing the government to dispatch South Korean troops to South Vietnam to cooperate with U.S. troops against the North Vietnamese. In August 1965, when violent demonstrations against these government actions broke out, the government declared martial law in the Seoul area.

The leaders in the opposition camps brought about the union of the Civil Rule Party and the Democratic Party "in order to strengthen the people's struggle against the corrupt and militaristic political power of the Park regime." Looking toward the 1967 presidential election, this and other parties merged to form the New Democratic Party(NDP) to challenge the ruling party and its government. However, in the February 1967 presidential election, the incumbent president defeated Yun Po-sŏn, the nominee of the NDP, by a large margin, and the ruling party won a substantial majority of seats in the National Assembly elections held in July. The South Korean voters clearly showed that they preferred to see the development of political stability and economy under a strong government which seemed to be doing well in both areas, fulfilling the goals of the first Five-Year Plan of 1962-66.

While the announcement in July 1967 regarding the arrest of a pro-North Korean espionage team consisting of over 100 members, whose main operational base had been located in East Berlin, shocked and dismayed the people, the attempt made in January 1968 by a North Korean commando team to assassinate President Park, the abduction of a U.S. intelligence ship, *Pueblo*, by North Korean naval vessels soon after that, and the arrest of an underground espionage group of the phantom "Unification Revolutionary Party" in South Korea in August increased tension and a sense of insecurity in South Korea, providing the government with ample excuses to tighten its control over the country. In April, the 2.5 million-man Homeland Reserve Forces were formed, and the government proceeded to give military training to college students in September.

The shift in U.S. Asian policy announced in the Nixon Doctrine of 1969, and Nixon's plan to withdraw half of the 40,000 U.S. troops from South Korea surprised the South Korean government, and further increased the sense of insecurity. In such a situation, the ruling party, despite strong opposition, amended the constitution in mid-September 1969, taking advantage of the fact that the members of the opposition party were boycotting the National Assembly session, allowing the incumbent president to run for a third term of office. A national refer-

endum held in October approved the amended constitution.

In the presidential election held in April 1971, President Park, by a narrow margin, defeated Kim Dae-jung,
the nominee of the NDP, who charged that President
Park's "highly militaristic" government had turned South
Korea into "a police state;" in the National Assembly
elections held in May, the ruling DRP won a large majority.

The two successive five-year economic development
plans (1962-66 and 1967-71) achieved much. (See Chapter 12) However, domestic and international situations
were not conducive for democratic development. While
anti-government student demonstrations became rampant, the Sino-U.S. détente led the South Korean government to seek direct contact with the North Korean government while increasing its control over the opposition
movement. Observing the development of the talks which
the South Korean Red Cross Society had initiated in
September 1971 with the North Korean Red Cross Society
to bring about the reunion of some 100,000 families
separated during the Korean War, President Park declared
a state of national emergency on December 6, 1971. This
was followed by the adoption of the Special Measure Law
on National Defense on December 26 by the National Assembly, giving extraordinary power to the president.

Secret negotiations that had been carried out between
Seoul and Pyongyang since early 1972 resulted in the
issuance of a statement by the two Korean governments
on July 4, 1972 regarding their agreement on a formula
for Korean reunification. The momentous statement
issued simultaneously by Seoul and Pyongyang on that
day announced the opening of a political dialogue between the two governments to achieve national unification by peaceful means whithout outside intervention.

Direct political dialogue between them began in the fall of 1972.

At this juncture, despite the opposition of some key party leaders, the ruling DRP proposed to prolong President Park's rule, and the president himself made a costly error by deciding to remain in power indefinitely. Thus, the government proclaimed a national emergency decree on October 17, 1972, dissolved the National Assembly, and suspended the constitution, bringing on the October *Yushin*, or "Revitalizing Reform." New constitutional amendments proposed by the government were approved in a national referendum held on November 21, enabling the incumbent president to run again. Needless to say, there was a strong negative reaction against such a move on the part of the ruling party, and student demonstrations erupted everywhere, bringing strong suppressive measures by the government against the students as well as the professors and political leaders who were behind them.

Martial law was lifted in mid-December, and the new electoral college known as the National Conference for Unification (NCU), whose 2,350 members were elected by popular vote on December 15, was established. The NCU elected the incumbent president to serve a new six-year term.

The Fourth Republic, December 1972–October 1979

With the inauguration of President Park on December 28, 1972, the Fourth Republic emerged. The new *Yushin* constitution was officially proclaimed three days later, followed by the promulgation of the new National Election Law and the Political Party Law.

After the elections of the National Assembly were held

in February 1973, a new political society, named Political Fraternal Society for Revitalizing Reform, commonly known as *Yujŏnghoe*, was set up as a companion political body of the ruling party. Under the new constitution, seventy-three of its members were elected by the NCU, on the president's recommendation, to serve three-year terms in the National Assembly.

The Fourth Republic encountered an increasing number of domestic and foreign problems. Unrest increased among dissident groups following the kidnapping of Kim Dae-jung, who had been conducting anti-government campaigns in the United States and Japan, in August 1973 from Tokyo by agents of the Korean CIA. As anti-government agitation and demands for the abolition of the 1972 *Yushin* constitution grew, the North Korean government abruptly suspended political talks with the South Korean government, against which it renewed its attacks.

Meanwhile, the government faced rising diplomatic problems with Japan and the United States in connection with the kidnapping of Kim Dae-jung and increasingly repressive measures against civil liberties. To cope with the situation, under the Presidential Emergency Decrees 1-4 of January-April 1974, the government banned all anti-government activities and agitation for constitutional reform, making the political situation only more unstable. In this tense situation, on August 15, a pro-North Korean from Japan attempted to assassinate President Park. Park himself was unharmed but his wife was killed. In late August, the Emergency Decrees 1-4 were lifted, but the NDP and other opposition groups relentlessly pressed for constitutional reform and the release of political prisoners. While a large number of college students were re-engaged in violent anti-government and anti-Japanese demonstrations in September and October, reporters of the

Korean daily newspaper, *Tong'a Ilbo*, and a group of 101 writers each issued their "Declaration for the Realization of Freedom of Speech and the Press," and in late November some seventy-one leaders formed the National Council for Restoration of Democracy.

As the demand for revision of the 1972 constitution grew, the government sought either rejection or reaffirmation of the constitution by the voters, and in a national referendum held in February 1975, some 73% of the voters re-affirmed the *Yushin* constitution. After this, the government released a large number of those who had been imprisoned for violation of the presidential decrees. Despite these actions, anti-government demonstrations and the movement for the revision of the constitution continued. Facing growing campus unrest and the voice of the opposition, the Presidential Emergency Measures No. 7 of April, and No. 9 of May 1975 were issued, imposing further restrictions on civil liberties as they banned student demonstrations and outlawed public criticism of the government.

The Fourth Republic carried out an ambitious military modernization program as it promoted the military industry. At the same time, in 1975, a Combat Reserve Corps was established under the Homeland Reserve Forces, and the Student National Defense Corps of university students was established, each university having its own unit. The Reserve Officers Training Corps (ROTC) program was also inaugurated.

The Civil Defense Corps, which was established in 1975 in every community to protect the lives and property of the people in times of enemy attack or in other emergencies, began to hold monthly mock air raid drills and other exercises. All able-bodied male citizens between the ages of 17 and 50 were obligated to serve in the Corps. The killing of American officers and wounding of

U.S. soldiers by North Korean troops at Panmunjom in August 1976, the increasing number of border clashes along the truce line (32,700 cases between 1970 and 1977), and the discovery in 1974, 75, and 78 of tunnels which the North Koreans had dug under the DMZ for the purpose of military invasion only increased the sense of insecurity in South Korea and the need for military preparation against possible North Korean aggression.

Following the issuance of a joint statement entitled the "Democratic National Salvation Declaration" by the three major opposition leaders in March 1976, the political situation in South Korea became more turbulent. Meanwhile, the South Korean government was troubled by the announcement made in March 1977 by U.S. President Jimmy Carter of a plan to withdraw all U.S. ground troops from South Korea within four years. Also of concern was the investigation carried out by the House of Representatives of the U.S. Congress in the spring of 1977 of the so-called "Koreagate" scandal involving a Korean rice dealer in the U.S. and a former South Korean diplomat to the U.S.

The re-election of President Park to serve another six-year term by the new members of the NCU in July 1978 only made the situation worse as student unrest, supported by opposition party leaders, became more troublesome for the government. In November 1978, as President Carter's plan to withdraw U.S. ground troops was being debated, the government was able to strengthen national defense by creating the U.S.-South Korean Combined Forces Command.

On December 27, 1978, President Park took the oath of office as the eighth president. One of his first moves was the release of some 1,000 political prisoners, followed by his call on North Korea for the resumption of the inter-Korean dialogue. When U.S. President Carter arrived in

Seoul in June 1979, President Park, while agreeing to re-open the dialogue with North Korea to reduce tension on the Korean peninsula, made serious efforts to persuade President Carter to cancel his proposed plan to withdraw U.S. ground troops from South Korea.

From August 1978, the dissident movement had grown stronger. The expelling in early October of Kim Young-sam, head of the New Democratic Party, from the National Assembly made the situation worse, bringing large mass student demonstrations in Pusan and Masan in mid-October. Martial law was declared in Pusan, followed by the imposition of a garrison decree in the Masan and Ch'ang'won area. The situation became more critical toward the end of October as college students in Seoul prepared for a large-scale uprising similar to that of April 1960.

In this situation, Kim Chae-gyu, director of the Korean CIA, shot and killed President Park on October 26, 1979. President Park's untimely death at the hands of one of his most trusted subordinates stunned the nation, as his *Yushin* rule was abruptly ended. Although his strong autocratic rule was detrimental to the promotion of political democracy, he had shaped South Korea's political economy and transformed an economically backward country into a prosperous, industrial nation, enabling the development of modern society and culture. Without such leadership, it is possible that the "miracle on the Han River" could not have occurred and the confidence of the people could not have grown.

As the nation faced an unprecedented national crisis, martial law was proclaimed, and Prime Minister Ch'oe Kyu-ha was named Acting-President by the NCU.

The Interim Period, October 1979–March 1981

Acting-president Ch'oe Kyu-ha attempted to restore political calm in a country stunned by the assassination of its
president while the Martial Law Commander Gen. Chŏng
Sŭng-hwa completed his investigation of the case of Kim
Chae-gyu and his accomplices. Ch'oe, who was elected by
the NCU as the new president of the republic on
December 6, announced that the *Yushin* rule would be
brought to an end with the adoption of a revised constitution that would promote greater democracy.

However, on December 12, scarcely a week after the
election of a new president, Lt. Gen. Chun Doo-hwan
(Chŏn Tu-hwan), commander of the Defense Security
Command of the South Korean Armed Forces, carried out
a bloody military *coup*, arresting the Martial Law Commander himself and gaining control over the military.

In February 1980, the new government of Ch'oe
Kyu-ha(Choi Kyu Hah) restored the civil rights of many
who had been purged, and in March it formed the Constitution Revision Deliberation Committee, but both the
opposition NDP and university students became impatient
with the slow progress in political reform. Conditions
deteriorated further when Gen. Chun was appointed as
acting-director of the Korean CIA in April without leaving
his army post. Many campus rallies were followed by violent street clashes between tens of thousands of students
and the police during the months of April and May as
hopes for democratization quickly faded away.

Troops were mobilized and on May 17 the government
proclaimed nation-wide martial law, followed by the issuance of Martial Law Decree No. 10. With this, some 30
political leaders, including Kim Chong-p'il(J. P. Kim),
head of the DRP, Kim Young-sam, head of the NDP, and

Kim Dae-jung were put under house arrest, and the National Assembly was closed, as were colleges. All political activities, assemblies, and public demonstrations were banned. In spite of these restrictions, the rebellious students and dissidents in the city of Kwangju and its vicinity rose up, bringing the bloody Kwangju Uprising of May 18-27, 1980, which caused a large number of casualties. According to some reports as many as 1,200 may have been killed.

The newly arrived troops stormed the city of Kwangju and recaptured it from the rioters after bloody fighting. On May 20 all cabinet members tendered their resignation, and a new cabinet emerged. Following this the Special Committee for National Security Measures (SCNSM) was formed on May 31 to cope with the crisis, with President Ch'oe as its chairman and Gen. Chun as chairman of its Standing Committee. Gen. Chun resigned as acting-director of the Korean CIA in June, but he and fifteen other generals in the SCNSM exercised absolute power, instituting many changes, including a drastic educational reform in July.

Upon the sudden resignation of President Ch'oe on August 16, Gen. Chun was elected by the NCU as president, and took the oath of office of September 1. In his oath of office he said that he would do his best to make the forthcoming government an "honest and efficient one, which can win the confidence of the nation," and he pledged that he would eradicate past ills and restore public faith in honest rule.

However, President Chun soon displayed despotic tendencies. Unlike President Park, Chun was not a reform-minded visionary, and it was soon apparent that he had no particular designs for national reconstruction. Former President Park had been a man of austerity and his personal honesty had not been questioned, and even those who disliked or despised him for his political practices had acknowledged his intelligence, sincerity, and economic achievement. President Chun, on the other hand, showed utter insensitivity to public opinion, and his character flaws were widely recognized. A writer said that "it required considerable effort to find anyone...who genuinely liked and respected Chun and his family."

No sooner had he taken the office of president than the police rounded up thirteen DNP members on dubious charges. Kim Dae-jung, a key opposition leader, was charged with instigating the Kwangju Uprising, and was given the death sentence by a military court. Meanwhile, the National Assembly, which had been suspended, was replaced by the 81-member Legislative Council for National Security (LCNS), whose members were appointed by President Chun himself.

On October 22, 1980, the new (8th) constitutional revisions proposed by the SCNSM were approved in a national referendum, replacing the *Yushin* constitution and paving the way for the Fifth Republic. Shortly after this, all political parties were disbanded, and on November 12, the government banned 555 persons from taking part in politics for the next eight years. At the same time, in October and November, the government brought about the dismissal of 937 journalists and editors of newspapers, and forced consolidation of civilian radio and television broadcasting companies and newspaper companies with those of the government, or semi-government agencies, causing what is known as "the massacre of the mass media." In December, the Korean CIA was renamed the Agency for National Security Planning, but its former power did not diminish.

With the partial lifting of Martial Law Decree No. 10 on November 15, 1980, political activity resumed, and in January 1981 three major parties emerged. They were the

Democratic Justice Party (DJP) with President Chun as its head, the Democratic Korea Party, and the Korean National Party. Meanwhile the new 5,278-member Presidential Electoral College, which was popularly elected on November 11, replaced the National Conference for Unification, and on February 25, 1981, the new electoral college elected the incumbent president to serve as the president of the Fifth Republic for a non-renewable seven-year term of office under the new constitution.

The Fifth Republic, March 1981–February 1988

With Chun's taking of office on March 3, 1981, the Fifth Republic emerged, followed by general elections for a new National Assembly in late March. The 11th National Assembly held its first session on April 11, replacing the short-lived LCNS.

The Chun administration remained unstable as he changed prime ministers several times during his rule: four times in 1982, once in 1983, twice in 1985, and three times in 1987. Meanwhile, many ministers and the directors of the Agency for National Security Planning were frequently replaced. Political and civil rights were restored for 250 blacklisted former politicians in February 1983, 202 in February 1984, and 84 in November 1984, leaving still on the list some 19 whose political and civil rights were not restored until March 1985. In January 1982, a 12 p.m.-to-4 a.m. curfew, a legacy of the postwar U.S. occupation of South Korea, and the strict requirements for uniforms and hairstyle of secondary school students, the legacies of the Japanese colonial rule, were finally removed. The administration brought about the exchange of hometown visiting groups between North and South Korea in September 1985, and it successfully hosted the largest Asian Olympic Games in the fall of 1986.

After completing the fourth five-year plan in 1981, the Fifth Republic successfully completed the fifth five-year plan of 1982-86. In 1987, it initiated the sixth five-year plan of 1987-91.

In foreign affairs, President Chun made state visits to five nations of the Association of Southeast Asian Nations (ASEAN) in June 1981, to four nations in Africa, as well as to Canada in August 1982, to Japan in September 1984, to the United States in February 1981 and April 1985, and to five European nations in April 1986. These state visits improved South Korea's diplomatic and commercial ties. His South Asian state visit in 1983 was cut short by a bomb incident brought about by North Korean agents in Rangoon, Burma on October 9, which killed eighteen ranking Korean officials, the deputy-premier, and three cabinet members.

Chun's accomplishments notwithstanding, the government of the Fifth Republic utterly failed to promote democracy as President Chun refused to revise the constitution of the Fifth Republic before 1989 despite a growing demand for the restoration of the direct election of the president and for freedom of the press. Not only that, the government used its power only to strengthen government control and to benefit the ruling party and those individuals and business firms which supported it. As a matter of fact, the Chun administration was regarded by the people as not only corrupt, but "the hotbed of illegality and irrationality." Rumors of the shady financial dealings of President Chun's wife, his brother and other relatives were rampant. Consequently, the democratic aspirations of the Korean people suffered, and frequent student riots and labor unrest, accompanied by violence, erupted as the demand for democratic reform increased.

Following the founding, in October 1984, of an under-ground radical student organization named the Committee for Promotion of Democracy, the student movement be-came more radicalized as it displayed an increasing de-gree of anti-American sentiments. Besides Communist propaganda, which promoted the anti-U.S. sentiments of Korean students, their anti-Americanism was intensified by their suspicion that the United States was behind Gen. Chun's seizure of power in the bloody *coup* of 1979 and that the U.S. approved Chun's brutal military action which crushed the Kwangju Uprising of 1980. Further-more, they were angered by a statement which Gen. John H. Wickham, then Commander of the U.S. Forces in South Korea, had made to the *Los Angeles Times* in August 1980, in which he hinted that the U.S. had de-cided to support Chun as the next president of South Korea. President Ronald Reagan's invitation for President Chun to visit the White House in February 1981 only strengthened their anti-U.S. sentiments. Underground societies promoted anti-Chun and anti-American student movements after 1981 as campus unrest increased. In October 1984, a large police force invaded the Seoul National University campus to control the rioting students, and in May 1985, a large number of students staged a three-day sit-in at the U.S. Information Service building in downtown Seoul, demanding that the U.S. apologize to the Korean people for what they called "U.S. involvement in the Kwangju incident." In October 1986, over 1,200 students staged a demonstration at Kŏn'guk University in Seoul shouting anti-government and anti-American slogans.

In January 1985, those former politicians who had regained their political and civil rights in November 1984 established the New Korea Democratic Party (NKDP), agi-tating for an immediate revision of the constitution and promotion of the struggle for democracy. In the general elections for the National Assembly held in February 1986, the opposition NKDP won the majority of urban votes, but it was unable to dislodge the ruling DJP from the majority.

Shortly after President Chun named Roh Tae-woo(No T'ae-u), a former Army general who had helped Chun in the December 12, 1979 *coup,* as new chairman of the DJP, the opposition party leaders formed the Council for the Promotion of Democracy, calling for a united front of all opposition groups under the leadership of Kim Dae-jung and Kim Young-sam. At this juncture, another radical student group named the Committee for the Three People's Struggle emerged, calling for the liberation of the masses, the attainment of democracy, and the unification of the Korean people. This student body clearly showed its pro-North Korean sentiments.

The political climate grew more turbulent in the spring of 1986 as the police placed 270 opposition politicians under house arrest and blocked a mass rally planned by the NKDP. Nonetheless, large-scale mass rallies were held in May in Seoul, Inch'ŏn, Kwangju, Taegu, and Pusan in support of the constitutional revision drive. While demonstrators even demanded the immediate resignation of President Chun, a group of 325 women leaders issued a statement calling for the promotion of social democracy and women's rights.

In this growing anti-Chun and anti-government climate, radical students organized the pro-North Korean Anti-Imperialist League, and the increasing activism of radical student groups created considerable internal instability. Meanwhile, the adoption by the ruling DJP of a resolution to permit the police arrest of opposition National Assemblymen, the passage of the 1987 national budget bill without participation of the opposition lawmakers, and the death by police torture of a university student further exacerbated the political situation, forcing the president to reshuffle his cabinet in January 1987.

President Chun's April 13, 1987 ban on any further talks for constitutional reform until after the 1988 Seoul Olympic Games only provoked a more violent reaction against the government and its party. While opposition lawmakers carried out their movement against the dictatorial rule of President Chun, hundreds of Protestant ministers and Catholic priests and nuns carried out hunger strikes, demanding Chun's resignation, as professors of many universities and many lawyers issued political statements, condemning the policy of the president and his party. Meanwhile, hundreds of thousands of students and others staged anti-government demonstrations throughout the spring and early summer, clashing with the combat police. The city of Seoul became a battleground between the demonstrators and the riot police.

In such a situation, President Chun reshuffled his cabinet six times in 1987 as some 71 lawmakers who defected from the KNDP formed a new Reunification Democratic Party (RDP) on May 1, with Kim Young-sam as its president and Kim Dae-jung as his mentor, declaring their determination to carry out their struggle for democratization.

The nomination on June 10 of Roh Tae-woo, chairman of the ruling DJP as presidential candidate, precipitated more violent reaction as the opposition RDP demanded an immediate revision of the constitution, restoration of full freedom of the press, release of all political prisoners, and restoration of full civil rights for Kim Dae-jung and others who were still on the blacklist. In the wake of this, on June 10, some 500 persons, including the president of the RDP, were arrested as bloody clashes between the combat police and protesters continued day after day. A total breakdown of law and order seemed imminent.

At this critical point, Roh Tae-woo, chairman of the DJP, realizing the inevitability of change and supported by his loyal followers in the party, proposed that drastic action be taken by President Chun. His proposal was also based on his realization that the 1988 Summer Olympic Games might be relocated from Seoul to elsewhere if the worsening situation in South Korea was not soon turned around. For such reasons, unlike other former army generals, Roh chose to pursue a constitutional means to solve the national crisis.

Thus, on June 29, he presented his "Democratization Declaration" to the people in a nationwide television broadcast. His eight-point reform proposal included an endorsement of an early constitutional reform to restore direct presidential elections, adoption of a new presidential election law, restoration of civil rights to all black-listed political leaders, protection of human rights, the lifting of press restrictions, the restoration of local and campus autonomy, the promotion of free political party activities, and a call for social reform. After disclosing his reform formula, he demanded that the president accept his proposals, or he would resign from chairmanship of the DJP and would not run for the presidency in the forthcoming election.

The nation was stunned by Roh's unexpected proposals, but welcomed them with cautious optimism in the midst of rumors of the possibility of another military *coup*. Following this, Roh met with Chun and convinced the president that the only peaceful way to defuse the crisis was to implement his reform policy. Persuaded by Roh, President Chun announced to the nation on July 1 that the revision of the constitution would be made before 1988 and that the next president would be elected under the new constitution. Following this, some 2,335 political prisoners were freed and civil rights for all those who had been purged were restored.

As the winds of democracy rose, labor unrest increased while radical students continued their anti-government demonstrations. More than 3,300 industrial disputes erupted involving workers' demands for higher wages, better treatment, and better working conditions. However, by mid-October, nearly all labor strikes ended with the government concession to some of their demands, including the revision of labor laws.

As the twilight of the Chun administration approached, the opposition leaders struggled to select a man who would run against and defeat the presidential candidate of the ruling DJP. It was their hope that Kim Dae-jung and Kim Young-sam would minimize their differences, and only one of them would run. However, when Kim Young-sam declared his candidacy for president in mid-October, Kim Dae-jung, taking twenty-seven of the RDP's lawmakers with him, formed his own Party for Peace and Democracy (PPD), and became its presidential candidate. Meanwhile, Kim Chong-p'il revived the DRP, which had been defunct with the death of former President Park, renamed it the New Democratic Republican Party (NDRP), and became its presidential candidate. For the first time in the history of South Korea, a woman member of the Socialist Democratic Party ran for the presidency, although she later withdrew from the race.

On October 12, the National Assembly passed the 9th constitutional amendment providing for direct presidential elections, and the new constitution was approved in a national referendum on October 27, to take effect on February 25, 1988. The new liberal constitution of South Korea increased safeguards for human and civil rights of the citizen; reestablished the system of direct, popular presidential elections; deprived the president of the right to dissolve the National Assembly; provided the power to the National Assembly to approve the appointments of prime minister and justices of the Supreme Court by the president; reinstated the power of the National Assembly to investigate affairs of state; enjoined the military from political activity; and deprived the president of the right to issue emergency decrees covering a whole range of state affairs, including judicial matters.

Under a supplementary provision of the new constitution, and in accordance with an agreement of the rival parties, the first direct, popular presidential election in sixteen years was held even before the new constitution went into effect. On December 16, 1987, some 23 million, or 89.2% of the eligible voters cast their ballots, electing Roh Tae-woo of the DJP as president for a non-renewable five-year term of office by 36.6% of the votes.

The Sixth Republic, February 1988-February 1993

With the inauguration of President Roh Tae-woo on February 25, 1988 the tortuous period of the Fifth Republic came to an end, bringing a peaceful transfer of power for the first time in South Korean history. As the Sixth Republic emerged, the new president proclaimed that the era of "ordinary people" had arrived, and the "day when freedom and human rights could be relegated in the name of economic growth and national security had ended."

The auspicious beginning of the Sixth Republic was marred by strong clashes between the ruling and opposition lawmakers when on March 8 the ruling party's lawmakers unilaterally passed an amendment to the parliamentary election law despite all-out opposition attempts to block it. The new National Assembly election law restored the single (small) constituency system for the first time in seventeen years as it increased the number of seats to 299.

In the general elections for the National Assembly held in April, for the first time in South Korean history, the ruling party (DJP) failed to win the majority as only 87 of its candidates were elected for 224 single constituent seats. The three major opposition parties (RDP, PPD, and NDRP) won a total of 126 single constituent seats. The 75 at-large, or "proportional" seats were distributed to each party according to the percentage of seats each had won. Thus, the DJP received 38, the PPD 16, the RDP 13, and the NDRP 8 seats.

The Sixth Republic faced numerous domestic problems. The most troublesome issues to be settled were those re- lated to the Kwangju Uprising and the wrongdoings of ex-president Chun and his officials of the Fifth Republic. In order to solve these thorny problems, President Roh appointed politically unstained academicians as premiers in February and December 1988 and December 1990; re- leased all political prisoners; restored civil rights to all those who had been blacklisted; liberalized the press law; adopted a cultural liberalization policy; and lifted a ban on the pre-1945 works of some 100 left-wing artists, musicians, and writers who had defected to North Korea before 1953. The study of Communism and North Korea was also allowed as the government permitted the circu- lation of some North Korean publications. Meanwhile, the government redesignated the Kwangju Uprising as "part of efforts for the democratization of the nation," offered an apology for the bloodshed, and agreed to provide mon- etary compensations to families of the victims.

While accepting gracefully the disapproval by the National Assembly of the appointment of Chief Justice of the Supreme Court nominated by the president, the Roh administration focused its attention on the promotion of national unity so that the XXIVth Olympiad could be hosted by Seoul as scheduled. In order to appease the students and academicians, the government promised to abolish compulsory military training for college students, and it restored the autonomy of colleges to select their own presidents and deans. It also promised to revise labor laws.

While the opposition party leaders clamored for a thorough investigation of the wrongdoings of the ex-president and his officials, President Roh managed to get the major opposition party leaders to agree to work jointly for the success of the Seoul Olympic Games. The student voice remained a problem and in May and June, thousands of students, who the previous year had been shouting "down with the military dictatorship," took to the streets and attempted to go to Panmunjom for joint meetings with their North Korean counterparts in order to bring about national unification. Their shouts were "drive out American imperialism" or "unite our motherland." At this juncture, in June 1988, the National Council of Representatives of University Students was formed, and it launched the Joint Masses Movement for Democracy and Unification.

In a vastly improved domestic environment from September 17 through October 2, 1988, Seoul hosted the most peaceful and largest summer Olympic Games ever, not only boosting the self-confidence of the South Korean people, but also creating a new image of the nation in the world. Only a handful of countries, such as Cuba and North Korea, refused to participate in the Seoul Olympic Games.

After fulfilling some of the hopes of the South Koreans, the government continued to democratize the nation by adopting many new measures. The students were allowed to organize their own associations and elect officials without outside interference, and most of the 3,749 labor strikes which had begun in 1987, were brought to an end by November 1988 as the government revised the labor law, legalizing collective bargaining and raising the minimum wage of workers.

Efforts made by the Roh administration brought about apologies to the nation by ex-president Chun on a nation-wide television broadcast in November 1988, and his testifying before the National Assembly in the evening of December 31, 1989. Although his apologies and explanations were not fully satisfactory to the Korean people as a whole, the government declared that the issues related to the Fifth Republic had been settled.

As a means of strengthening the ruling party, in early February 1990, President Roh brought about the merger of his Democratic Justice Party with the Reunification Democratic Party of Kim Young-sam and the New Democratic Republican Party of Kim Chong-p'il, thus creating a large Democratic Liberal Party. Following this, some members of the Reunification Democratic Party who disapproved of the merger, along with others, formed their own Democratic Party. Meanwhile, the Democratic Coalition, which was formed in 1989, joined the opposition movement of the Party for Peace and Democracy of Kim Dae-jung and the newly formed Democratic Party against the vastly expanded conservative, ruling party.

As party politics became more active, in December 1990 the National Assembly passed the law proposed by the government to restore in 1991 the local autonomy which had been abolished in 1961. Under this law, all provincial governors and provincial, municipal, and county assemblies would be elected by popular vote.

While promoting democracy and making efforts to fulfill the goals of the sixth five-year socioeconomic development plan of 1987-91, President Roh expanded summit diplomacy and initiated what is called "northern diplomacy." Thus, immediately before, during and after the Seoul Olympic Games, the South Korean government promoted cultural exchanges with China, Hungary, and the Soviet Union. Efforts made by the government under this new diplomacy, which had been advocated by the late President Park in 1979, brought about the establishment first of official trade relations in 1988, and then diplomatic ties in 1989 with Hungary, Poland, Yugoslavia, and with Algeria, East Germany, Czechoslovakia, Mongolia, and finally with the Soviet Union in 1990. Although diplomatic ties with China have yet to be established, South Korea's economic relationship with China has grown enormously since 1988.

Expanding summit diplomacy, President Roh made state visits to the South Asia-Pacific nations in November 1988 after addressing the U.N. General Assembly in October, clarifying South Korea's foreign policy to the world body. He then became the first South Korean president to visit a former Socialist country when he made a state visit to Hungary in December 1989. Although memories of the shooting down of a Korean Air Lines passenger plane by a Soviet fighter plane in September 1983 near Sakhalin Island were still vivid, the South Korean government cultivated goodwill with the Soviet Union. In July 1989, Kim Young-sam, president of the Reunification Democratic Party, was allowed to visit Moscow, meeting Soviet leaders, as well as a North Korean leader, and in March 1990 he again visited Moscow as a top leader of the newly formed Democratic Liberal Party. In June 1990, President Roh himself met Soviet President Mikhail Gorbachev in San Francisco, paving the way for the establishment of diplomatic relations between the two countries in November 1990, and President Roh made a state visit to Moscow in December. Meanwhile, South Korea carried out talks with Vietnam.

While President Roh's state visit to the United States in October 1989 improved the ties between the two countries, his state visit to Japan in May 1990 prepared the ground for the settlement of many pending problems for Koreans residing in Japan. Apologies were received from the Japanese emperor and the prime minister for exploitation and mistreatment of the Koreans at the hands of the Japanese during the 1905-1945 period.

The government of the Sixth Republic also endeavored to relax tensions on the Korean peninsula and establish amicable relations with North Korea. In his address to the National Assembly in September 1989, President Roh announced a new unification formula which called for the founding of a commonwealth of the Korean nations as "an interim stage toward unification." In it, he also called for a north-south summit meeting at an early date.

After announcing its decision to allow authorized South Korean citizens to visit North Korea, the South Korean government called for the convening of a premiers' conference of the north and the south, as well as cultural exchange and economic ties for the purpose of promoting new, peaceful and cooperative relations between the two states, taking advantage of the rapidly changing conditions in Eastern Europe and the ending of the Cold War. As a result, many South Korean citizens and groups from both South Korea and abroad visited North Korea in 1990, and in October, after a South Korean soccer team played in Pyongyang, a North Korean soccer team played in Seoul. Although no satisfactory agreements has reached after the three meetings of the respective premiers which were held between September and December 1990, the two governments agreed to continue their talks.

Meanwhile, when the leaders of the citizens' groups in

South Korea learned of the dire food shortage in the north, they collected funds, purchased some 51,000 bushels (800 tons) of rice, and handed them over to North Korea in July 1990. In December the South Korean government indicated its willingness to donate 510,000 bushels of rice to the north if the North Korean government would accept them.

Thus, at the end of 1990, South Korea at last witnessed growing democratic trends at home, improving relations with formerly hostile Socialist countries, and slowly cultivated ties between the peoples of the north and the south.

As the end of President Roh's term of office approached, party politics associated with the selection of presidential candidate became active. On February 8, 1992 Chung Ju-yung, founder and honorary chairman of the Hyundai Business Group, formed the United People's Party with Prof. Kim Dong-gill, a long-time critic of authoritarian regime as co-chairman, and announced his candidacy in the upcoming presidential election.

Following several months of intense intra-party maneuvering, on May 19, 1992 Kim Young-sam won the nomination of the ruling DLP as its presidential candidate over his rival. The defeated candidate eventually defected from the DLP, formed his own New Korea Party in November, and became its presidential candidate. Soon after that, however, he merged his party with that of Chung, abandoning his own presidential ambitions. Meanwhile, President Roh stepped down from the DLP presidency which was won by Kim Young-sam in August. On October 9, President Roh formed a politically neutral cabinet under a new premier. Meanwhile, other presidential candidates appeared. Among them were Kim Dae-jung nominated by his Democratic Party as its candidate and Pak Ch'an-jong, who formed the Party for New Political Reform and became its candidate.

Throughout the election campaign, President Roh and his administration kept political neutality as he promised. On November 18, he invited the candidates of three major parties (the two Kims and Chung) to the Blue House, and urged them to make the 14th presidential election "the cleanest one" in South Korea's political history.

In the presidential election held on December 18, 1992, 81.9% of the 29,422,658 registered voters cast their ballots for seven candidates. Kim Young-sam was elected to serve a single five-year term by receiving 9,977,332 votes. Kim Dae-jung received 8,041,284 votes, Chung Ju-yung 3,880,067 votes, and Pak Ch'an-jong 1,516,047 votes. The other three candidate received a combined total of 360,669 votes. After his defeat, Kim Dae-jung resigned his National Assembly seat and "retired" from politics. Chung also left the political scene, leading his party in disarray in the hands of Kim Dong-gill and others.

The Seventh Republic, February 1993 –

On February 25, 1993, Kim Young-sam took the oath of office as president of the Seventh Republic, restoring the government to the hands of civilians after some 37 years of rule by military men. The inauguration of the new administration under the president who had championed democracy for nearly a half century signaled the coming of a new age for the Koreans in the south. Various reform measures which he rapidly and successfully put into effect created high expectations and new hopes for many beneficial results. The process of building a democratic and just society that began in the late 1980s after decades of often violent struggle is certain to bring about many visible changes.

12

Development and Modernization of South Korea, 1953-

ALTHOUGH the realization of democratic political aspirations only began in 1988, with arduous and tenacious efforts made by the Koreans themselves, together with assistance given to them by the United States and other democratic nations, as well as the United Nations, the South Korean people have brought about a remarkably rapid national development and modern transformation of the society. While achieving what they proudly called "the miracle on the Han River" in economy, they promoted modern education and culture as they transformed their feudalistic, tradition-bound society into a modern, urban and industrial one.

Economic Development

Economic Conditions Prior to 1961. The young republic faced many economic problems. The shortage of capital, raw material, electricity, scientists and technicians, skilled workers, food, housing, commodities, and the run-away inflation seemed utterly insurmountable problems. The South Korean economy was prevented from total collapse by the U.S. economic assistance of $110 million, however small it was, given in the fiscal year of 1949-50, together with the U.N. aid.

The land reform the government carried out was the most significant economic change. Under the Land Reform Act of June 22, 1949, the government purchased all farmlands not cultivated by the owners, as well as holdings of more than 7.5 acres by owner-cultivators, excluding fields where such crops as tobacco and ginseng were grown, and sold them to landless peasants on a 15-year installment plan without interest on the price of the land. The poor farmers were given 30% of the purchase price as government subsidy.

Some 1.7 million acres of farmlands were sold to 1.5 million farm households by 1957. The average size of farms they bought was a mere 2.25 acres, but this reform ended the exploitative absentee landlordism. Many former landlords who sold lands invested capital in commerce or industry. Some of them became successful entrepreneurs themselves.

Following the land reform, and with the importation of chemical fertilizers with the U.S. aid, the agricultural output grew by 11%, and the amount of grain produced rose from 4.6 million tons in 1948 to 5.2 million tons by 1950. Meanwhile, coal production was accelerated, and was increased by 40% by June 1950. In 1950, the per capita gross national product (GNP) reached the $86 mark with the gross national product of less than $1.8 billion.

The little economic improvement made was wiped out by the Korean War, making the economic situation far worse than that of the prewar period. The damage inflicted was estimated at three billion dollars. The rice production decreased from 2.3 million tons in 1949 to 1.9 million tons in 1953 as inflation grew and the number of jobless people increased vastly. The gross national product dropped from $1.8 billion in 1949-50 to $1.4 billion in 1952-53. The urban retail price index was 197.8 in 1949 (1947 = 100), and it more than doubled between June and September 1950, increasing to 2,128 in 1951, 5,243 in 1952, and 7,618 in 1953. In 1954 it jumped to 10,319.5 and in August and September 1955 it reached the staggering 20,000 mark. The GNP in 1953-54 was $1.7 billion.

The postwar economic recovery plans which were carried out with some $1.8 billion U.S. economic aid between 1953 and 1960, and $150 million aid of the U.N. Korean Reconstruction Agency, brought about some improvement. Grain production increased to 5.9 million tons in 1960, the amount of coal produced grew to 5.3 million tons, the amount of electricity generated reached the 1,686 million kilowatt hours (kwh) by 1960. More railways were rebuilt, and by 1960, South Korea's economy barely recovered the prewar level. The growth rate of gross national product increased from one percent in 1953 to 5.9% in 1960 when the per capita GNP was slightly below $100. However, the steady population increase from 21 million in 1953 to 25 million by 1960 made any economic improvement less effective.

Economic Development after 1961: An Overview. South Korea's significant economic improvement came only after 1961 when the Supreme Council for National Reconstruction established the Economic Planning Board and implemented the first five-year economic development plan of 1962-66. After the Third Republic was established in 1963, another five-year economic plan of 1967-71 was carried out, with an average annual GNP growth rate of

9.1%. The Fourth Republic carried out two successive five-year socioeconomic plans of 1972-76 and 1977-81 with an average annual GNP growth rate of 10.2%. After successfully completing the goals of the fourth five-year plan in 1981, the Fifth Republic carried out the fifth five-year socioeconomic development plan of 1982-86, and initiated the sixth five-year socioeconomic development plan of 1987-91.

Whereas the first two five-year plans were aimed at the construction of a self-sustaining economy, development of heavy industries without sacrificing the consumer economy, and modernization of the economic structure, the particular aims of the third and other plans were to promote export-oriented industry, to bring about social development, and to equalize income distribution between rural households and urban wage earners.

Although state planning and guidance played an important role in economic growth, the initiatives taken by private corporations and businessmen under the principle of free market economy contributed enormously toward South Korea's economic transformation. The other factors which enabled South Korea's achievement of rapid economic development were U.S. economic aid which was terminated in 1976, loans from the World Bank and the International Monetary Fund, and the $350 million reparation paid by Japan along with a $350 million commercial loan. The importation of the latest industrial technology and equipment also played a key role in the economic growth. Needless to say, the sacrifice and hard work of the people, particularly the workers, for the sake of national development made an important contribution.

By 1975, South Korea's GNP grew to $18.8 billion from $2.3 billion in 1962 with the average annual GNP growth rate of 10% between 1962 and 1975 despite the oil shock of 1973. Meanwhile, the rate of inflation (wholesale price) was brought down from 42% in 1962 to 8% in 1977. Although the annual average GNP growth rate between 1972 and 1978 was 10.8%, the GNP growth rate of the fourth five-year plan period of 1977-81 at 5% was the lowest since 1962 due to the aftermath of the oil shock of the late 1970s, the world-wide recession, as well as political turmoil brought about by the assassination of President Park in 1979. However, the GNP grew to $57.4 billion in 1980 with per capita GNP of $1,735.

An important aspect of economic development was the growth of average annual income of farm households from $147 in 1962 to $4,830 in 1979 while the average annual income of urban wage earners increased from $190 to $5,460 during the same period.

Economic growth continued after 1980 with the successful completion of the fourth five-year socioeconomic plan of 1982-86, and by 1986 the GNP grew to $95.1 billion with per capita GNP of $2,296. In 1987, the sixth five-year socioeconomic development plan of 1987-91 was launched, achieving satisfactory results. The GNP growth rate of 1986-88 was 12.6%, bringing the GNP up to $150 billion and per capita income of $4,738 in 1988. Some 500,000 new jobs were created, bringing the unemployment rate down to an unprecedentedly low 2.5%. Its exports grew by 28.3% to $60.7 billion in 1988 from $47.3 billion in the previous year, and the trade surplus was $8.9 billion in 1988. With this, South Korea was able to reduce its foreign debts from $45 billion in 1986 to $30 billion in 1989.

However, South Korea's economic growth has slowed down since 1988. The consumer price rose by 7.1% in 1988, 5.7% in 1989, and 9.4% in 1990. The domestic savings ratio dropped from 38.1% in 1988 to 36.3% in 1989, and 35.5% in 1990, while the private consumption rate rose from 8.7% in 1987 to 9.8% in 1988 and 1989, and 10% in 1990. South Korea's exports grew by only 6.6% to $76.6 billion in 1992, but its imports increased by 13.9% to $70 billion, producing a trade deficit of $2.5 billion in 1990. The causes for such economic changes were the growth of inflation and rising labor costs, decline of exports due to the world-wide recession, soaring consumer prices, and over-importation. However, the rates of inflation decreased from 20.1% in 1988, to 15.5% in 1989, and to 4.5% in 1992. Labor disputes at such places as Hyundai Shipyard, Hyundai Motors and KBS in 1989 and others in 1990, also contributed to the down-turn in the economy.

Be that as it may, South Korea's economy continued to grow with an annual growth rate of GNP of 6.6% in 1989 and 8.4% in 1991, bringing the GNP to $295 billion and per capita income to $6,749 in 1992.

The expansion of South Korea's economy was accompanied by dramatic changes in its structure. The mining and manufacturing sector grew much faster than the agriculture, forestry and fisheries sector between 1962 and 1989. As a result, the share of the latter sector in South Korea's GNP declined from 37% in 1962 to 20.6% in 1989. This sector accounted for 63.1% of all jobs in 1963, but the percentage fell to 15.6% in 1989. Meanwhile, the mining and manufacturing sector grew to make up 34.5% of the GNP, up from 16.3% in 1963, and jobs in this sector swelled to 29.5% of South Korean employment, up from 8.7% in 1963. The social services sector in GNP grew from 28.2% in 1963 to 44.9% in 1988.

In 1988, 16.9 million people out of 17.3 million economically active population were gainfully employed. The number of unemployed persons stood at 435,000 (2.5% of the entire work force) in 1988. In 1992, there was a work force of 19.7 million people. Of this, 19.3 million were gainfully employed while 450,000, or 2.4% of the total work force were unemployed. Some 3 million people were engaged in agriculture, forestry, and fisheries, 4.8 million in manufacturing, 94,000 in mining, and 11 million were engaged in service industries. Of the latter, 1.7 million were in construction, and 3.9 million were in commerce.

The make-up of South Korea's manufacturing sector was also changed as the nation's economy grew. During the 1960s and early 1970s, South Korea based its economic growth on light industries, producing wigs, footwear, textiles and other labor-intensive products. After the implementation of the third socioeconomic development plan in 1972-76, the share of primary industries in the total industrial structure decreased from 42.5% in 1966 to 10.2% in 1989. On the other hand, the share of secondary industries increased from 13.4% in 1966 to 31.9% in 1989. The tertiary industries' share remained relatively high: 44.1% in 1966 and 57.9% in 1989.

Structural change is reflected in the composition of export commodities. Exports of manufactured goods comprised 62.4% of the total in 1966, but it increased to 95.4% in 1986, primarily as a result of the increase in export of heavy industry and chemical products, as well as electronic products and ships.

Key Aspects of Economic Development. The achievement of self-sufficiency in rice supply by 1987 was one of the most significant aspects of economic development. With modernization of agriculture by introducing modern farm machines such as power tillers, farm tractors, rice transplanters, reapers, and harvesters, together with an abundant supply of chemical fertilizers and introduction of high-yield rice seeds, the amount of rice produced increased from 3 million tons in 1962 to 5.9 million in 1989 although the total area of cultivation decreased. The production of barley, the second major grain, dropped from 1.3 million tons in 1962 to 579,176 tons in 1989, but the total amount of grains produced rose from 5 million to 7 million tons during the same period. In 1989, 5 million bushels of surplus rice was produced.

Meanwhile, the amount of apples produced grew from 118,000 tons in 1962 to 676,016 tons in 1989, pears from 27,000 to 198,852 tons, and peaches from 20,000 to 137,000 tons during the same period.

In 1989 some 1.8 million farm households comprising a population of 6.8 million, cultivated 3.3 million acres of paddy fields where rice was grown and 1.9 million acres of dry fields where potatoes, wheat, barley, fruits and vegetables, and other crops were grown.

Another significant aspect of the economic change of South Korea was the development of industry. In 1948, and even as late as 1960, South Korea was basically an agricultural nation, producing no steel, petrochemical products, ships (tankers), automobiles, or plate glass. It had old systems of paper manufacturing and textile industry. Its electronic industry was in an infant stage, producing only light bulbs and vacuum tubes for radio receivers in the 1950s and early 1960s. It generated only 1.2 billion kilowatt hours (kwh) of electricity in 1961, manufactured only 97,000 tons of cement, and produced only 69,799 tons of cotton yarn and 1,731 tons of nylon fabrics as late as 1966.

Only after the implementation of the first five-year economic development plan of 1962-66 did the growth of modern industry begin, changing the character of South Korea's economy. Following the establishment of the Korea Oil Corporation (now Yukong Ltd.) at Ulsan in 1964, and the adoption of the Integrated Development Plan for the Petrochemical Industry in 1966 and construction of the petrochemical complex at Ulsan, South Korea's petrochemical industry developed rapidly, producing many beneficial side effects. The petrochemical industry continued to grow with the establishment of Honam Oil Refinery Company in 1969 and the Kyŏng-In Energy Company in 1971. In 1980, the Korea-Iran Petroleum Company (renamed later as the Ssangyong Oil Refining Company) was established, increasing the petro-industry. The amount of petroleum produced increased from 4.8 million barrels in 1964 to 257.5 million barrels in 1985. Of this, 35.8% were bunker crude, 27.7% diesel, 14% naphtha, 5.4 each of kerosene and jet oil, and 4.9% gasoline.

The development of the petrochemical industry was followed by that of machine industry under the Promotion of the Machinery Industry Act of 1967. Since then the production pattern of machine industry has shifted from manufacturing of farm implements such as power tillers, reapers, tractors, and water pumps to heavy machinery. The promulgation of the Electronics Promotion Law in 1969 and implementation of the Eight-Year Electronics Industry Development Plan (1969-76) led to the rapid development of the electronics industry, and by 1980 South Korea became one of the world's top ten producers of electronics goods, exporting $4.2 billion worth in 1985.

With the completion of the first iron and steel mill of the P'ohang Integrated Iron and Steel Company (POSCO) in 1973, South Korea's development of heavy industry moved forward, becoming the 14th largest producer of crude steel in the world. In 1988, South Korea produced 17.3 million tons of steel. With the establishment of the Kwangyang Steel Works in 1988 South Korea's steel industry supplied in 1989 some 78% of the domestic need while exporting $28 million worth of steel.

Following the establishment of the Hyundai Motor Company in 1968, South Korea's automobile assembly plants became automobile manufacturing plants. After

A computerized production line turns out automobiles for both domestic and overseas markets.

this, the Daewoo Motor, the Kia Motor, and the Ssang-yong Motor companies joined the field, increasing the number of cars, buses, trucks, and motor-bicycles manufactured in South Korea. With the exportation of Hyundai's small car (Excel) that began in the early 1980s, followed by exportation of a mid-size car (Sonata), South Korea became an auto-exporting country while meeting the entire domestic demand. Thus, South Korea, which had only a few hundred passenger cars in the early 1960s, became a nation with more than 14 million cars, manufacturing 1.5 million vehicles and exporting 347,000 cars or trucks in 1990.

With the rapidly developing heavy and light industries, the demands for coal and electricity increased dramatically. While importing a growing amount of oil for fuel, the production of coal and electric power was stepped up. As a result, the amount of coal production grew to 24 million tons in 1988, and the amount of electricity generated in 1988 grew to 58,007 million kwh. Meanwhile, the amount of cement produced in South Korea increased from 728,000 tons in 1962 to 20.5 million tons in 1985.

The development of the shipbuilding industry is another important aspect of the phenomenal economic development. Following the promulgation of the Shipbuilding Encouragement Law in 1962, the Hyundai Shipyard was constructed at Ulsan in 1974, followed by the construction of the Samsung Shipyard on Kŏje Island. By 1985, South Korea had become the fourth largest shipbuilder in the world, exporting 2.5 million tons of ships (mostly tankers and cargo ships) in 1988.

The production of chemical fertilizer grew from 83,000 tons in 1961 to 1.5 million tons, production of pulp and paper from a negligible amount to 1.7 million tons by 1985, and manufacturing of plate glass from 527,000 cases in 1966 to 2,157,000 cases in 1976.

The development of industry brought about the rise of industrial parks under careful government planning. The Seoul-Inch'ŏn area had been a large industrial zone, consisting mostly of light industry. But after 1962, several industrial centers emerged, first in the southeastern region and then in the southwest. The first industrial park to emerge was that of Kumi, and then such industrial centers as P'ohang, Ulsan, and Pusan, followed by those of Masan-Ch'ang'wŏn, Kŏje Island, Kwangyang, and Kwangju. As these centers were established, a growing number of people migrated from rural regions into these areas, becoming industrial workers.

In order to bring about rapid economic development, as well as to facilitate large-scale mobility of people and goods, and as industrial centers emerged, the government launched ambitious plans for highway and railway construction, harbor expansion and modernization, and other rapid transit and air traffic system. As a result, the mileage of roads increased from 11,738 in 1961 to 35,111 in

1989. Of these, 23,115 miles were paved, and 960 miles were four-lane divided expressways such as the Seoul-Pusan Expressway. The nation is served by Korean Air Lines and Asiana Air Lines, which also have some 41 foreign routes.

In 1945, South Korea had 2,318 miles of railway. During the Korean War most of the railway tracks were destroyed along with over 61% of the locomotives, 60% of the passenger cars, and 57% of the freight cars. The railway reconstruction that began in 1953 brought about not only a recovery, but also an increase in railway mileage and modernization of rail transportation. The progress made since 1963 has been substantial, increasing the railway mileage to 3,976 by 1988. Of this, 528 miles were double-track, and 327 miles were electrified. Today, all parts of the country are connected by modern highways, railways, and air routes.

Labor Movement. With the collapse of the leftist labor movement after 1948, the rightist General Federation of Korean Labor Unions grew in size, but it soon became a tool for the government and the Liberal Party after 1952. In 1959, a new National Council of Labor Unions was formed with some 100 labor unions to promote a "pure and democratic labor movement." However, labor strikes of the 1950s were crushed by the police and the development of a healthy labor movement was prevented.

When the May Military Revolution took place in 1961, the two existing federations were merged into a single federation. Although South Korean labor unions struggled for the right of labor and for the increase of wages and the improvement of working conditions, as of 1987 nothing significant had been accomplished as their membership dropped to about 900,000. With the radically changing political situation, the number of labor strikes in

1987 increased to 3,749 and the number of labor unions grew to 5,598 with a total membership of 1.7 million in 1988. In 1988, the number of labor disputes dropped to 1,874 and in 1989 to 1,616.

With the revision of the Labor Standard Act and the enactment of the Equality Law of Male and Female Employees in 1989, the daily minimum wage increased by 23.5% while that of miners rose by 20.5%, of construction workers by 15.8%, and of social and individual services by 15.8%. The average monthly fixed income of production-line workers rose by 24.4% to $395.12 and that of an office worker to $696.00. However the National Teachers' Union, which was organized in 1989, has been unable to obtain legal status because of the government ban against the organization of labor unions by teachers.

The founding of the new National Alliance of Labor Unions (*Chŏnnohyŏp*) in January 1990 by some 600 labor unions (300,000 workers) opened a new chapter in the labor history of South Korea. The new alliance of labor unions claimed that its aim was to promote a "genuine democratic labor movement," charging that the existing Federation of Korean Trade Unions (7,455 unions with 1.8 million members) is both "pro-government" and "pro-management," and speak for the bosses rather than to promote the rights of workers.

Social Transformation

Population. South Korea underwent a rapid social transformation after 1953. The population grew from 21.5 million in 1955 to 43.7 million in 1992 with a population density of over 1,100 persons per square mile, ranking the 11th most populated country in the world. The population growth rate up to 1960 was 3.0% per year, 2.7% between 1960 and 1966, and it dropped to an average of 1.9% during 1977-80, 1.24% during 1980-81, and to 0.99% after 1986. One of the modern features of South Korea's pattern of population growth was a rapid decline in the birth rate and gradual lowering of the mortality rate. In 1991, the birth rate was 17 per 1,000 and the death rate was 5.9 per 1,000. The average woman had 6.1 children in 1961, 4.2 in 1970, 2.8 in 1980, and 1.7 in 1991. The ratio of the age group from 1-14 to the total population fell from 42.5% in 1970 to 24.8% in 1992 while that of the age group over 65 increased to 4.5% in that year from 3.4% in 1970. The average life span of the South Koreans increased from 52.4 (51.1 for men and 53.7 for women) in the 1960s to 72 in 1989 (69 for men and 75 for women) as public health and welfare programs improved and living standards rose. Some 5.2% of the total population in 1992 was above the age of sixty-five.

Urbanization. The growth of educational and commercial institutions, as well as industrial facilities in and around large cities brought about rapid urbanization, attracting an increasing number of people away from rural areas. The urban population grew at an annual average rate of 5%, increasing the percentage of urban population from 28 in 1960 to 74.4 in 1990. The population of Seoul, which was about 700,000 in 1945, grew to 10.6 million in 1990, that of Pusan from 350,000 to 3.8 million, that of Taegu from less than 250,000 to 2.3 million, and that of Inch'ŏn grew from about 250,000 to 1.8 million during the same period. The population of Kwangju and Taejŏn also increased to a little over one million each, and some eight other cities had more than 500,000 inhabitants as of 1990. In 1990, about 25% of the nation's population lived in the metropolitan area of Seoul while 48% were in the six largest cities.

The most populated province was Kyŏnggi with 6 million in 1989, followed by South Kyŏngsang with 3.7 million, North Kyŏngsang with 3 million and North Chŏlla with 2.3 million. The island province of Cheju had the smallest population of a half million in 1989.

Social Change. The most conspicuous pattern of social structural change in South Korea was the rise of the middle class. Although some members of the former *yangban* families became political and intellectual leaders, the once privileged *yangban* class as such completely disappeared as the new elite class of educated people emerged from the former commoner class as political, cultural, and economic leaders. The new class of *nouveau riche* in South Korea consisted mostly of former members of the commoner class. The rise of education and economic development were the two most influential factors which brought about such a social transformation. Economic improvement in rural regions also gave rise to a distinctive new class with a "middle class outlook." In 1988, a survey showed that 61.5% of the population regarded themselves as "middle class."

Accompanying the structural change, a new pattern of life developed with the construction of high-rise apartment buildings and Western-style houses. Forms of dress also changed drastically. Although most women, particularly older women, prefer traditional costumes, Western clothes and hair-style became popular among both sexes and all ages. On holidays and certain other occasions women, including young ones, wear the traditional Korean dress, but very seldom do men in urban areas appear in traditional costumes in public.

A significant social change was the decline of the extended family system. Not only in urban areas, but even in rural areas one saw the break-up of the once prevalent extended family system, to be replaced by the nuclear family. The conjugal family has become popular, birth control has become widely practiced, and the number of apartment-dwellers has increased rapidly.

Under the law, parental consent for marriage had been required for couples until January 1979. Although most marriages are still arranged by parents or go-betweens, the choice by individuals has become increasingly important. With the rise of the modern family system, relationships, between husband and wife, parents and children, and wife and in-laws have changed also. Equality before the law increased women's rights greatly, and parental control over children has weakened, although authoritarianism on the part of the father still remains strong.

Status of Women. Although meaningful and satisfactory sexual (social) equality is yet to become a reality, the status of women in South Korea has improved considerably, thanks to determined efforts made by various women leaders and women's organizations. South Korean women demanded full human and civil rights as well as full social equality, as more women were educated, and an ever increasing number of women became judges, lawyers, physicians, dentists, artists, writers, educators, scientists, and technicians, as well as wage-earners, social leaders and politicians, reporters, and athletes. At the same time, the notion for the attainment of happiness of individuals rapidly replaced the traditional concepts of obedience, chastity, and propriety among women. The concept of women as child-rearing and home-making people has been weakened considerably.

A significant aspect of the new trend among women is the increase in the percentage of women who receive higher education. At the same time, the percentage of unmarried women aged 20-24 increased from 6.1% in 1960 and to 22.6% in 1985. Unlike in the past when young girls married before the age of 20, the new trend shows that an increasing number of young women delay their marriage while becoming working women after their graduation from either high schools or colleges. In 1960, only 2.7% of girls graduated from middle and high schools, but the percentage grew to 85% in 1989. Some 40% of girls who graduated from high schools advanced to colleges and universities in 1989.

In 1989, 46.5% of the economically active population were female, and 7.1 million women were working. Some 500,000 were professional administrators, technical or managerial staff, 850,000 were clerical workers, 1.2 million were sales workers, 1.2 million were service workers, 1.5 million were engaged in agriculture, forestry, and fisheries, and 2 million were production workers and equipment operators.

The determined and concerted efforts made by various women's organizations had brought about the revision of the Family Law in 1977. However, dissatisfied with the new law, they continued to push for the complete legal equality of women. As a result, in 1989, the Family Law was revised again, increasing property rights of women, as well as their right to become heads of household.

The New Community Movement. A most successful social engineering that brought about both economic and social benefits to the rural population was the New Community Movement which the Third Republic launched in 1971. Benefitted by the two successful five-year development plans of 1962-66 and 1967-71, the urban population was moving ahead socially, culturally, and economically, but the countryside was still sunk in poverty and lethargy. Growth rate in the agricultural sector lagged far behind that in the industrial sectors. As the economy grew, the gap between the annual income of farm households and urban wage earners widened. Such a situation brought about the exodus of the young rural population into urban areas, leaving the rural areas without adequate man power or leaders and creating population pressure on urban areas.

In view of this, in 1970 President Park provided the initial impetus to the New Community Movement as "a spiritual pillar for Korea's modernization," and in 1971 experimental projects were carried out. Meanwhile, the third five-year plan of 1972-76 was designed as a socioeconomic development plan, stressing a balanced growth between industry and agriculture.

The social objectives of the New Community Movement were to enlighten the rural people through "New Community education" so as to transform the outlook and habits of the tradition-bound and poverty-stricken rural population, help them develop diligence and thrift; a spirit of self-help and cooperation, and modernize rural society.

In order to accomplish these objectives, the Ministry of Home Affairs created the New Community Planning Division, and the New Community Central Consultative Council was established under the Home Ministry. Following this, a $2 billion budget for the 1972-76 period was adopted. Soon after that, the Central Consultative Council encouraged the rural population to adopt individual projects, village projects, and inter-village projects with or without the government's financial support. At the same time, it provided administrative and technical guidance, financial support to village and inter-village projects, and established the New Community Movement Training Institutes to train local leaders.

The New Community projects brought about modernization of rural housing, reconstruction of roads and waterways, and development of sanitary systems and scientific and technical know-how among the villagers. Such programs also expanded the role women played, as income and living standards improved and villages became modernized.

The New Community Movement which brought about these beneficial results in the rural areas was also extended into the urban areas, making it a nation-wide movement as a means of promoting unity and a cooperative spirit.

Other Social Programs. Ever mindful of the need to promote social welfare programs for children and the elderly, the Third Republic converted a golf course in Seoul, which had been constructed during the Japanese colonial period, into a 200-acre Children's Grand Park equipped with facilities not only for amusement and recreation, but also for scientific and artistic education for children. It was disclosed that behind this project was Mrs. Yuk Yŏng-su, wife of President Park. Meanwhile, the government relocated and expanded the zoo and a botanical garden, which had been established by the Japanese on the grounds of Ch'angdŏk Palace.

The government of the Third Republic also encouraged the formation of the societies for honoring the elders (*kyŏngnohoe*) and the organization of local residents and business groups as a part of the New Community Movement so as to promote solidarity of and cooperation among the people. This organization called *pansanghoe*, along with the aforementioned *kyŏngnohoe*, was established throughout the country.

The only significant social legislation that the Fifth Republic implemented was a welfare program for the aged in June 1981, constructing the old folks homes and sanitoria, and providing special favors such as free bus rides and discounts at public facilities for those 65 years of age and older. The Sixth Republic abrogated the 1981 social legislation, but in 1988 it inaugurated a mandatory national pension system, bringing 4.5 million people into it by December 1989. In December 1990, the National Assembly approved a revision of the law to provide special monetary support to destitute senior citizens but only a small number of elderly people were expected to receive such aid for the time being because of budget restraints.

When a revised Family Law was adopted in 1989, the Maternal Child Welfare Act adopted by the National Assembly in 1989 provided welfare benefits for widows, divorced, separated or out-of-wedlock mothers and their children under 18 years of age. Another important piece of social legislation that the Sixth Republic adopted in July 1989 was that which established the medical insurance system for all Koreans.

Sports. In sports, South Korea came a long way after participating in the Olympic Games for the first time in London in 1948. Memories were yet vivid of the 1936 Berlin Olympics in which two Korean runners, wearing Japanese uniforms, took first and third place in the marathon race.

Because of lack of funds and facilities, the development of modern sports was slow. However, after 1963 as the government emphasized the strengthening of physical education along with other subjects, the development of sports was rapid as intermural sports of high schools and colleges became more competitive. Physical education was required at all levels of schools, as professional sports teams were organized and modern sports arenas and stadiums were built in the 1970s. The inauguration of the annual Children's National Sports Festival in 1972, and expansion of the annual athletic meet of primary and secondary schools established significant milestones in the development of sports. As primary and secondary school students competed in the annual national athletic meet in all categories of sports for the honor and prestige of their schools, colleges promoted intermural sports, producing athletes who could compete in world-wide sport events.

In 1982, the Sports Ministry was established to promote sports, sponsoring the annual National Athletic Meet, the Winter National Sports Festival and other events. Both the government and private organizations encouraged the revival, promotion, and further development of traditional sports such as Korean-style wrestling called *ssirŭm* and archery. Western archery was also introduced as was Western wrestling.

The hosting of the Asian Olympic Games in Seoul in 1986, and the XXIVth Olympic Games in 1988 marked high points in the history of South Korea's sports. The hosting of the largest and most peaceful 1988 Olympic Games in Seoul at newly constructed, ultra-modern sports facilities was of particular pride to the South Koreans. The winning of fourth place in the games by capturing 12 gold, 10 silver, and 11 bronze medals put South Korea squarely on the main stage of the sports world. Shortly after the ending of the Seoul Olympic Games in October, South Korea hosted the 8th Paralympics in which some 3,200 athletes from 65 countries participated.

In September 1989, South Korea held the first World Korean Ethnic Sports Festival, strengthening the solidarity of Koreans around the world while promoting sports as a means of goodwill diplomacy. Participating in this festival were some 1,300 athletes from 50 countries including the United States, Japan, China, and the Soviet Union.

Educational and Cultural Development

EDUCATIONAL DEVELOPMENT

The government promulgated the Educational Law in December 1949, making elementary education compulsory for children aged six to eleven. At the same time, the Ministry of Education adopted the principle of education which stressed the development of national spirit, the concept of righteousness, obligation, and duty, the promotion of knowledge and technical skills, and unity and harmony of all the people. It also set forth the ideal of education stating that all nations and people must contribute to the common prosperity of mankind by developing democracy.

The educational process that had just begun to have an impact was abruptly arrested by the Korean War that destroyed over half of the schools. During the war, educational activities were carried out in tents and makeshift barracks in those areas not occupied by the Communist troops.

After the war, rehabilitation of the educational system was undertaken vigorously with the help of the U.S. and the U.N. Korean Reconstruction Agency. The physical facilities were rebuilt and the quality of instructional programs was improved within a few years to prewar levels. Carefully controlled planning, supported by traditional zeal for education, brought about rapid educational development. Although the improvement of the quality of education lagged far behind the quantitative growth, by 1960 the number of primary schools had grown to 4,496 with a total enrollment of 3.6 million pupils, the number of secondary liberal arts schools stood at 1,400 with 692,116 students, the number of vocational secondary schools was 252 with 99,076 students, and the number of higher educational institutions increased to 85 with 101,045 students. The establishment of national universities in the provinces was a significant aspect in the development of education for men and women. As in the days of Japanese colonial rule, all secondary schools were segregated.

The Third Republic promulgated the Charter for National Education in December 1968. It defined the following goals: (1) the construction of a spiritual base for regeneration of the nation (2) the creating of a new image for the Korean people, and (3) the promotion of knowledge of national history and issues. It emphasized the importance of educating the people to counter the aggressive schemes of the North Korean Communists.

In 1969, the entrance examination for middle schools was abolished and a nine-year education was made compulsory. With this step 99.2% of primary school graduates advanced to middle schools. The high school entrance examination was also abolished in 1973, but the college entrance examination system was retained.

The Korean government made great efforts to develop scientific and technical education. As a result, in 1967 the Ministry of Science and Technology was created, and in 1971 the Korean Advanced Institute of Science and Technology was established followed by the establishment of Science Town near Taejŏn in 1974. These institutes were created to promote scientific research and develop new technology, and in close cooperation between the ministries of Education and Science and Technology, science education at all levels of schools was improved as they produced a rapidly growing number of scientists, technicians, and skilled workers.

As before, private educational institutions played a significant role at all levels. Of some 302 colleges and universities (including 120 junior vocational colleges) some 80% were private institutions as of 1989. Most primary schools were public institutions, but there were some 730 private liberal arts middle schools, 623 private liberal arts high schools, and 246 private vocational high schools in 1989.

Quantitative Growth of Korean Education, 1945-1988

A. Number of Schools
(the 1945 figures include both zones)

	1945	1960	1970	1980	1992
Primary Schools	2,834	4,496	5,961	6,487	6,122
Middle Schools	166	1,053	1,608	2,100	2,539
High Schools	97	353	408	748	1,058
Vocational High Schools	68	282	481	606	677
Higher Educational Institutions*	19	85	191	224	298
4-year Colleges & Universities	19	56	71	85	121

B. Number of Students
(the 1945 figures include both zones)

	1945	1960	1970	1980	1992
Primary Schools	1,366,024	3,621,267	5,749,301	5,658,002	4,560,128
Middle Schools	83,514	528,614	1,318,808	2,471,997	2,336,284
High Schools	50,343	164,492	315,367	932,602	1,313,081
Vocational High Schools	33,171	90,071	272,015	764,187	812,492
Higher Educational Institutions*	7,819	101,045	201,436	611,394	1,491,669
4-year Colleges & Universities	7,819	92,934	146,414	402,979	1,070,169

Sources: Ministry of Culture and Information, Republic of Korea, *A Handbook of Korea*, 1982, pp. 686, 689; 1987, pp. 450, 456; 1993, pp.461; Yonhap News Agency, *Korea Annual*, 1989, pp. 232-234.

*Included 4-year colleges and universities, junior colleges, teachers' colleges, and junior technical colleges.

As of 1989 there were some 200 other schools such as civic high schools, trade high schools, and miscellaneous middle and high schools with a total enrollment of 1.2 million students. In 1989, the total number of students in South Korea was 12.2 million.

CULTURAL DEVELOPMENT

The South Koreans have made great strides in cultural development, although certain restrictions have been imposed on freedom of speech and the press, mainly for reasons of national security and as a defense against propaganda of the North Koreans and their agents in South Korea. In general, however, cultural progress has not been hampered.

Mass Media. Korean journalism has come a long way from those dark days of Japanese colonial rule when no Korean newspapers except that of the government existed. A large number of newspapers which had emerged between 1945 and 1948 collapsed during the Korean War, and they were consolidated into a half dozen major national daily newspapers such as *Tong-a Ilbo, Chosŏn Ilbo, Chung-ang Ilbo, Kyŏnghyang Shinmun, Seoul Shinmun,* and *Han'guk Ilbo.* Two English-language dailies, *The Korea Times* and *The Korea Herald,* emerged in 1950 and 1958, respectively. As Koreans began to emigrate to the United States and other countries, branches of these national papers were established in those countries and provided news about the homeland.

During the Fifth Republic, in 1980, these papers were further consolidated under government order into the four major national dailies of *Tong-a, Han'guk, Chosŏn,* and *Seoul.* The government also reduced the number of periodicals from 800 to 645 by revoking publication rights of 155 periodicals. However, when the Sixth Republic implemented its cultural liberalization policy in 1988 and revised the press law, many new newspapers were published while those which had been abolished were revived, raising the integrity of journalism in South Korea. Among the new newspapers published were *Hankyŏre* ("One People"), published in 1988 by those journalists who had been purged in 1980, the *Segye Ilbo* in 1990, and *Munhwa Ilbo* in 1991.

The state-run Korean Broadcasting System (KBS) which took over the Japanese installed radio broadcasting system in 1945, was joined by a privately-owned Christian Broadcasting System (CBS) in 1954 and the Munhwa Broadcasting Company (MBC), the nation's first commercial radio broadcasting system, in 1959. Other commercial radio broadcasting systems that emerged after 1959 were the Dong-A Broadcasting System (DBS) in 1963 and the Tongyang Broadcasting Company (TBC) in 1964. In 1966, FM broadcasting began in South Korea.

After KBS-TV was set up as the first full-scale television broadcasting system in Korea in 1961, other radio broadcasting systems began television programs. Thus, TBC-TV and MBC-TV emerged in 1964 and 1969, respectively, thereby promoting a new culture.

In 1980, under government order, the KBS-Radio-Television System took over two major private broadcasting systems (the DBS-Radio and the TBC Radio-TV) and three privately run provincial radio stations, leaving only one non-government MBC Radio-TV system. In December 1980, KBS-TV began color television broadcasting. As of 1989, there was a total of 53 AM radio stations, 58 FM radio stations, and 44 television stations in South Korea. In 1991, two more TV networks were established in Korea—the Educational Broadcasting System (EBS) and the Seoul Broadcasting System (SBS). These newly founded broadcasters operate their own radio channels EBS-FM and SBS-AM. Other broadcasters in Korea are PBC for the Catholics and BBS for the Buddhists. On the other hand, TBS, a public corporation operated by the Ministry of Home Affairs, is airing traffic-related programs only.

The number of television sets grew from 25,000 in

1961 to 8.5 million by 1989, or one TV set per 1.2 households. The Far East Broadcasting Company and the Asia Broadcasting Company are currently engaged in foreign language broadcasting in Chinese, Japanese, and Russian.

Religious Development. Under religious freedom, the growth of religion was rapid. While the number of Buddhists decreased from over 14 million in 1960s to 8.59 million (15% of the population) at the end of 1989, the number of Christians grew from some 6 million in the 1960s to 9.5 million (20% of the population) by the end of 1989. Of this, 8.2 million were Protestants and 1.3 million were Roman Catholics. There were a total of 31,954 churches and 8,101 Buddhist temples in South Korea. The *Chogye* sect of Buddhism had the largest number of followers. The newly introduced Islam had won some 5,000 converts by 1989.

Some 787,000 South Koreans were registered as Confucianists in 1987, and they maintained 231 shrines under their national association. Sŏnggyun'gwan in Seoul had been the main Confucian shrine in Korea. The *Ch'ŏndogyo* (formerly *Tonghak*) maintained its order with 52,350 followers, as *Taejonggyo* that worships Tan'gun had a small number of followers in 1989.

Development of National and Western Cultures. As Western culture inundated South Korea, whose traditional culture had been suppressed during the Japanese colonial period, both the government and the people felt the need to revive and nurture their national heritage. Thus, the Ministry of Culture and Information increased its budget for the National Classical Music Institute and encouraged musicians of traditional music and dance to elevate their standards. At the same time, the Ministry of Education instituted a curriculum in traditional music and dance at primary and secondary schools and many private institutes and groups of people, engaged in traditional music and dance, fostered such art as *p'ansori* (traditional operatic narration of epic stories accompanied by music) while training young Koreans in their respective fields. As a result, Korea's traditional music and dance not only revived, but also made great strides in gaining popularity.

While old masters of traditional painting produced new masterpieces of fine art and trained young artists at their studios or galleries, ceramic artists revived the interest in traditional ceramic art by establishing new kilns and producing many superior quality ceramic wares in the green celadon ware style of Koryŏ and the blue and white porcelain style of the Yi period.

In the field of drama and theater, South Koreans revived and popularized traditional puppet plays and masked dances. Several groups of young people, interested in this area, formed associations and societies and

Dancers of the Pongsan Masked Dance

performed puppet plays and masked dances to open theaters called *madang,* bringing back the age-old *kwang-dae* and *namsadang* plays in which puppets, masked players, and public entertainers took part. In the rural areas, the puppet plays of Hahoe, near Andong in North Kyŏngsang Province, became increasingly popular.

The government instituted the national festival of traditional plays and games so as to revive Korea's national culture. At the annual festival, provincial representatives performed traditional music and dance while introducing new styles in games and plays.

The government also encouraged the development of Western culture. Thus, classes in Western painting, music, dance, philosophy, and literature, as well as theater, were instituted. At the same time, it put emphasis on the development of foreign language instructional programs. As Western culture developed, such cultural halls as the Sejong Cultural Center in Seoul was established in 1978. Attached to it were the Seoul Philharmonic Symphony Orchestra, the Seoul City Orchestra of Traditional Music, the Seoul Municipal Dance Corps, the Seoul Municipal Music Company, the Seoul Municipal Choir, and the Seoul Municipal Junior Choir. The National Theater and its performing groups such as the National Drama Company, the National Traditional Opera Company, the National Dance Company, the National Ballet Company, the National Choir and the National Opera Company promoted modern as well as traditional culture. In February 1988, the massive Seoul Art Center was dedicated for the promotion of native and foreign culture. Meanwhile, many private cultural societies such as the Korean Cultural and Arts Foundation, the Hoam Cultural Hall, the Folk Art Puppet Theater, and others contributed greatly to the development of traditional and Western culture.

A vastly increased number of music programs at secondary schools and colleges of music trained many young musicians in both the vocal and instrumental fields, producing several internationally acclaimed violinists, pianists, and vocalists. A large number of young musicians trained in Korea received further training abroad and became members of foreign symphony orchestras of high reputation. Meanwhile, composers produced a large number of lyric songs with poems written by the poets of the by-gone days. Among them were "Azaleas," "The Hills Have Flowers," "Mother's Heart," and "Love." Among more recent poems which became lyrics of beloved songs were "Wheat Field" and "The Pioneer." A composer used "Dream," a *shijo* poem written by Hwang Chin-i, a female poet of the sixteenth century, as lyrics for his song, linking the early cultural heritage with the present-day culture. Meanwhile, some young composers wrote protest songs such as "The Morning Dew" and "Jesus Wearing a Golden Crown."

Although the quality and standard of South Korean films can still be improved, many film companies that emerged in the 1960s competed for excellence and market with limited funds and a small pool of talented actors and actresses. In doing so, they produced many films with historical and social themes. After two decades of experiments and growth, South Korean filmmakers and directors became more sophisticated and their techniques improved, and in 1989 the film *Why Did Bodhi Dharma Go to the East?* won best film award at the Locarno Film Festival in Switzerland. In that year, a Korean actress in *Surrogate Mother* received best actress award at the Venice Film Festival and another in a film with a Buddhist theme entitled *Aje Aje Para Aje* ("Come, Come, Come Upward") also received best actress award at the Moscow Film Festival.

Kang Su-yŏn, left, won the best actress award at the 16th Moscow International Film Festival in 1989 for her role in Come, Come, Come Upward.

Two important aspects emerged in the 1980s in the development of the South Korean film industry. One was the rise of a group of young avant-garde filmmakers who emphasized the dark side of Korean society, focusing their attention on people living on the margins of society, inhumanity, and oppression. The other was the emergence of women filmmakers who championed "defiant feminism," producing such films as *Even a Little Grass Has a Name.*

In the 1950s, novels and short stories which expressed realism were produced. The first such novel to appear was *The Free Woman,* which depicted contemporary reality of social conditions, morality, and human desires. However, the dominant theme of the "postwar literature" was man's inhumanity to man. Such novels as *Shower, The Rainy Day,* and *Fireworks* represented such a trend as they dealt with the Korean War.

In the 1970s, after recovering from the nervousness of the post-Military Revolution era of the 1960s, new writers promoted what is called national literature in which nationalism was expressed in "search for the total meaning of the life of the nation and the recovery of its wholeness." In the late 1970s and 1980s, young writers brought about the rise of what is known as "people's literature," emphasizing the masses as "the principal elements in society, as consumers of literature, and as a powerbase." As the avant-garde filmmakers and dramatists had done, the writers in this group dealt with psychological problems in the postwar South Korean society when a rapidly changing social and economic environment, especially modernization and industrialization, created numerous new and unfamiliar situations. These writers dealt more with the problems of the marginal urban population, alienated farmers, disgruntled laborers, activist youth, and revolutionary intellectuals. Other novelists and short story writers dealt with the problems associated with the breakdown of traditional social order and human relations, as well as the political struggle in which young Korean students were involved. Among the works of these avant-garde writers were *Small Ball Launched by a Dwarf* and *City of Machine*.

Women writers joined the new literary movement, producing many novels and short stories depicting irrationality and contradictions of the South Korean society, as well as the problems which women encountered in a rapidly changing social and economic situation. Such works as *Song of the Reeds Beyond the Rear Gate* (translated into English as *Lullaby*), *Days and Dreams, Evening Game,* and *A Room in the Woods* are representative works of women writers. These stories portray the wretched lives of Koreans in general and women in particular. In *A Room in the Woods* the writer depicts a young rebellious, resentful, anti-establishment, anti-bourgeoisie coed, who, after vainly searching for new meaning of life and a new mission in the 1980s, ends her life in a tragic death.

As recently as the late 1980s, the novelists dealt with the trying times of before and during the Korean War, producing such novels as *The Southern Army* and *The T'aebaek Mountain Range*. Meanwhile, dissident poets wrote poems of protest following the footsteps of Kim Chi-ha, who championed political democracy and social justice in his protest poetry in the 1960s and 1970s.

With the rise after the Korean War of the Korean Fine Art Association and the Contemporary Korean Art Exhibition for Invited Artists, a remarkable diversity in style and techniques in ceramic art and sculpture developed. The competition between the traditional school of academic realism which campaigned for the preservation of "all natural forms," and the artists belonging to the Korean Avant-Garde Art Association, who repudiated all natural forms and sought to give spontaneous expression in their works, gave a new impetus to the rise of sculptural art in South Korea.

Modern architects joined the new breed of literary figures, painters, sculptors, and ceramic artists, and designed spectacular buildings, changing the face of urban South Korea. New cultural halls, cathedrals, churches, schools, stadiums, and commercial buildings which they designed and built brought about a certain universalism in South Korea's architecture.

In the field of modern drama, the New Drama Society, an organization of the National Theater, emerged shortly after the Korean War and the Korean National Center for International Theater Institute, which emerged in 1958, popularized Western plays. They were joined by other theater groups which were organized in the 1960s and 1970s, promoting modern drama with Korean experience.

Preservation of National Cultural Treasure. In order to take charge of the preservation of cultural relics and national treasure, the Law on Conservation of Cultural Assets was promulgated in 1961 and the Bureau of Supervisory Administration for the Preservation of National Cultural Assets was established. Under the law, antique art products, ancient buildings, and even certain individuals such as folk dancers, musicians, artists and craftsmen were designated as "cultural treasures." As of 1989, the government has named some 1,249 places and items as cultural and historic spots, 271 items as national monuments, 221 items as folklore materials, and selected some 90 men and women as "intangible cultural assets." Meanwhile, the government undertook many projects to restore cultural properties while some ancient tombs were excavated under government supervision.

Thus, both traditional and modern culture flourished in South Korea after 1953 while spiritual and material cultural assets were preserved. A most significant aspect of cultural development of the recent past was the adoption of a new cultural policy by the government which liberalized the press law that had prevented the circulation of those works of Korean artists who had defected to North Korea, as well as those of Socialist countries. Such a step taken by the government enabled the people to enjoy once again those songs, literary works, paintings, poems, and other artistic works which had been forbidden by law.

Other Cultural Developments. While the National History Compilation Committee increased its research and publication activities to promote the study of Korean history, the National Museum, which was established in 1972 on the grounds of the Kyŏngbok Palace, and the National Museum of Modern Art, established at Tŏksu Palace, provided a greater opportunity to more people to appreciate

Korea's traditional and modern culture. Other public museums such as those of Kyŏngju, Puyŏ, Kongju, and Kwangju, along with privately established museums such as the Emille Museum, brought cultural enrichment while providing opportunities to gain a greater knowledge of historical legacy and heritage. Meanwhile, in 1973 the privately established Folk Village near Suwŏn became one of the most important open museums in South Korea with its display of various aspects of Korean traditional life, including architecture and methods of production.

South Korea Today

South Korea, with its population of 44 million, is a nation with a growing democracy in the political sector, rising expectations in the economic sector, increasing social equality, and an expanding cultural horizon. In politics, the multi-party system was replaced by a bi-partisan one as human and civil rights have grown and the press law has been liberalized. The National Assembly has gained its constitutional power as it better reflects the opinions and attitudes of the people. The steps taken by the National Assembly prepared the legal ground for the reestablishment of local autonomy that was realized in 1991. The relationship between the executive and the legislative branches has improved greatly as the judicial branch exercises an increasing degree of independent power. The political situation has improved in such a way that ex-president Chun and his wife, who had gone into self-imposed exile at a remote Buddhist temple in November 1988, returned to their former residence in Seoul at the end of 1990.

Student unrest still exists, mainly because of the persistence of subversive propaganda of North Korea among students who are led by radical organizations such as the National Council of Representatives of University Students, which sustains anti-government and anti-American sentiments. As late as 1989, students belonging to that group fire-bombed the U.S. Cultural Center in Kwangju, shouting anti-American slogans. However, the popularity of radical student movements somewhat diminished after 1989 as their radicalism and activities alienated their supporters, including ordinary citizens.

South Korea's national defense is strong, and it is well prepared to meet the North Korean aggression if and when it comes once again. Its 550,000-man Army, 60,000-man Navy, and 45,000-man Air Force are well trained and equipped, augmented by some 40,000 U.S. ground troops and Air Force units. In addition, some 1.4 million men in the active reserve, 3.5 million in the Homeland Reserve Forces, and 3.5 million in the Civil Defense Corps are adequately prepared to meet any eventualities of a renewed North Korea attack. South Korea's defense industry is well developed, producing tanks, firearms, and light military aircraft and naval craft.

Although South Korea's economic growth slowed down after 1988 and euphoria and optimism have subsided, the chronic rice shortage has ended, the job market is still growing, especially in industries, the unemployment rate is at its lowest in history, and the tourist industry is expanding. The Economic Planning Board stated at the end of 1992 that the goals of the sixth five-year socioeconomic development plan were fully achieved in 1991. It also announced that the new five-year socioeconomic development plan of 1993-98 would raise the GNP to $667.8 billion and per capita GNP to $14,500.

Although labor disputes in the future are likely to be troublesome, the South Korean people are resolutely making efforts to maintain the momentum in the economic growth which had been initiated in the 1960s.

As Korean society became modern with the increasing urban population and the rising middle class, social equality has made great stride, and today South Korean women enjoy a greater degree of rights and equality following the second revision of the Family Law in 1989. However, the gender equality is yet to be fully realized if greater social equality is to be achieved and the feudalistic attitudes of the male sex toward the opposite sex are to be eradicated.

Under the flourishing freedom of religion and the press, Christianity is growing with more than 10 million adherents, although the popularity of Buddhism is in decline. The press enjoys the greatest amount of freedom so far in the history of the republic as more newspapers and magazines are published. The cultural liberalization policy adopted in 1988 has an enormously beneficial effect, enabling the citizens to be better informed and interested in public affairs as intellectual and cultural development has become more rapid.

Today, all South Korean school-age children up to fourteen receive nine years of education and nearly 85% of all middle school graduates advance to high school. More than 300 institutions of higher education with more than 1.3 million students make South Korea one of the most educationally advanced nations in the world.

The newly established ties with the former Socialist countries have improved South Korea's international status while increasing its cultural diversity. The agreement reached between Seoul and Washington to sign a new Status of Forces of U.S. troops in South Korea in 1991 and to relocate U.S. military bases in Seoul to elsewhere has reduced problems which had existed between the two countries. Meanwhile, efforts made by the South Korean government and private citizens have brought about increasing contacts between the people of the two Korean states as indirect trade between the two states has grown.

South Korea, which gained its independence from Japanese colonial rule in 1945 and suffered the Korean War, has risen from the ashes like a phoenix, bringing about dramatic economic and social modernization, cultural development, and growing democracy in recent years. Despite some unsolved domestic and foreign problems, optimism and hopes are still high in South Korea for a better future. It is a country of energetic people with resilience, tenacity, a positive outlook, and a rich cultural heritage, which looks forward with confidence to the twenty-first century.

Selected Bibliography

THIS is not a selected bibliography in ordinary sense. Only those books which are considered to be helpful to the general reader to gain further knowledge about particular aspects of Korean history, culture, and society are included in this list.

ANTHROPOLOGY AND SOCIOLOGY

Vincent S.R. Brandt. *A Korean Village Between Farm and Sea.* Cambridge: Harvard University Press, 1971.

Sung Hwan Ban. *The New Community Movement in Korea.* Seoul: Korean Development Institute, 1975.

Seiwha Chung ed. *Challenge for Women: Women's Studies in Korea.* tr. by Chang-hyun Shin and others. Seoul: Ewha Woman's University Press, 1986.

Laurel Kendall and Mark Peterson ed. *Korean Women: Views from the Inner Room.* New Heaven: East Rock Press, 1983.

Yung-chung Kim ed. *Women of Korea: A History from Ancient Times to 1945.* Seoul: Ewha Woman's University Press, 1977.

Man Gap Lee. *The Social Structure in a Korean Village and Its Change.* Seoul: Seoul National University, 1973.

Edward S. Mason et al. *The Economic and Social Modernization of the Republic of Korea: Studies in the Modernization of the Republic of Korea, 1945-1975.* Cambridge: Harvard University Press, 1980.

Sandra Mattielli ed. *Virtues in Conflict: Tradition and the Korean Women Today.* Seoul: Royal Asiatic Society, Korea Branch, 1977.

Robert J. Moose. *Village Life in Korea.* Nashville: Publishing House of the Methodist Episcopol Church South, 1911.

Ki-hyuk Pak and Seung Yun Lee. *Three Clan Villages in Korea.* Seoul: Yonsei University Press, 1963.

———— and Sidney D. Gamble. *The Changing Korean Village.* Seoul: Royal Asiatic Society, Korea Branch, 1975.

Research Center for Asian Women. Sookmyung Women's University. *Women of the Yi Dynasty.* Seoul: 1986.

ARTS AND CRAFTS

Edward B. Adams. *Korean Folk Art and Craft.* Seoul: International Publishing House, 1987.

Jon C. Covell. *Korea's Cultural Roots.* Salt Lake: Moth House and Seoul: Hollym Corp., 1983.

G. St. G. M. Gompertz. *Korean Celadon and Other Wares of the Koryo Period.* London: Faber and Faber, 1963.

————. *Korean Pottery and Porcelain of the Yi Period.* London: Faber and Faber, 1968 and New York: Praeger, 1968.

Dong-hwa Huh. *Crafts of the Inner Court: The Artistry of Korean Women.* Seoul: The Museum of Korean Embroidery, 1987.

Hyung-mi Pub. Co. *Korean Folk Painting.* Seoul: 1980.

International Cultural Foundation. *Buddhist Culture of Korea.* Korean Culture Series, No.3. Seoul: 1960.

————. *Folk Culture in Korea.* Korean Culture Series, No. 4. Seoul: 1974.

————. *Upper-class Culture in Yi-dynasty Korea.* Korean Culture Series, No.2. Seoul: 1973.

Chewon Kim and G. St. G. M. Gornpertz. *The Ceramic Art of Korea.* London: Faber and Faber, 1961.

Chewon I im and Lena Kim Lee. *Arts of Korea.* Tokyo: Kodansha International, 1974.

Won-yong Kim. *Art and Archeology of Ancient Korea.*

Seoul: Taegwang Pub. Co., 1986.

Korean National Commission for UNESCO. *Modern Korean Painting.* Seoul: 1971.

Evelyn G. McCune. *The Arts of Korea: An Illustrated History.* Rutland, VT: Tuttle, 1962.

Robert R. Paine, Jr. ed. *Masterpieces of Korean Art.* Boston: 1957.

Zayong Zo ed. *Introduction to Korean Folk Painting.* Seoul: Emille Museum, 1977.

AUTOBIOGRAPHY AND BIOGRAPHY

Richard C. Allen. *Korea's Syngman Rhee: An Unauthorized Portrait.* Rutland, VT: Tuttle, 1960.

Sung-do Joh. *Yi Sun-shin: A National Hero of Korea.* Chinhae, Korea: Choongmu-kong Society, 1970.

Young-gill Kang. *The Grass Roof.* New York: Scribner's, 1931.

Agnes Davis Kim. *I Married a Korean with Sketches of the Author.* New York: The John Day, 1953.

King Sejong Memorial Society. *King Sejong the Great: A Biography of Korea's Most Famous King.* Seoul: 1970.

Peter H. Lee tr. *Lives of Eminent Korean Monks: The Haedong kosung chon.* Harvard-Yenching Institute Studies, No. 25. Cambridge: Harvard University Press, 1969.

Miruk Li. *The Yalu Flows: A Korean Childhood.* tr. by H. A. Hammelmann. East Lansing: Michigan State University, 1956.

Ilhan New. *When I was a Boy in Korea.* Boston: Lithrop, Lee and Shepard, 1928.

Robert T. Oliver. *Syngman Rhee: The Man Behind the Myth.* New York: Doo Mead, 1954.

Induk Park. *September Monkey.* New York: Harper, 1954.

Louis Yim. *My Forty Years Fight for Korea.* Seoul: International Cultural Research Center, Chungang University, 1951.

DRAMA AND THEATER

Oh-kon Cho. *Traditional Korean Theatre.* New York: Asian Humanities Press, 1988.

Sang-su Choe. *A Study of a Korean Puppet Play.* Seoul: Korea Book Pub. Co., 1960.

John Kardose. *An Outline History of Korean Drama.* Greenville, NY: Long Island University Press, 1966.

Korean National Commission for UNESCO. *Traditional Performing Arts of Korea.* Seoul: 1975.

ECONOMY

Irma Adelman ed. *Practical Approaches to Development Planning in Korea: Second Five-Year Plan.* Baltimore: Johns Hopkins University Press, 1969.

Larry L. Burmeister. *Research, Realpolitik and Development in Korea: The State of the Green Revolution.* Boulder, CO: Westview Press, 1988.

Oh-hyun Chang. *Land Reform in Korea: A Historical Review.* Madison: University of Wisconsin Press, 1973.

Davis C. Cole and Princeton N. Lyman. *Korean Development: The Interplay of Politics and Economics.* Cambridge: Harvard University Press, 1971.

Korea University. College of Agriculture. *A Study of the Regional Characteristics of Korean Agriculture.* Seoul: 1967.

J. P. Lewis. *Reconstruction and Development in South Korea.* Washington, D.C.: National Planning Association, 1955.

David I. Steinberg. *The Republic of Korea: Economic Transformation and Social Change.* Boulder, CO: Westview Press, 1988.

South Korea Today / **361**

HISTORY
(Books on general history of Korea are not included)

Before 1945

Chin-young Choe. *The Rule of the Taewŏn'gun, 1864-1873, Reconstruction in Yi Korea.* Cambridge: East Asian Research Center, Harvard University, 1972.

Won Sang Choi. *The Fall of the Hermit Kingdom.* Dobbs Ferry, NY: Oceania Publications, 1963.

Hillary Conroy. *The Japanese Seizure of Korea, 1868-1910 — A Study of Realism and Idealism in International Relations.* Philadelphia: University of Pennsylvania Press, 1960.

JaHyun Kim Haboush. *A Heritage of Kings: One Man's Monarchy in the Confucian World.* New York: Columbia University Press, 1988.

Homer B. Hulbert. *The Passing of Korea.* New York: Doubleday, Page, 1916.

Eugene C.I. Kim and Han-kyo Kim. *Korea and the Politics of Imperialism, 1876-1910.* Berkeley: University of California Press, 1967.

Eugene C.I. Kim and Doretha E. Mortimore ed. *Korea's Response to Japan: The Colonial Period, 1910-1945.* Kalamazoo: Center for Korean Studies, Western Michigan University, 1975.

Dae-yeol Ku. *Korea under Colonialism: The March First Movement and Anglo-Japanese Relations.* Seoul: Royal Asiatic Society, Korea Branch, 1985.

Gari Ledyard. *The Dutch Come to Korea: An Account of the Life of the First Westerners in Korea (1653-1666).* Seoul; Royal Asiatic Society, Korea Branch, 1971.

Chong-sik Lee. *The Politics of Korean Nationalism.* Berkeley: University of California Press, 1965.

Percival Lowell. *Choson: The Land of the Morning Calm — A Sketch of Korea.* Boston: Ticknor, 1988.

George A. McCrane. *Korea's Tragic Hours: The Closing Years of the Yi Dynasty.* ed. by Harold F. Cook and Alan M. Macdougall. Seoul: Taewon Pub. Co., 1973.

Frederick A. Mckenzie. *Korea's Fight for Freedom.* New York: Revell, 1920. Reprinted by Yonsei University Press, Seoul, 1969.

_____. *The Tragedy of Korea.* London: Hodder and Stoughton, 1908. Reprinted by Yonsei University Press, Seoul, 1969.

Andrew C. Nahm ed. *Korea under Japanese Colonial Rule — Studies of the Policy and Techniques of Japanese Colonialism.* Kalamazoo: Center for Korean Studies, Western Michigan University, 1973.

Michael Edwin Robinson. *Cultural Nationalism in Colonial Korea, 1920–1925.* Seattle: University of Washington Press, 1988.

Dae-sook Suh. *The Korean Communist Movement, 1918–1948.* Princeton: Princeton University Press, 1967.

Edward W. Wagner. *The Literati Purges: Political Conflict in Early Yi Korea.*

Post-Liberation Period

Soon-sung Cho. *Korea in World Politics. 1940–1950: An Evaluation of American Responsibility.* Berkeley: University of California Press, 1967.

Henry Chung. *The Russians Came to Korea.* Seoul and Washington, D.C.: Korean Pacific Press, 1947.

Donald N. Clark ed. *The Kwangju Uprising: Shadow Over the Regime in South Korea.* Bulder, CO: Westview Press, 1987.

Bruce Cumings. *The Origins of the Korean War: Liberation and the Emergence of Separate Regimes, 1945–1947.* Princeton: Princeton University Press, 1981.

Sungjoo Han. *The Failure of Democracy in South Korea.* Berkeley: University of California Press, 1981.

Se-jin Kim. *The Politics of Military Revolution in Korea.* Chapel Hill: University of North Carolina Press, 1971.

George M. McCune and Arthur Grey Jr. *Korea Today.* Cambridge: Harvard University Press, 1951.

Grant Meade. *American Military Government in Korea.* New York: Columbia University Press, 1951.

Andrew C. Nahm ed. *Studies in the Developmental Aspects of Korea.* Kalamazoo: Graduate College and Institute of International and Area Studies, Western Michigan University, 1969.

John K. C. Oh. *Democracy on Trial.* Ithaca: Cornell University Press, 1968.

W.D. Reeve. *The Republic of Korea: A Political and Economic History.* London: Oxford University Press, 1963.

The Korean War

Carl Berger. *The Korean Knot: A Military-Political History.* Philadelphia: University of Pennsylvania Press, 1957.

Mark W. Clark. *From the Danube to the Yalu.* New York: Harper, 1954.

Lloyd C. Gardner ed. *The Korean War.* New York: Quadrangle Books, 1977.

Max Hastings. *The Korean War.* New York: Simon & Schuster, 1987.

David Reese. *Korea: The Limited War.* New York: St. Martin's Press, 1964.

Allen A. Whiting. *China Crosses the Yalu: The Decision to Enter the Korean War.* New York: Macmillan, 1960.

William H. Vatcher. *Panmunjom: The Story of the Korean Military Armistice Negotiations.* New York: Praeger, 1958.

Diplomatic History / Foreign Relations

Jongsook Chay. *Diplomacy of Asymmetry: Korean-American Relation to 1910.* Honolulu: University of Hawaii

Press, 1990.

Frederick Foo Chien. *The Opening of Korea: A Study of Chinese Diplomacy, 1876–1885.* Hamden, CONN: Shoestring Press, 1967.

Bruce Cumings ed. *Child of Conflict: The Korean-American Relationship, 1943–1953.* Seattle: University of Washington Press, 1983.

Martina Deuchler. *Confucian Gentlemen and Barbarian Envoys: The Opening of Korea, 1875–1885.* Seattle: Washington: University of Washington Press, 1983.

Fred H. Harrington. *God, Mammon and the Japanese: Dr. Horace N. Allen and Korean-American Relations, 1884–1905.* Madison: University of Wisconsin Press, 1944.

Young-nok Koo and Dae-sook Suh ed. *Korea and the United States: A Century of Cooperation.* Honolulu: University of Hawaii Press, 1984.

Tae-hwan Kwak et al, ed. *U.S.-Korean Relations, 1882–1982.* Boulder, CO: Westview Press, 1983.

Manoo Lee et al, ed. *Alliance under Tension: The Evolution of South Korean-U.S. Relations.* Boulder, CO: Westview Press, 1989.

Yul-bok Lee. *West Goes East: Paul Georg von Möllendorff and Great Power Imperialism in Late Yi Korea.* Honolulu: University of Hawaii Press, 1988.

─────── and Wayne Patterson ed. *One Hundred Years of Korean-American Relations, 1882–1982.* University, AL: University of Alabama Press, 1986.

Andrew C. Nahm ed. *The United States and Korea: American-Korean Relations, 1866–1976.* Kalamazoo: Center for Korean Studies, Western Michigan University, 1979.

Robert R. Swartout, Jr. *Mandarins, Gunboats, and Power Politics: Own Nickerson Denny and the International Rivalries in Korea.* Honolulu: University of Hawaii Press, 1980.

GOVERNMENT AND POLITICS

Pyung-choon Hahm. *The Korean Political Tradition and Law: Essays in Korean Law and Legal History.* Seoul: Royal Asiatic Society, Korea Branch, 1967.

Gregory Henderson. *The Politics of the Vortex.* Cambridge: Harvard University Press, 1968.

Young Whan Kihl. *Politics and Policies in Divided Korea: Regimes in Contrast.* Boulder, CO: Westview Press, 1984.

Ilpyung Kim and Young Whan Kihl ed. *Political Change in South Korea.* New York: Korean PWPA, 1988.

Joungwon A. Kim. *Divided Korea: The Politics of Development, 1945–1972.* Cambridge: East Asian Research Center, Harvard University, 1975.

Se-jin Kim and Chang-hyun Cho ed. *Government and Politics of Korea.* Silver Spring, MD: Research Institute on Korean Affairs, 1972.

Byung Chul Koh ed. *Aspects of Administrative Development in South Korea.* Kalamazoo: Korea Research and Publications, 1967.

Koon Woo Nam. *South Korean Politics: The Search for Political Consensus and Stability.* Lanham, MD: University Press of American, 1989.

James B. Palais. *Politics and Policy in Traditional Korea.* Cambridge: Harvard University Press, 1975.

Chi-young Pak. *Political Opposition in Korea, 1945-1963.* Honolulu: University of Hawaii Press, 1980.

Dae-sook Suh and Chae-jin Lee ed. *Political Leadership in Korea.* Seattle: University of Washington Press, 1975.

Yong-pil Rhee. *The Breakdown of Authority Structure in Korea in 1960.* Honolulu: University of Hawaii Press, 1982.

Edward Wright ed. *Korean Politics in Transition.* Seoul: Royal Asiatic Society, Korea Branch, 1974.

Sung Chul Yang. *Korea and Two Regimes: Kim Il Sung and Park Chung Hee.* Cambridge: Schenkman Pub. Co., 1981.

LITERATURE

Tok-sun Chang comp. *The Folk Treasury of Korea: Sources of Myth, Legend and Folktale.* tr. by Tae-wung Kim. Seoul: Society for Korean Oral Literature, 1970.

Francis Carpenter. *Tales of a Korean Grandmother.* Garden City: Doubleday, 1947.

International Cultural Foundation. *Humour in Korean Literature.* Korean Culture Series, No. 1. Seoul: 1977.

————. *Korean Folk Tales.* Korean Culture Series, No.7. Seoul: 1979.

Chong-un Kim tr. *Postwar Korean Short Stories.* Seoul: National University Press, 1974.

Korean National Commission for UNESCO. *Modern Korean Short Stories.* Seoul: Si-sa-yong-o-sa Pub. Co., 1983.

Peter H. Lee. *Anthology of Korean Literature from Early Times to the Nineteenth Century.* Honolulu: University of Hawaii Press, 1981.

————. *Anthology of Korean Poetry from the Earliest Era to the Present.* New York: John Day, 1964.

————. ed. *Flowers of Fire: Twentieth Century Korean Stories.* Honolulu: University of Hawaii Press, 1974.

————. *Korean Literature: Topics and Themes.* Tuscon: University of Arizona Press, 1965.

David R. McCann. *Form and Freedom in Korean Poetry.* Leiden: E.J. Brill, 1988.

Mashall R. Phil. *Listening to Korea: A Korean Anthology.* New York: Praeger, 1973.

Richard Rutt. *The Bamboo Grove: An Introduction to Sijo.* Berkeley: University of California Press, 1971.

———— and Chong-un Kim tr. *Virtuous Women: Three*

Masterpieces of Traditional Korean Fiction. Seoul: Korean National Commission for UNESCO, 1974.

W.E. Skillend. *Kodae Sosol: A Survey of Traditional Korean Style Popular Novels.* London: School of Oriental and African Studies, University of London, 1968.

In-sob Zong. *A Guide to Korean Literature.* Seoul: Hollym Corp., 1986.

MUSIC AND DANCE

Sa-hun Chang. *Glossary of Korean Music.* Seoul: Korean Musicological Society, 1972.

Won-kyung Cho. *Dances of Korea.* New York: Norman J. Seaman, 1962.

Keith Howard. *Bands, Songs and Shamanistic Rituals.* Seoul: Royal Asiatic Society, Korea Branch, 1989.

Hey-kyu Lee. *An Introduction to Korean Music and Dance.* Seoul: Royal Asiatic Society, Korea Branch, 1977.

Keith Pratt. *Korean Music: Its History and Its Performance.* Seoul: Jeong Eum Sa, 1987.

Si-sa-yong-o-sa Pub. Co. *Traditional Korean Music.* Seoul: 1984.

PHILOSOPHY AND RELIGION

Min-hong Choi. *A Modern History of Korean Philosophy.* Seoul: Songmunsa, 1980.

Charles A. Clark. *Religions of Old Korea.* New York: Revell, 1932, reprinted by Seoul: Christian Literature Society, 1961.

Alan Carter Covell. *Folk Art and Magic: Shamanism in Korea.* Seoul: Hollym Corp., 1989.

J.H. Grayson. *Early Buddhism and Christianity in Korea: A History in the Explanation of Religion.* Leiden, Netherlands: E.J. Brill, 1985.

William T. de Bary and JaHyun Kim Haboush. *The Rise*

of Neo-Confucianism in Korea. New York: Columbia University Press, 1985.

Everett H. Hunt. *Protestant Pioneers in Korea.* New York: Orbis Books, 1980.

Roger Janelli. *Ancestor Worship in Korean Society.* Stanford: Stanford University Press, 1982.

Laurel Kendall. *Shamans, Housewives and Other Restless Spirits.* Honolulu: University of Hawaii Press, 1985.

──────── and Griffin Dix. *Religion and Ritual in Korean Society.* Berkeley: Institute of East Asian Studies, University of California, 1987.

Spencer J. Palmer. *Confucian Ritual in Korea.* New York: Asian Humanities Press, 1984.

Benjamin Weems. *Reform, Rebellion and the Heavenly Way.* Tuscon: The University of Arizona Press, 1964

SOURCE ON NORTH KOREA

Tae-sung An. *North Korea in Transition from Dictatorship to Dynasty.* Westpoint, CONN: Greenwood Press, 1983.

Ellen and Jacques Hersh Brun. *Socialist Korea: A Case Study in the Strategy of Economic Development.* New York: Monthly Review Press, 1976.

Joseph S. Chung. *The North Korean Economy: Structure and Development.* Stanford: The Hoover Institution Press, 1974.

Peter Hyun. *Darkness at Dawn: A North Korean Diary.* Seoul: Hanjin Pub. Co., 1981.

Eugene C.I. Kim and B.C. Koh ed. *Journey to North Korea: Personal Perceptions.* Berkeley: Institute of East Asian Studies, University of California, 1983.

Chung-sun Kim. *Fifteen-year History of North Korea.* Washington, D.C.: Joint Publications Research Service, 1963.

Ilpyung J. Kim. *Communist Politics in North Korea.* New York: Praeger, 1975.

Byung-chul Koh. *The Foreign Policy of North Korea.* New York: Praeger, 1969.

Chong-sik Lee. *The Korean Workers' Party: A Short History.* Stanford: The Hoover Institution Press, 1978.

Lim Un (pseud). *The Founding, of a Dynasty in North Korea: An Authentic Biography of Kim Il-sung.* Tokyo: Jiyusha, 1982.

Andrew C. Nahm. *North Korea: Her Past, Reality and Impression.* Kalamazoo: Center for Korean Studies, Western Michigan University, 1978.

Koon Woo Nam. *The North Korean Communist Leadership, 1945-1965: A Study of Factional and Political Consolidation.* University, AL: University of Alabama Press, 1974.

Jae-kyu Park and Jung Gun Kim ed. *The Politics of North Korea.* Seoul: The Institute for Far Eastern Studies, Kyungnam University, 1979.

Philip Rudolph. *North Korea's Political and Economic Structure.* New York: Institute of Pacific Relations, 1959.

Robert A. Scalapino and Chong-sik Lee. *Communism in Korea.* 2 vols. Berkeley: Institute of California Press, 1972.

_____ and Jun-yop Kim ed. *North Korea Today: Strategic and Domestic Issues.* Berkeley: Institute of East Asian Studies, University of California, 1983.

Dae-sook Suh. *The Korean Communist Movement, 1918-1948.* Princeton: Princeton University Press, 1967.

Index